SHI CHARLOTTE

*A Mother's Physical, Emotional, and Spiritual Journey
with Her Child with Medical Complexities*

Emily K. Whiting

Blue Heron Book Works, LLC

Allentown, Pennsylvania

This is a true story. Some names have been changed to protect privacy.
All Bible references from New Revised Standard Version (NRSV) Catholic Edition

ISBN:978-1-7354019-9-7
Book One of the Charlotte's Hope Series
Cover image by: Bonnie Roberts Krueger
Cover design by: Angie Zumbrano
www.CharlottesHopeFoundation.org
www.EmilyKWhiting.com
www.blueheronbookworks.com

"She is Charlotte is the journey of a mother in her quest for meaning and purpose. Emily K. Whiting did not fully realize how or where she would find that fulfillment, but through the trials and struggles of dealing with Charlotte's multiple health diagnoses, God revealed himself in the greatest of ways. You will be blessed by this beautiful story of true faith."

Anne DeSantis, author of Love and Care for the Marginalized, podcaster of Sewing Hope and Journeys of Faith, and nonprofit Executive Director of Saint Raymond Nonnatus Foundation

"This book will inspire you! Guaranteed. As Emily K. Whiting shares this deeply personal journey with you, your heart will expand as you experience love, courage, and the grace of God in ways you have never experienced before. A rich treasure."

Allen Hunt, best-selling author of Everybody Needs to Forgive Somebody

"She is Charlotte is a powerful story of how God uses the life of a medically fragile little lady to impact the hearts and lives of a NICU and family. Emily does an incredible job of portraying the perspective a parent gains from tenaciously fighting for the life of their child. You cannot walk away from this book unchanged."

Judy Hostetler, fellow warrior mama

"Emily has an authentic and extraordinary way of taking you on a journey through her eyes into a sacred time and space. It's a journey no mother should have to experience, and is fueled by her faith, family, and the extraordinary little warrior we come to know as Charlotte. An experience that transforms the reader's heart, and shows the fiercest, bravest, and gentlest kind of love."

Teresa Koch, RN, specialized in Maternal Fetal Medicine

"Emily beautifully brings you along the behind-the-scenes journey many parents of medically complex kids go through. Displaying how deep the brokenness gives way to a desperate faith and surrendered peace is adorned throughout the words and prayers found within these pages. You will feel privileged to witness such joy within the depths of the difficult circumstances."

Erica Ryan, author of <u>Hospital Stay Notebook</u> and <u>Medical Appointment Notebook</u>, founder of <u>Strengthening by Fire</u>

"This book shares an inspiring and heart-felt journey of a little girl and her family. It puts a spotlight on the challenges, dedication and love that goes into dealing with a special child. I would encourage everyone, especially those in the healthcare field, to read this to gain an empathetic understanding of these special families."

Elaine Foster, PhD, MSN, RN

"She is Charlotte is one of those rare books that inspires, challenges, captivates, and gives hope, regardless of the reader's own life experiences. The honesty and vulnerability Emily K. Whiting shares in every chapter is written in such a way that one can't help but be pulled into the story and feel the enormity of its message. As a mother of my own daughter with medical complexities, I can't recommend this book enough, especially for anyone who is facing challenging times. She is Charlotte is more than a book, it is an experience with the potential to positively change one's perspective and provide hope, even when all hope feels completely lost."

Ashlyn Thompson, co-founder of Charlotte's Hope Foundation, Inc.

To the man I'm blessed to call husband. Daniel, without you none of this is possible. Your selflessness, steadfastness, and support is extraordinary. God really knew what he was doing when he brought us together.

Contents

Foreword

This journey with my daughter—her diagnoses, prognosis, the fight for her life and her progress toward healing—it's changed everything.

How I think, how I perceive life and love, how I interact with God. Nothing is the same.

It's changed my perspective on what matters, and perhaps more importantly, what doesn't. My dreams and personal aspirations are nothing like what they used to be. I now see a greater purpose and cause for life than I ever dreamed possible.

This journey has flipped my life upside down, inside out, and ultimately transformed me into a different person. A better person, I hope.

I always knew I wanted to do something to help people. To love people. But how? There are countless ways to help people. What is the way I am meant to bring love to those around me? What is my calling? My purpose in life?

I remember getting really serious about this question shortly after I broke up with my then-boyfriend, now-husband, back in college. Yup, it took us dating twice to get things right. More on that later.

What was I meant to do with this one life I was given? I started diving into any books and resources I could find. I was hungry for meaning—meaning for all the hurt this world brings, all the struggles and all the joy this life has to offer. What does it all mean? And what is my role in it?

This seems to be the journey we all are on, a journey of seeking meaning and purpose. I used to think if I sought hard enough, dug deep enough, and asked the question often enough, eventually I would just know my purpose. Like my calling would just fall from the sky in a grand ah-hah moment and I would say, "That's it! That's what I'm supposed to do with my life!"

It turns out that's not how life works. Life is ever evolving, ever revealed one faithful step (and misstep) after the other. It's waking up each day and saying, "Yes, Lord, I will follow you," and then seeing where the day takes me.

And wow, I never would have guessed life would lead me here, sharing my story with you and my work would lead me to serve parents of children with medical complexities. If God would have revealed that to me in my college apartment when I was sitting on my twin-sized bunk bed pouring over different degree paths and praying fervently for clarity, I would have said no. No way was I going to be equipped to help parents with medically complex children. I had no experience in the medical world. All I'd known in life thus far was health. Never mind was I going to be able to parent a child with major medical complexities myself.

I suppose there's a reason the future is not divulged to us. Instead, God beckons us to simply hold his hand and take one step, then another, learning to grapple with fear, letting it become a propelling agent rather than a stopping force.

Fear. I was laced with it when we first received that diagnosis. And even before, I was riddled with fear when I first heard God calling me to ministry work. He beckoned me, gently, lovingly, and steadily. I wanted to ignore him and stay comfortable in my suitcase and blazer lifestyle, earning a dependable wage and making a positive difference in a very tangible way in my small circle of influence. That was good, wasn't it?

Yes, very good. But it wasn't what God had in store for me for long. I wasn't going to be the executive who worked her way up through the ranks at the same company since college graduation and proved herself professional and capable, though that seemed like the dream I wanted. I knew it deep in my soul that somehow my life's work lived outside office walls and a busy travel schedule. But what was it?

And I was so comfortable. Dare I step out and follow the Lord's call to put it all on the line? I would sing in church on Sundays, "Here I am Lord. Is it I Lord? ...I will go, Lord. Will you lead me?" My soul would stir into a fiery passion to live these verses in the daily realities of life. The allure of adventure and entering the unknown beckoned. But the gravitational pull of predictability and comfort kept me planted. It's far easier to sing about going where the Lord leads than it is to actually follow.

Fear. It was my stumbling block. How could I walk away from the life I've built for a life that is blurry, unknown and scary as hell? Yet each day on my drive through Wayne County, Ohio's mild version of rush hour traffic, I ached for something more. As I turned off State Route 585 and pulled into my quiet, comfortable small-town home, God whispered to the dormant corners of my heart, "Come, follow me, and see. Come. See my people. Love my people."

What did that even mean?

I spent hours praying about it, arguing about it with God.

Lord, what do you want me to do?

He didn't provide much clarity. Only to "*See his people. Love his people.*" Over time, one thing led to another, and the way he wanted me to follow him became a bit clearer, even if still fuzzy and distant. He wanted me to use my professional training of speaking and writing to share his love with his people. An agricultural communication degree might not seem like obvious training for this kind of work, but God knew what he was doing.

He wanted me to share with others my witness to his passionate pursuit, how he loved me through my darkest hours and my greatest failures and spoke knowing love and mercy to me when I thought I was beyond recognition and repair. How he told me, "*I have heard your call for me. I have remained with you through the darkness, and you have reached out for me once more. Don't let go of me, Emily. I will carry all of your worries and fears, loneliness and dissatisfaction on my shoulders so that you may live for me.*" He extends the same unfailing love to you.

He wants a truly deep, personal relationship with each of us, and he pursues us with such tender and fierce love it will bring you to your knees when you recognize it. When you recognize him. He wanted me to share how he seeks an intimate relationship with you and me that surpasses any level of intimacy we may dream of. True, true intimacy.

In-To-Me-See. That's what we all want, right? To be seen and known at the depths of our being and loved for who we really are.

He wanted me to share how intimacy between man and woman here on earth is meant to simply be a beautiful, albeit broken in our sinfulness, foreshadowing, a great sign and symbol, that points us to the deep, deep intimacy we truly desire with him. Not that God is sexual, but that he does truly see you for who you are, and he loves you so very deeply right there. He does see you in all your nakedness and brokenness, and he loves you all the more. He sees you, beautifully, wonderfully, fearfully made. Made out of love and for love. He gives himself so completely and faithfully to you, even in your and my unfaithfulness. He can't help himself. He is love.

But…fear.

What would others think of me? I'd spent my life trying to brand myself as professional. A career woman. Now God was asking me to stand in front of crowds and talk about two things seemingly far from professional, and seemingly unrelated—faith and sex.

My very first talk I delivered in an effort to answer God's call was titled "Five Truths about God and Sex." Talk about fear. How am I supposed to openly talk about faith and sex and still maintain professionalism? And to tell of all my mishaps and mistakes to boot! Would I be shunned by my coworkers and colleagues? Would people think I'm crazy? Would anyone even listen to what I have to say? I didn't have a degree in theology. Did I even know what I was talking about?

Crippling fear.

Worse than the fear of others' judgment and rejection was the fear of not following God. Not because I thought he would condemn me, but because I knew my soul would die more each day if I said no to his invitation to follow him. I was made for an adventure that far surpassed the pretty little box I'd put my life in, and if I said no to God's beckoning, I would be saying no to my very soul. I'd made that mistake before. I could not do it again. Not to mention, it would be selfish for me to keep all these things to myself out of fear and complacency. He didn't meet me in my time of need only for me to keep his love to myself. No, his love was meant to be shared far beyond this one girl in rural Ohio.

And so, with deep fear and reservation, I began taking one faithful step after another, speaking, and writing about God's design for relationships, his design for our desires to point us to him, and how he desires a deeply personal relationship with you and me.

There's a reason the Bible says "do not be afraid" on repeat. Fear is part of the natural human condition. Faith does not exist in a vacuum separate from fear. Rather, they often go hand-in-hand.

The black leggings did a poor job hiding shaking knees at my 1st talk in Columbus, Ohio, March 2017. I had given countless presentations before, stood before hundreds of audience members as the main speaker. But never about anything so personal, so private and so revealing. I kept wanting to find some reason why I couldn't do it. Surely the date wouldn't work with my schedule, or no one would show up to the Young Adults event, or a huge storm would cancel the thing entirely. No such thing happened, and something propelled me forward and granted me the courage to follow through.

Then just a couple weeks after that event, two pink lines announced our lives were about to change forever. My husband and I were overjoyed but it wasn't long into the morning sickness and cravings before we learned of our precious child's seemingly terminal diagnoses from head to toe.

How could this possibly be part of God's plan? Didn't I follow him faithfully? Did I mishear him? Did I misunderstand his call on my life toward ministry, or was this part of it? How could this possibly be part of it?

A realization of just how little control I had in life piled on top of my fear. I could not control my child's health nor her outcomes. I could not control that nothing about my motherhood journey and her infancy was normal. I could not control whether she lived or died, whether she needed XYZ surgery or whether her liver enzymes behaved in the latest lab results. Whether she endured unthinkable pain or not.

In the midst of my wavering sense of control, I learned early in the pregnancy that life is a gift, not a given. Life is a precious, treasured, fragile gift that is not to be taken for granted because it's here today and gone tomorrow, and it's not up to us when life comes and when it goes.

I learned that I had two options. I could either live in fear each day, awaiting my daughter's death and sucking the joy right out of this gift that is her life. Or, I could embrace the gift that she is, loosen my death grip on my illusion of control, and keep taking one step at a time saying, "Yes Lord, I will follow you."

Then there was my ever-evolving understanding of providence. I often heard mentors say, "God will provide." I didn't give this much thought until I was brought to the depths of my inability to provide for my own child that I began to truly understand what this might mean. The day I recognized and accepted that his answer to my prayer for my daughter's healing may very well mean that she dies, that was the day I began to really understand providence. If I really believed in a good God who makes all things new and who uses all things for his glory, then even my daughter's death would not go wasted. And perhaps her true healing would be done with him in heaven and not here with me. The heartache was intangible and immeasurable. Yet somehow acceptance eventually accompanied that heartache like a quiet friend extending a warm hand saying, "it will be okay," and the meaning of "okay" is not what it once was.

The story that unfolds in the following pages is, yes, the story of my daughter's incredible, and almost unbelievable journey toward healing. It's also the story of this mom's fear evolving from crippling to propelling, and this mom's journey from the illusion of control toward the realm of acceptance. Even more so than acceptance, a newfound resolve to embrace the call God's placed in my life, now as a mother of a courageous, life-filled and hope-filled child. This is the story of how my walk to the edge of life and back knocked me out of complacency and comfort and into something so much more. To embrace the call God's placed on my heart in ministry, leading me to see his people and love his people in a whole new way I never saw coming. To extend a loving hand of help to other parents and caregivers who find themselves in the devastating, traumatizing, yet sometimes surprisingly beautiful trenches of raising a child with medical complexities. To be that friend who extends the hand and says, "It will be okay. Let me be here with you in the pain."

Looking back, I see how God invited me to the depths of my fears, first asking me to openly speak about something so very personal as faith and sex, then asking me to face the reality of my child's seemingly never-ending series of pain and the looming threat of her death, so I could wrestle with fear and walk away realizing just how little power fear truly has over me, and how little say it has over the impact my life can make in this world.

You know, at first I thought this mission to support parents and caregivers of medically complex children was a complete divergence from the original one God called me to a few years ago, when my ministry started with that talk about God and intimacy. It turns out they are not all that different, and actually complement each other beautifully. Maybe not at face value, but it boils down to this: God wants a deeply personal loving relationship with each of us, each and every one of us, no matter our past or mistakes, our abilities or disabilities, our diagnoses or prognosis. I am humbled and honored to spend my days making his invisible love visible for the world to see, by seeing his people and loving his people to the best of my limited ability, one faithful step (and misstep) at a time.

Chapter 1   The Big Reveal

Journal Entry - Saturday, April 8, 2017

Baby Whiting #1,

We just learned about you last night, 12 hours ago, when the pregnancy test read positive. Yet, I knew two weeks ago you were coming. God told me you were coming. While I believed, a part of me doubted whether I heard God's voice or my own. I was Peter stepping out of the boat among crashing waves, walking on water toward outstretched Jesus. Walking on water one moment, then sinking with disbelief the next. But God is strong through our disbelief. He always delivers his promises. And now you're here. We love you already. You are a miracle baby after months of trying and hoping we'd get pregnant. God loves you more than you or I can fathom.

> *Love,*
> *Your Mama*

Wednesday, July 26, 2017

Heat radiates from the asphalt and envelopes my calves as I jump out of my black Ford Escape—the car I jokingly refer to as the Tin Can because it rattles so much—and walk to Dan's truck in the Women's Health Clinic parking lot. My cheeks burn. Is that from the 86-degree Fahrenheit weather or my growing excitement?

"Hey Babe!" I give him a quick peck on the lips. "How's your workday going?" Our fingers entangle in the way I've grown so familiar with, and we start walking toward the clinic's glass doors. We both took our lunch breaks to meet for this appointment.

"Good," he simply says, his mind clearly not on the question at hand. Neither is mine.

"Are you excited?" I probe, getting to the topic on both our minds.

"Yeah," he answers, almost flippantly. I know better. He's anxiously awaited this day much like I. But he's always been a man of few words. At least until you get him one-on-one and start asking him about the intricacies of how something works. Then he has much to say.

He opens the door for me, quickly walks past me and opens the next one before I can do it myself. He knows I forget to let him be a gentleman. I always appreciate it, but usually move so fast to get wherever I'm going that I just do it myself.

My eyes adjust to the indoor lighting, and I go to the front desk to check myself in. "Emily Whiting, here for my appointment." My phone buzzes in my work slack's pocket. It's probably a customer asking about the latest point of sale order or a team member calling to plan our next sales meeting trip. I silence the phone. I'll call them back as soon as I return to the office this afternoon.

I go over insurance and contact information with the receptionist. "You're all set," she says with one of those bored smiles that gives away she's had this exact conversation 40 times already today. "You can be seated, and someone will come get you shortly."

Dan's already perched next to the television which is playing some kind of house flipping show. He's ignoring it, mindlessly scrolling through his phone, passing the time and distracting himself.

"So ... do you think it's a boy or girl?" I ask the question we both have wondered ever since we got the positive pregnancy test a few months ago. I smile at him coyly as he puts his phone away. We both know it really doesn't matter whether we are pregnant with a boy or girl, but it is still fun to guess.

"Well, if it's a girl she has no name," he says with a laugh and reaches out to give my hand an anticipatory squeeze. I've always loved the strength of his hands. They remind me of my dad's, big, calloused and yet gentle and loving. Though my own hands fill an extra-large size glove, Dan's are even bigger. I find comfort in that.

I pull out my phone with my free hand to look at the list of possible names we've noted. There are nearly ten contending boy names, William, James, and Silas among them, but not one for a girl. We don't prefer a boy. We just don't like any girl names we've thought of yet.

I look up from our list to see Dan's excitement mixed with anticipation and a little bit of apprehension written all over his face. The weight of this immense responsibility is in his eyes. He takes his role as a father very seriously. He's going to be incredible with our baby.

He's so handsome. His brown hair is sprinkled with just enough gray to make him look wise, yet still youthful. It's thick and wavy and currently a little longer than he likes. He says he's due for a haircut, but I think this length is perfect, when the curls start to form. Will our baby have his hair or mine, straight and blonde?

Maybe our kiddo will have his blue eyes, or will he or she inherit my green? I hope the baby doesn't get Dan's scalp ... he has this strange ability to move his entire scalp from the top of his head to his eyebrows back and forth. Whenever he wants to make me laugh, he starts raising his eyebrows and making his whole head move backward and forward. The thought makes me smile. There could be worse things to inherit, right? Like my tendency to create a new mole every 20-minutes. The dermatologist has a heyday with my skin, chopping away new dark spots and oddly shaped beauty marks at each routine visit. I wonder if she enjoys my appointment days because it gives her exciting specimens to biopsy. There's one thing for sure, this baby is guaranteed to be tall because Dan and I both hover around six feet.

A woman dressed in green scrubs comes into the waiting room and calls my name, breaking my train of thought. This is it! My stomach flips as I stand and walk with her to the ultrasound room. Dan follows.

"You can lay down right there," the woman points to a hospital bed with fresh white paper pulled across it and a white pillow at the top. She closes the sonography room door behind us and turns off the lights. I fumble onto the bed. She stands next to me and presses a button with her foot to raise the bed so she can more easily reach me. She lifts my shirt up over my swelling stomach and squeezes blue gel onto an ultrasound probe.

By the way she goes about everything, obviously she's done this hundreds of times. I'm glad she knows what she's doing. I have no clue. This is my first pregnancy and first ultrasound.

This is the greatly anticipated routine anatomy scan, the one they apparently do for all babies at 20-week gestation, halfway through a woman's pregnancy. This is the original gender reveal party before that was even a thing.

"The gel is going to feel warm," she says, gesturing to the probe as she places it on my abdomen and squishes the slimy substance around. While she moves the probe with her right hand, she focuses intently on the ultrasound screen and clicks a bunch of buttons with her left. After watching her work for a moment, I glance over at Dan and follow his gaze to find a monitor on the wall. It projects the images she's seeing on her computer. Breath catches in my throat. That's my baby up there on that screen. It's one thing to know you have a human growing inside you. It's another to see it. My chest pounds. I strain to see if I can make out any features.

As if reading my mind, "there's the head, stomach, arms and

legs," she points, orienting me. Ultrasound images make the baby look funny, like a black and white alien. I see a leg twitch in the image and simultaneously feel a kick inside my abdomen.

"That's our baby!" I state giddily. Dan's expression matches how I feel, a look of awe and wonder mixed with a little terror. Becoming a parent is no joke. To think we are solely responsible for this kid's care ... it's hard to imagine we are ready for that. But then, is anyone, ever?

"Do you want to know the sex?" the sonographer asks. I bite my tongue so Dan can answer. I have become increasingly aware of the fact that I tend to be the first to talk in most circumstances. I'm trying hard not to always be so dominating in conversations, both in my relationship with Dan and in my work relationships. It's hard for me, though, to not respond right away and instead wait for him.

When he realizes I'm not answering, he looks at me for confirmation and nervously says yes. She clicks the sonograph and moves the probe around for several more minutes before saying anything more. Anticipation builds.

After what seems like ages, she finally states, "It's a girl!" It's hard to see the baby's image anymore through my tear-filled eyes. A wave of exhilaration hits me. I'm a girl mom! Then anxiety hits. I have no idea what I'm doing being a girl mom. I grew up with only brothers. I shrug off the anxiety so I can focus on the amazing news. I guess I'll figure it out as we go.

Color flushes Dan's cheeks. He shakes his head in disbelief. The corners of his lips curve up into that explosive smile of his that he reserves for big occasions. "Oh boy," he chuckles, processing this news. I can almost see his mind flashing ahead to skinned up knees, chasing teenage boys off, and walking her down the aisle. His protectiveness over this currently six-and-a-half-inch long child is beautiful.

I give his hand a squeeze and start thinking through various girl names to see if any might seem fitting now.

"How about Norah?" I ask.

"Hmmm … maybe," he replies skeptically.

While Dan and I playfully banter back and forth about different names the sonographer quietly continues measuring and analyzing seemingly every organ and limb of our little girl. I suppose that's why they call this the anatomy scan, since beyond announcing the gender, they are looking over every body part in as great of detail as possible on a sweet-potato sized human.

My phone buzzes again in my pocket, reminding me I need to get back to work soon. I look at the sonographer to see if she's close to done. She is quietly concentrating on the job at hand, not giving much hint of wrap up anytime soon. I point to a mass on the screen. "What is that?" I ask.

"The doctor will be in to review everything with you soon," she simply answers. Her demeanor seems to change, going from joyful and lighthearted to serious and intent. Odd. But all these tiny measurements must be challenging to make accurately and she needs to focus on the job at hand.

"What about Gwenevieve, Gwen for short," Dan says. I

wrinkle my nose and shake my head before catching myself and saying, "I don't love it. But maybe I'll warm up to it."

Dan and I fall silent as we run out of name ideas. While we revel in this incredible news of having a girl, the sonographer puts more gel on my belly, shifts her weight from one foot to the other and continues measuring. It looks like we are going to be here a while. I hope my coworkers aren't waiting on me for a meeting. I can't remember my afternoon schedule now, though I reviewed it just this morning.

"I'll be back with the doctor to go over the scan," the sonographer finally says, breaking the silence as she hangs the probe back in its place and wipes the gel off my belly with a dry, scratchy, over-bleached wash cloth. She hands me an extra cloth to finish the cleanup and then leaves the room. I sit up on the exam table, wipe my belly a few more times and roll my maternity shirt back down. After the door clicks closed, Dan slides his chair closer to me. We wait.

I assume by the way the sonographer spoke that she will be back any minute with the doctor. Five minutes go by. Then another five. And another. Did they forget which room we are in? Is the doctor stuck with another patient? I reach for my phone to text my boss that I'll be gone for longer than planned. I know she'll certainly understand since she has several kiddos of her own. I am grateful I work for a company that is so supportive of family life. But I still feel bad for leaving the team this long. I had expected this appointment to be short and sweet.

Whispers float under the hallway door. The doctors and nurses must be excited we are having a girl! Finally, the door opens and Doctor Greenwood walks in. She comes straight over to me and puts her right arm around my shoulders in an embrace. She seems sad.

"Did you see we are having a girl?" I ask excitedly, hoping our good news can brighten her seemingly bad day. "She was kicking during the ultrasound, and I saw her cute little arms and nose."

Is that sympathy I see in her expression? Panic rises as she begins to rub my back. What is going on here? Why isn't she excited for me?

"I see you're having a girl," she gives a pained smile. "Congratulations." She clearly has more to say, so I bite my tongue again and sit quietly, waiting.

She takes a deep breath. "Emily and Dan, we see on this ultrasound that the fetus has various anomalies. We've assessed the anatomy, measured, and remeasured, and we can see several organs have not developed appropriately."

Anomalies?

She continues, "Unfortunately the baby seems to have several malformations which we can already see today in the ultrasound, and there may be more problems which we cannot see yet in her development."

Malformations? Surely she's mistaken. Maybe she's mixed us up with a couple in another room. I can feel my little girl kicking and I just watched her do a flip on the ultrasound screen twenty minutes ago. How could our baby possibly have *malformations*?

Dan clenches my hand hard and clears his throat, "What kind

of anomalies?" For a moment I had forgotten he was even there, lost in trying to wrap my head around the doctor's words.

"Well, it appears her brain is malformed," my world is spinning and everything around me seems to go black. *Brain? Malformed?* There's that word again. I want to spit it as far away from me as possible. "There is something with the heart that's not pumping blood correctly. We think maybe it's something with the valves, but we need to do more testing to know for sure. There is a mass filling her lower right abdomen and it appears to be something other than an organ. Her kidneys seem abnormal, and they don't appear to be attached to the bladder." She takes a deep breath and continues, "the upper lip didn't form fully, and she has what's called a cleft lip. Often when there is a cleft lip, a cleft palate is present as well, meaning the roof of her mouth didn't form. But we don't know that for sure."

Dr. Greenwood is still rubbing my back. I want to throw her arm off me and run. Instead, I'm paralyzed.

"So, what does all this mean?" I hear my voice as if I'm having an out of body experience. My palms are sweating. My chest hurts. I put my hand on my swelling abdomen.

She sighs, clearly not enjoying delivering such devastating news. "Unfortunately, we don't know. But it doesn't look good. From what we can see, this baby has many physical abnormalities and very well may have mental as well. Her quality of life is unknown, if she survives."

If? If she survives? This cannot be happening.

"What do we do now?" Dan asks, looking pale and frightened.

"Well, we have a couple options. We can do more testing to see if a genetic condition is the root cause. We can get you in to see a Maternal Fetal Medicine doctor who specializes in high-risk pregnancies and can provide more answers."

Goosebumps rise on my arms and my body shivers to fend off the cold starting to consume me.

"Or you may choose to terminate."

Chapter 2 Very Much Alive

Journal Entry - Thursday, July 27, 2017

Oh God, yesterday we got the most devastating news. While we are having a beautiful baby girl, she is not likely to survive outside of the womb. We aren't even sure how long she'll survive inside the womb.

She has an under-developed brain, her heart valves don't close, she has a cleft lip and a cyst on her pelvis, her kidneys aren't attached to her bladder. But she has ten beautiful fingers and toes, the cutest little button nose and her mama and papa love her more than we can say. We are likely going to have either a stillbirth or she will pass away soon after.

I want to hold her. I want to love her and tell her everything is going to be okay. Oh God help us. I pray you heal our baby if that is your will. I know in you all things are possible. I trust in your goodness. But God, if you don't heal her, I pray you love her home to you and grant us the grace to do the same. We know this little life was never ours to keep, but ours to love.

Thank you for one more day I get to carry her. Help me to count my blessings each day and cherish the time we have with her here on earth.

Thank you for the blessing of my husband. This baby is blessed with the best dad ever. God please be with his heart. Love him and lead him closer to You in his pain. Teach me to love him the way you call me to love and the way he deserves. We are beyond blessed to have Dan as our husband and father. Help him to know it's okay to hurt and it's okay to cry.

Thursday, July 27, 2017

One lane turns to two, then two into four. The drive seems eons long though it's only forty minutes to Independence, Ohio, from our house. As highway median lines blur, I cut the silence. "What questions do we want to make sure we ask?" I know if they are not written down we will forget in the heat of the moment. In the heat of intense emotion.

After some time to think it over, Dan says, "I want to know how this happened and what are the chances of it happening again."

I cannot fathom worrying about the next baby when we are actively mourning our current one. I write his question down anyway. Everything is hazy through my red-rimmed eyes. The lines blur on the paper. My hands shake.

Dan pulls in the parking garage and puts the small SUV in park. We sit for a moment, peering out our windshield at the looming glass building, trying to gather courage to enter. We know full well we are walking into a parent's nightmare.

"Can we pray quick, Babe?" I ask awkwardly. Saying an impromptu prayer together in the middle of the day, in the middle of a parking lot, feels uncomfortable. Ad-lib prayer is not something I remember our family doing growing up. I mean sure, we prayed, but at predictable and safe times like at church, before a meal, before bed. Clasping hands and bowing heads at any other time, in public and praying out loud, that feels entirely too … vulnerable. If God is truly the king of my heart and the center of our family, then I want to live that truth out authentically, vulnerability and all. If there is ever a time to put awkwardness aside and cling to faith, it's now.

Lord, help me.

We cling to each other and say a furtive prayer of desperation. Renewed with a slight sense of peace amidst the fear and pain, we clamor out of the car, clasp hands, and walk in.

The receptionist reminds us at check-in it may be a while before Dr. Carvalho, a maternal-fetal medicine OBGYN, can see us since we aren't technically on his schedule. After yesterday's devastating news at our regular OB appointment, Dr. Carvalho graciously said he could work us in today.

All that's left to do is wait. We sit and I find myself staring blankly at a toddler who waddles around the waiting room, his exhausted and very pregnant mother trying to remain patient with his antics. "Don't play by the door," she warns. "It could open any minute and you'll get hit."

She must think we are basket cases. I know full well we look as wrung out as we feel. Does she know what it's like to receive devastating news about her child? Or is she pregnant with a perfectly healthy kid? I thought I was too, until yesterday.

"Emily Whiting?" A nurse finally calls, long after this mother and countless others go back for their appointments before me. She leads us to the ultrasound room where a sonographer and Dr. Carvalho analyze our little girl on the small black and white screen. I watch intently, looking for any detectable sign my untrained eyes can see of an unhealthy baby. I have no idea what I'm looking for. All I see is my beautiful baby girl with a head, two arms, two legs, ten fingers and ten toes. She looks perfect to me. I can't help but feel relieved that she is still moving and alive.

The silence could be cut by a knife as the two medical professionals assess every detail, measurement, and movement of our 20-week-old fetus. Before either gives us a clue what they are seeing or thinking, the sonographer wipes the blue jelly off my growing belly, helps me sit up and walks us to a neighboring conference room. Dr. Carvalho isn't far behind, bringing us Dixie cups of cold water and a box of scratchy hospital tissues.

"I see what Doctor Greenwood told me about yesterday." Dr. Carvalho says as he shuts the door and sits down across the aluminum coffee table from Dan and me. "The fetus has various abnormalities. I see the cleft lip. I cannot get a good image of the brain to say if it's affected so it may or may not be malformed. There is clearly a heart defect. There is a mass in the right portion of her abdomen, but I don't know what it is. It's fluid-filled so not likely a tumor. Both kidneys are obstructed and may have blockage in both ureters. The good news is the amniotic fluid around the fetus is normal, so kidneys appear to be functioning for now."

Relief and pain simultaneously cross Dan's face, expressing

what I'm feeling, too. Relief that there is no more or worse news than we heard yesterday. Pain that the news hasn't improved. I realize now that I came into this appointment holding onto the hope that maybe, just maybe, this was all a horrible nightmare and yesterday's news was a result of inaccurate imaging. Maybe this appointment would confirm our daughter is in fact as healthy as can be.

Now I recognize how naive a thought that was. In high school health class I recall learning the stages of grief, and I note in this moment I am most definitely in denial.

"I see you have a list of questions," Dr. Carvalho points to the crinkled paper in my hand. "Can I have it?" I reluctantly slide the college-ruled scribbles across the cold metal table. Do I really want to know his answers? My body tenses. I put my hands on my knees, willing them to stop shaking.

"What is the worst-case scenario?" he reads aloud.

He sighs and stares distantly at the bleach white wall behind us, probably thinking this is the worst part of his job, having to tell expectant parents their child is not well and may never be. No one goes to medical school hoping they get to be the person delivering the bad news.

This is the real question, far beyond her heart issues or a missing part of her lip. I want to know what's going to happen to my baby and how bad it's going to be. My heart rate quickens, and I lean in to make sure I hear his every word.

"The worst-case scenario is she passes away before birth or she is born alive but is unable to survive for long," he says bluntly and moves on quickly to the next question, "What is the best-case scenario?" He pauses to think for a moment. "That each of these issues we see on ultrasound is isolated and treatable."

"How long do you think she could live?" he reads on.

"It depends on her heart defect. I don't know yet," he sighs. "You'll probably carry her for a while longer at least. The issues we can see are all survivable in utero. The question is, is Baby viable once she's not dependent on you, Mom. I really don't think she'll pass away in utero, so we have some time to figure things out, do some testing."

I'm shocked at this revelation. Just yesterday we were told she wouldn't likely survive much longer. Now we are being told she likely will make it full-term. I'm hesitant to get excited, not sure which doctor to believe.

He patiently continues through each question. There are 18. "Is this genetic? Could it happen again in future pregnancies? What is the cause of the issues? If she dies in utero, do we have a funeral? What happens to her body—from a legal standpoint do we get it or does the hospital dispose of it?" The questions go on like an interrogation.

My stomach does somersaults as he answers us as honestly as he can. I might throw up. My lap dampens with tears as they stream down my face, the scratchy tissue rubbing my cheeks raw. It's fitting, really, for my cheeks to be raw, since that's how I feel. Raw.

"Now having answered your questions, I'd like to talk about testing. We might need to move quickly before it becomes illegal."

I look at Dan, wondering if he's as confused as I am. Did I just hear what I thought I heard?

"Illegal? Before what becomes illegal?" Dan asks, voicing my same question.

"Terminating the pregnancy. In the state of Ohio, you can no longer terminate after 22-weeks, so we have two weeks to make some big decisions," he simply states. Is it just me or is he avoiding eye contact?

It takes me a minute to wrap my head around what he's saying. But as soon as I realize he's talking about abortion, my hands cover my swollen belly as if that could protect our child from the cruel realities of this world. I never really knew what the expression mama bear meant before this moment.

No one is going to touch my baby. I feel adrenaline pumping through my veins. I thought my heart rate was high before; now it's through the roof. If anyone so much as comes within five feet of me and my baby, I think I might kill *them*. I want to run. My instant defensive reaction surprises me.

I'm shocked the option to abort is even on the table. It's offensive and repulsive to think *killing* my child is being discussed right now. It's one thing to discuss her dying naturally. But abortion? That's a whole other thing. Dan and I look at each other and know instantly we are on the same page. Dan breaks the silence, staring at his hands saying, "We will not terminate the baby. If she dies on her own, so be it." Dan looks back up at Dr. Carvalho. "But that's not up to us. Abortion is not an option for us." Dan concludes.

"Yes, we plan on giving her every chance at life," I say firmly, as if to say, "back off!"

Relief seems to wash over Dr. Carvalho's face. Or does he think we are crazy? It's hard to tell.

He gives a half smile, sits back, and looks like he's in a different world with his thoughts for a moment. Then he leans in, slides the questions back across the table toward Dan and I, looks us each in the eyes and says, "Now, we've spent this appointment talking about your daughter's developmental anomalies and her potential death. But the baby I saw on that ultrasound is very much alive. I chased her around with the ultrasound probe because she was moving around so much. And it sounds like you two want to give her every opportunity to live. I don't know what tomorrow brings, but for today, she is alive. So, let's focus on her life rather than her death. Okay? Let's talk about what we are going to do next to help her live."

Finally, oxygen re-enters my lungs and my heart rate comes down a beat or two.

Hope.

I take a deep breath, flip over the list of questions and start taking notes on the blank page as Dr. Carvalho runs through the litany of tests we need to do in the coming weeks and months ahead to prepare for her birth.

Chapter 3   Everything Dims

Thursday, July 27, 2017

The free-standing metal love swing squeaks with each rock, back and forth, back and forth. Mosquitoes buzz around my ankles and the cool evening air ushers the hot summer day away. The swing posts are rooted in the dirt where we busted up old concrete in anticipation of building a patio. Stones are stacked around me, waiting to be placed.

I watch Dan throw a tennis ball for Gracie over and over and over on our little half-acre village lot, working out the tenseness of the situation with each thrust. Meanwhile, Petey paces my swing and whines with his usual dose of anxiety. The two border collie mixes couldn't be more opposite in personality, one playful, carefree and queen bee, the other anxiety ridden and loyal to the core. Petey senses we aren't okay and therefore is falling apart himself.

Apparently, my coworkers sense everything's not okay too because my phone is flooded with texts, calls and emails from them, wondering where I was today and what's going on. I just don't have the energy to answer them yet. How do I answer them? Nothing is okay, and I don't know how to begin explaining why.

I'm not even sure I want them to know. Not yet at least. This seems private, something between Dan and I and the select few family members in our inner circle. We just told everyone we were expecting a mere six weeks ago, and now we face telling them we might be burying our baby soon. A vision of thrusting a shovel full of dirt on a tiny burial box, the thud of dirt meeting box sending a jolt up my spine, passes through my mind before I can stop it. I just can't muster the strength to explain, nor the fortitude to face their sympathy. No, I can't tell them yet. My hand rests on my abdomen as I swing, silently begging the baby to move so I can feel her life within me and reassure myself we aren't burying her, yet.

I can't help but fight this overwhelming feeling of guilt, too. Guilt that somehow I did something while pregnant with this child that caused her to malform. Will my coworkers, family and friends think the same thing? Will they judge me as a bad mother? Illogical as it is, the guilt hangs over me like a thick cloud. I'd rather not tell anyone what we learned at yesterday's and today's appointments. Yet I know they all eagerly await the gender reveal. As if that matters at all at this point. Boy. Girl. Who cares, if the baby isn't even compatible with life?

 Guilt

One of the first emotions that hit me upon our baby's diagnoses was guilt. Crushing guilt.

What did I do to cause this? What was wrong with my body that I didn't carry a healthy baby? What would others think of me and my baby? Many parents experience this guilt when they first learn of their child's diagnosis.

Of course, the truth is there is nothing I or any other parent did to cause their child's challenges. Aside from the obvious culprits of drug or alcohol abuse, there is nothing a parent does or does not do that's going to cause their child's anomalies. Nonetheless, logical or illogical, the guilt can be all consuming.

After years of navigating the persistent and resurfacing bouts of guilt, I've learned to get them out of my head by sharing my thoughts with a trusted friend, family member, spiritual director, or a doctor, and with God himself, too. It is scary to voice my thoughts because what if the person I'm confiding in, or even God, agrees I caused my child's unthinkable suffering and challenges, or judges me as a bad mother? But, the truth is, we are the ones unfairly judging ourselves, rarely the one we tell.

When we stay in this place of guilt and then the resulting fear, it can start to fester into anxiety, loneliness, isolation and the list goes on. Give voice to your thoughts of guilt and then let the person you confide in reassure you that there is nothing you have done or not done that caused this.

Not knowing what to say, this morning I sent my boss a text saying something is wrong with the baby and I won't be in today. Thankfully she didn't ask any questions and canceled my appointments and meetings for me. She told me to take all the time I need.

More immediately, we have to figure out how to handle this weekend. I'm supposed to board a plane in less than 24 hours.

"What should we do about the bachelor party and the wedding?" I ask Dan. He stops throwing the ball, ruffles Gracie's ears and comes to sit beside me on the green outdoor cushioned swing. He doesn't respond right away, running his fingers through his hair and thinking. Early in our relationship I used to take his silence as disinterest or disengagement. Now I know he's quiet because he's

EMILY K. WHITING

thinking.

"If you still want to go to the wedding, I support you in that," Dan finally utters. I've never witnessed him in so much deep pain like I have in the last 24 hours. Last night when we called his parents to inform them, they answered the phone and were met with silence. Dan struggled to find his voice without sobbing.

"I really want to be there for Emma and Byron on their wedding day, but I cannot fathom leaving you now. And even if you still go to the bachelor party like we planned, I can't imagine facing all those people at the wedding by myself," I admit. This weekend was double-booked long ago, so we had decided to divide and conquer, each of us going our separate ways to support our old college friends' new marriages. But now the idea of leaving Dan and being surrounded by people, even loving and caring people, sounds like I might drown in my effort to paint on a happy face. I can't bear the thought of facing anyone. I want to hide in the safe sanctuary of our home and not come out. Ever.

He let out a sigh of relief. "I can't imagine being apart right now either," Dan agrees and wraps his arm around my shoulder.

"Maybe you could come with me to the wedding," I think out loud. "We'd have to buy you a plane ticket to Iowa."

"I don't want to tell you what to do, but I'd feel more comfortable if you didn't travel right now," he says. "I know flying is not going to hurt the baby, but I'd just feel better if you stayed here where you are near the doctors."

"You're right. It's probably best we just cancel everything and stay home," I agree, thankful. This weekend is Dan's birthday too, though. What a birthday celebration, hiding from public and mourning the loss of the healthy child we thought we had.

A kid squeals with laughter from a distant neighbor's porch. A crack of a baseball bat echoes through the air from the ballfield a few doors down. Cheers follow. Squirrels and birds flit around the large old trees in our backyard. Life goes on around us as if nothing has happened. Yet, our world has stopped spinning.

I keep wavering between devastation, despair, denial and numbness. All the while, people return to their homes from their work days, cook dinner for their families and do all their normal routines.

I was supposed to be at the office today preparing my two main session talks for our upcoming Annual Conference. I was supposed to spend tonight packing for a fun weekend away. I had planned on working tonight on follow up from the *She Speaks* conference I attended last week.

Was that just last week? It feels like a lifetime ago. I recall meeting with the publisher at the conference and pitching my book idea. I was so filled with hope and excitement for this ministry venture God was calling me to. I stood in the large conference room during the main session with one hand raised high in praise and the other hand resting on my growing belly, singing aloud with the worship band. I was so filled with peace and a deep knowledge that God was doing big things in my life, even in light of the fear that seemed to tag along with my excitement like an unwelcome companion. God was preparing me for a speaking and writing ministry and he was leading me to something I couldn't quite see or explain but I just knew he was taking me somewhere big. Somewhere important.

Now I don't even know which way is up, let alone what I'm supposed to be doing with my life. The pain rings so loud in my ears that the joy I felt last week seems a faint echo. It's like the world that just yesterday morning was still so full of color and spinning so fast as we walked into our gynecology appointment is now dark and quiet, moving in slow motion. Nothing else matters besides the news of our baby's diagnoses. What used to seem like a busy, important, purposeful life is now dim, irrelevant, quiet. Like the eerie calm before a devastating storm, when you know it's coming and there's nothing you can do to stop it, there's nowhere to hide or take cover. There's no hoping the storm will blow over. It's heading straight for me.

Journal Entry – Friday, July 28, 2017

God, I know you will carry out what you started, and I rejoice in that truth.

"I am confident of this, that the one who began a good work among you will bring it to completion by the day of Jesus Christ." (Philippians 1:6)

"And this is my prayer, that your love may overflow more and more with knowledge and full insight to help you to determine what is best, so that on the day of Christ you may be pure and blameless, having produced the harvest of righteousness that comes through Jesus Christ for the glory and praise of God." (Philippians 1:9-11)

Chapter 4   Amniocentesis

Journal Entry - Friday, July 28, 2017

Good morning Lord,

 Praise Your name! So many blessings rained on us in the last twenty-four hours. You blessed us with loving parents who went out of their way to be here for us. You faithfully provided a doctor's appointment to get us answers yesterday afternoon. You comforted us with hope that this might not be as severe as we were originally told. You performed a miracle in that our baby girl does not have visible brain deformation like we thought. You provided a friend that spoke love, hope and faith into our hearts. You brought Daniel and I together and drew us closer than ever before. You calmed our hearts and provided peace, trust, and hope where fear, anxiety and anger resided. Praise Your name, oh God. We are so grateful. Grant us faith that only grows and matures from here. Forgive us for our lack of faith.

 Amen.

Tuesday, August 1, 2017

The needle seems as long as my forearm. Dan hands me a little red stress teddy bear to squeeze. It has our alma mater logo on it, The Ohio State University. My knuckles go white from my death grip on the poor little fella, the block O bulging from the pressure. I'm beside myself with nerves. This massive needle is about to be inserted into my abdomen, but that is not what's causing my angst.

Dr. Carvalho pulls on his sterile gloves and begins preparing the site on my swelling stomach with a cold antiseptic. A nurse stands at the ready, handing him whatever he needs. She adjusts the lighting to help him see. I will my eyes to stop staring at my baby on the ultrasound screen. I cannot watch. I look up to the ceiling, searching for anything I can fix my eyes on that will keep the world from spinning. My left-hand squeezes Dan's. My right squashes the beads in that stress bear.

This room is becoming all too familiar. It's the same room we were in less than a week ago, learning our baby is a girl. A girl who is not healthy. I was afraid to walk back in today, wondering what other devastating news we might receive. Am I going to have posttraumatic stress disorder (PTSD) when I walk through the door and lay on the elevated hospital bed, again? Or, when I roll up my shirt and the ultrasonic waves reveal my child's developmental challenges?

I remember I'm not here for myself. I'm here for my baby. PTSD or not, I am determined to go through with this procedure.

"Okay Emily, I know we went over this before, but just to remind you, this is a hollow needle which I will insert through your abdomen and your uterine wall, into the amniotic sac," Dr. Carvalho explains. "Once there, I'll collect a small sample of the amniotic fluid and then remove the needle. You're going to feel uncomfortable, and you might feel cramping. The entire amniocentesis procedure is pretty quick. Then you just need to take it easy for the rest of the day."

"Is the baby going to feel anything? How do we know you won't accidentally prick her?" I ask shakily. Everything in me screams that I need to get up and run, protect the baby from that needle. Protect her from this horrible situation. But logic keeps me rooted in the hospital bed. This is meant to help her, not hurt her.

"There is a very, very small chance I will poke the baby. I am following her with this ultrasound right now and I'll be able to see my needle as I guide it in. I will make sure it doesn't touch her. I just need some of the fluid that's around her, so I can send it off for genetics testing." His attempts to reassure me are futile. Surely he can see the mistrust written all over my face. He adds, "I've been doing this for twenty years and I've never once accidentally touched a baby."

The goal of the genetics test is to learn if our baby's anomalies are from a genetic condition, which will help us prepare for her birth and know if there are any interventions that can be done in utero to give her every chance at life.

"And the risk for miscarriage?" I ask.

"It's certainly a risk," he says. "But with every procedure or intervention we have to weigh risk versus benefit and the potential benefits for learning what Baby is up against outweighs the risk of miscarriage from my experience." He moves the ultrasound probe around to follow Baby as she wiggles.

"What if she moves right into your needle?" I ask again, petrified I'm going to cause my unborn child to get poked with this insanely aggressive needle while she's still in my womb. While I'm supposed to be protecting her from the outside world.

"I'm following her closely, Emily. I'll take good care of her. But, if you are having second thoughts, we don't have to go through with this," he says, looking at me with empathy and reassurance.

I think about it for a minute, torn. I look to Dan. After all, this baby is his, too. I've noticed doctors and nurses keep talking to me as if I'm the sole guardian and parent of this child. Yet, Dan is just as much her parent as I, and I need his input, guidance, and support now more than ever.

"What about risks to Emily from the procedure?" Dan asks.

"There is of course risk of infection, and as we said, miscarriage, but again, we have to weigh risk versus benefit," Dr. Carvalho responds.

"If this is truly what's best for the baby and will give us answers, if this is what you would do if this was your wife and baby, then I think we should do it," Dan says.

I nod in agreement.

"Okay then, you're going to feel a pinch and some pressure," he says as he positions himself to begin.

Journal Entry - Tuesday, August 1, 2017

Today was the amniocentesis. God you were with us all day. Praise Your name. Our little lady is still squirming and kicking! She kept getting in the way and the doctor had to find a new place to get amniotic fluid so he wouldn't poke her. God, Daniel and I were so nervous and still are that the amnio will cause us to miscarry.

But you are bigger than a needle and syringe. God we trust you. Help us for our lack of trust.

Now we wait. We get results in two weeks. Grant us the grace to accept and take on whatever challenges lie ahead, Lord. Thank you for our daughter. Thank You for another day to love her. Be with us, Lord. I know you are, and I know you will be.

Amen

Chapter 5 Grandma's Gravesite

Thursday, August 3, 2017

The cows must think I'm crazy. There are brown, white, and black ones all mixed together. Some dairy. Some beef. I know because I work in the beef industry and was raised by parents with dairy science degrees. The cows chew their cuds amicably and stare at me curiously over the fence.

I am sitting at the foot of my grandma's gravesite, weeping. This place struck me as absolutely beautiful in a simple and odd kind of way nearly a year ago when I stood right here with my family, burying our matriarch. Leave it to her to choose such a small cemetery surrounded by a cow pasture as her final resting place. She even requested a beautiful but plain wooden box handmade by Franciscan Monks to be her coffin before she died. She was a woman of no frills. I admire that.

Somehow, I find myself back here today. I'm not really a visit-the-gravesite kind of person. Grandma's not here anyway. In fact, I don't know if I've ever visited a graveyard of a loved one before today.

I'm not sure how I got here either. All I know is I was driving home from work trying to wrestle with all my thoughts and emotions and I wound up here. My chest hurts from trying to remain professional all day in the office, meeting with team members, restaurant and retail partners, as if life was normal. As soon as I sink into the green grass and look at the mounded dirt in front of me, the dam breaks. I can't hold the flood of tears back any longer. They come in waves, in sobs and wails. My diaphragm hurts from the strain. No one can hear me out here besides the cows and the headstones, so I let my guard down and cry as ugly and obnoxiously as I need. This is probably not the first time these cows have seen big emotion. The difference is, I'm not crying for my deceased relative.

I start praying, mumbling my thoughts aloud between moans. "What am I going to do, Grandma?" I cry. "How am I going to do this?" I know she's not here in this field but, man, I wish she was. I could use her wisdom and strength right about now. Surely she would know what to do. She raised seven kids and was an Emergency Room head nurse, for crying out loud. "I don't know how I'm going to do this," I repeat as if saying it over and over could help her hear.

Grandma was a petite but mighty woman. The kind of woman who you knew loved you fiercely and would always be there for you.

A couple years ago, I returned home from a work trip and discovered I didn't have a house key and Dan was still at work. I called Grandma who lived ten minutes down the road. I told her I was going to get out a ladder and climb to the second floor to get the AC unit out of the window so I could climb in.

"I'll call you once I'm in, so you know I'm okay, and if I don't call you in a few minutes then you know something's wrong," I said, somehow thinking this was a brilliant idea and I was being safe by letting someone know.

Of course, being much more sensible than I, and already having a paralyzed brother from a ladder situation gone awry, she firmly told me not to dare do such a thing and she would be over in a few minutes. Me being stubborn and Miss Independent I didn't listen, and by the time she showed up ten minutes later I was proudly waiting for her inside the house, the ladder and AC unit propped on the ground. Her less-than-impressed reaction wiped the grin off my face immediately.

"You'd better never pull a stunt like that again," she told me with fear in her voice and a sternness that would have made a dog pee down his leg. "Next time when I say wait, you wait," she looked one-and-a-half feet up at me with such intensity.

Yes ma'am. I absolutely will never pull a stunt like that again.

She was an independent lady who had strong faith and took no nonsense from anyone. She was full of common-sense wisdom. I remember once asking her what the secret to financial success was, observing that somehow, she and Grandpa successfully raised all seven kids and seemed to be comfortable in retirement years. How did she do it?

She laughed, "There is no secret, Emily. Just don't spend more money than you have. Period, end of story." I was disappointed at first, expecting a profound insight like where I should invest my money or something of that sort. But then I recognized the truth of her statement. In a world where credit cards and debt are commonplace, she bucked the system and lived on what she had. No more. No less.

That is the kind of wisdom I need today.

A fence lines three sides of the graveyard, keeping the cows from stepping on burial sites, and a country road lines the fourth. Clouds blow overhead wistfully while cars roll by the hilly field. Where could those people be driving that could mean anything worthwhile when my baby is not well? They go about their day, these clouds, these cars, these cows, as if life is normal. But life is not normal. Life is upside down, twisted. My baby is not okay. I might have to bury her soon like I buried Grandma. Accept this time the box will be tiny, holding a child who never breathed her first breath or took her first step. And what if she lives but her life is full of pain and struggle? I don't know if I can bear the burden either way. They say God doesn't give you more than you can handle. That simply cannot be true because I cannot handle this. Not on my own, anyway. Not without him.

After twenty minutes of letting all my emotion drain out of me and down my face, I finally melt into the grass with no tears left to cry. My face feels crusty, my lips salty.

Now what? I should go home to Dan. He's probably wondering where I am. But something keeps me here. I linger. The soft summer breeze dries up my cheeks while the humidity sticks to my arms and legs. An ant crawls over my barefoot. I had kicked my work heels off so I could feel the cool of the grass, though it is dry and a bit crunchy from the drought of the summer. I bet this ant has no idea what it's like to have a sick child. I envy him. His life is as simple as collecting food and avoiding getting trampled. Sounds luxurious.

I flick the ant off and pray for a few more minutes, this time with more control and focus. I need help. I don't know how to do this.

Then, peace. It washes over me like a fresh summer rain, and I hear in the back of my mind the unmistakable voice of Grandma, "You'll do it the same way I did, Emily. You'll do it one day at a time." And just as fast as she came, she was gone.

I smile. I should have known she could hear me. After all, she is in the presence of our Lord. Why wouldn't she be able to hear me?

I have a deep sense of knowing. Knowing beyond a shadow of doubt that God spoke to me through Grandma just now. For the first time since the original diagnosis, I feel real peace.

Grandma is right. I am going to do this the same way she did, one day at a time and with God's help. I stand up, brush the grass clippings and dirt off my skirt, slip my heels back on and walk to my car, waving goodbye to the cows, who have returned to grazing.

Chapter 6   A Whole New World

Journal Entry - Tuesday, August 15, 2017

Praise your name, Lord! Hallelujah! I don't even know how to thank you for your blessings. Today we learned that the amniocentesis test came back negative! I believe we are part of a miracle you're working. We will learn more tomorrow, and we know that doesn't necessarily mean we are in the clear. But it does mean we are one BIG step closer!

Wednesday, August 16, 2017

Notes float through the air. I spot the source of the beautiful sound. A piano in the corner of the vast reception area at Main Campus Cleveland Clinic. The sign beside it reads, "Music Therapy." It seems out of place amidst the buzz of people everywhere. Some walk briskly in various directions, others converse in small groups, still others are stretched out and lounging in stiff leather chairs. Some are in wheelchairs, others on crutches. Some on oxygen, others wearing masks. There is every race and nationality, every size and shape. I hear a couple speaking in a foreign language nearby. Some people are clearly just arriving at the hospital, looking around to find which direction they need to go, like us. Others are leaving, bags hanging off wheelchairs filled with discharge paperwork and bedside equipment.

I wonder about each of their stories. Besides the doctors and staff who work here, what required each of these people to spend their Wednesday afternoon at this enormous hospital? Where would they be if they didn't have to be here? Cleveland Clinic is acclaimed to be world-leading in many specialties, so I imagine they are each here for different reasons, different diagnoses. They all must have stories. Now we are one of them—people with a medical story who spend their days here, in the hospital.

This is a whole new world for us. Dan and I both have very healthy family members. We are, generally speaking, quite naive to the realities of major medical diagnoses. I'm on the edge of a whole new territory which no one in our family has journeyed, and I'm not sure which way to turn.

This place is a maze. I don't know where to go to find our appointment location. It took us a while to even figure out where to park after we drove the hour North. We went around and around in the parking garage until we reached the fifth floor and found an open spot. Then after taking an elevator, crossing a four-lane street, a bus lane, then hoofing it into the glass hospital doors, I was still sweating when Colleen Pope showed up. She told us to meet her here at the piano so she could escort us to our Genetics and Cardiology appointments.

Just two weeks ago, shortly after our amniocentesis, Colleen called me while I was on lunch break at work.

"Hi Emily, this is Colleen Pope. I'm a Fetal Care Coordinator and Dr. Carvalho connected me to your case. I understand your baby has been diagnosed with several medical anomalies," she paused. Her voice became soft and gentle, "I am so sorry. No parent should ever have to experience what you're going through." I sensed her true empathy and compassion, and it brought me to tears. I was at a loss for words for a moment. She said what I had been thinking but hadn't yet expressed. No parent *should* have to go through this. So, why was I?

Yet, here we are, preparing to meet with the Genetics department to review the amniocentesis results, followed by a Cardiology appointment to have a fetal echo of our baby's heart. I wish I'd paid more attention in my high school health and college animal reproduction classes when we learned about DNA and genetics.

Phenotype and genotype, X and Y chromosomes. Words come to mind, but I cannot remember exactly what they mean or how they affect a person's development. I'm not sure I even know what a fetal echo is. I suppose I am about to learn more medical terms than I ever thought I'd need to know. It feels like I'm back in my undergrad, this time earning my mom M.D.

Chapter 7 Echo Chamber

Tuesday, September 12, 2017

The sound alarms me. It's no wonder Baby keeps jumping and moving around. She must be practicing her somersaults in there because I keep feeling kicks and punches, butt scrapes and flips.

It sounds like I'm in a loud pinball machine one minute, then inside an old box computer with dial-up the next. The high-pitched squeals and beeping are giving me a headache. I've been inside this Magnetic Resonance Imaging (MRI) machine for what feels like hours, though it may very well have only been twenty minutes so far. They said this could take up to forty-five minutes, depending on how active the baby is. They need her to be still so they can get clear images of her brain and heart. Obviously, she's not complying. I'm glad she's active, though. That's a good sign that she's full of life.

My left arm tingles as it falls asleep. This would be an awkward and uncomfortable position for anyone to maintain on this rock-hard plastic table, let alone someone twenty-six weeks pregnant. My left hip aches and my big belly feels like it's hanging off me, pulling the muscles and tendons in my back with it. I'm lying on my left side with the flimsiest pillow to support my head. Some support. I could use about ten more pillows before I could get remotely comfortable in this big white tube.

Oh Lord, please let this be over soon! Please let them get the images they need.

"Uh, Emily, Baby seems to be very excited today, so I apologize but we haven't gotten the images we need. It's going to be a while longer. How are you doing?"

I can't see the technologist, but I know he's just a few yards away from me. He's in the corner of the MRI room standing behind glass windows, running the computer which controls this loud contraption.

"Fine," I lie. He told me before this miserable test started that if I move they have to start over with the imaging and it will take even longer. While I can't hold my baby still, I can hold myself still. If I can just lay here for a little longer, we can get this over with. If I tell him I'm uncomfortable he'll pull this table I'm lying on out of the machine, rearrange me and start over. There's no way I'm doing this again.

My face itches, like a little fine hair is tickling my cheek. I don't dare move to scratch. When I'm not allowed to move, I obsess with the desire to itch, twitch, adjust. My skin seems to crawl.

Goose bumps form on my arms and legs. This hospital gown doesn't do much in the way of warmth. Could they have created a more uncomfortable process to diagnose my baby's anomalies?

Looks like I'm going to be in here for a while. My thoughts shift away from my discomfort to my active baby. I hope her movement is not because she's scared from these noises. Oh, how I wish I could tell her everything will be alright. That there is nothing to fear. But, even if I could comfort her, I can't honestly say that. I don't know if everything will be alright. I am more scared than I've ever been.

It's been nearly seven weeks since that horrible twenty-week-gestation ultrasound when we discovered our baby is not well. All this time I have worked hard to keep certain thoughts at bay. But, lying here in this echo chamber with nothing left to distract me, I can't resist them any longer. They rush in like a flood.

Why is this happening to me, God? Why is this happening to a sweet innocent baby? To my sweet innocent baby?

I cannot fathom what it will be like if our child is stillborn. Holding my cold, blue baby in my arms. Her coffin the size of a shoe box. Or what it will be like if our child is alive and she dies right in front of us, shortly after the exhilarating high of giving birth to a breathing, crying, pink baby.

How will I ever survive her death, Lord?

Or suppose she survives. How can I possibly care for a child with major medical needs? I can barely take care of myself and a couple of rambunctious dogs. Just a few short months ago one of my Border Collie mix rescues bit the local veterinarian during a routine checkup and the doctor had to get stitches. That just about sent me over the edge with anxiety and worry, feeling like I'm a horrible dog mom. How can I possibly handle wheelchairs and feeding tubes, oxygen and medications for a *human*? Not just any human, for my child!

The now familiar sense of guilt jolts through me. How can I mourn the loss of my child when I haven't lost her yet? How can I moan about having a physically or mentally handicapped child when she's my child. I should be joyful. Does it mean I love her any less because I'm sad about her diagnoses and potential prognoses? The guilt drowns me, and I can't stop my tears. They flow freely and pool onto the cold white plastic table as the MRI machine whirs on. I stifle a sob and attempt to rein in the flood that threatens to overtake me, commanding the tears to stop.

They don't listen. They just keep flowing as if I am made of water.

Why, Lord? Why?

Journal Entry - Wednesday, September 13, 2017

Lord, help me to believe you. Teach me to overcome fear and anxiety with hope and trust in you. I have no idea how this will turn out for us and Baby Whiting, but I know you love us and will not forsake us. I have no idea what her health will look like, what our financial strain will be, how it will affect our marriage, our home or our work. But, God, none of that matters because it's all in your hands, and you already know how the story will unfold. Lord, teach Daniel and I full and complete trust. Help us to take our words of faith and turn them into true faithful belief. Only you can make "all things good for those who love you." Use this for your glory God and grant us the courage and faith to follow you day-by-day. Decision-by-decision.

Chapter 8   Testing Versus Trusting

Journal Entry - Friday, September 22, 2017

Good morning God,

Praise your name! Thank you for my husband's heart, for your loving encouragement, for never leaving or forsaking me, for Baby Girl's life, and for our family and friends.

Lord, doctors still think we may have to choose comfort care (aka end of life care) for our daughter when she's born, and they want to pursue more tests to find out what she may have so we can know before she's born. But part of me doesn't want to keep testing. I know she's in your hands. I know she'll be beautiful and is beautifully and wonderfully made. How far do we test before we simply trust? And, what good does it do to keep testing and worrying when in three short months she'll be here, and we will be able to see her for ourselves? Oh Lord, lead us. Guide the doctors, Daniel, and I that we may provide the care you want us to and that she needs, without depending so heavily on doctors and tests that we forget to simply have faith in you. Help us to know when to say enough is enough.

Oh God, I know you love Baby Whiting more than Daniel and I do, which is crazy. I know you are forming her in my womb. I know she's beautifully and wonderfully made. I know she was made so that she may have a relationship with you and so she may have life abundantly.

I don't know what her future holds. I don't know if you'll choose to heal her or not. I don't know if she'll survive and if she does, I don't know what survival looks like. But I do know you're capable of radical healing and I know you will use this for your glory and all our good. Oh God lead us. Help us to trust you. Teach us. Your will be done.

Amen.

Testing Versus Trusting

There is a fine line between testing and trusting, though they are not mutually exclusive.

Sometimes, testing is trusting.

Testing is trusting that God places people, science, and medicine in our lives to help us care for our children to the best of our ability.

Other times, testing is not trusting, but an attempt at controlling an otherwise uncontrollable situation.

So, how do you know the difference? After endless testing with our baby, here's what I've learned about the line between testing and trusting—when the results of the test can potentially help you care for your child best and when the benefits of the gained knowledge outweigh the risks to the mother and child, then testing is trusting.

Conversely, when the results of the test are simply for information's sake and when the risks outweigh the benefits, or when gaining the results is intended to help determine if a parent will intentionally terminate their child's life, then testing is no longer trusting, but grasping at control.

It's a fine line, this testing and trusting, and one that each parent has to discern for themselves in their given situation. For instance, when we chose to proceed with the amniocentesis, we understood the results could help us save our baby's life by helping us prepare any intervention needed for her well-being. The potential benefits outweighed the risks. So, at the time, going forward with that particular test was an act of trust. Knowing what I know now, however, the amniocentesis ultimately did not show us helpful results for our baby's particular developmental challenges and the mental and emotional toll on me over the risk of inducing labor and miscarriage was, in hindsight, absolutely not worth it. The benefit in our specific situation, in hindsight, did not outweigh the risk in my opinion. We of course had no way of knowing that until we did it.

If ever found in a similar situation again with a future pregnancy, I would not choose to proceed with an amniocentesis. But another family might choose otherwise due to their own special circumstances and that's okay.

The bottom line is this—so long as we are making our decisions from a place of love and care for ourselves and our children, then testing can and is a very helpful tool in the process toward healing, and it does not signify you trust God any less.

Chapter 9   Fear

Journal Entry - Tuesday, September 26, 2017

Good morning Lord,

We humans are so frail. I read about the Israelites and how they doubted you over and over and over again. We are no different. Our flesh gets in the way of our faith. Our fears overwhelm us and lead us to doubt and resentment.

Oh Lord, Daniel is very afraid about our finances and the potential cost of Baby Whiting. I fear the unknown, too. Oh Lord teach us not to cling to the false security of money and possessions but to cling to hope in you alone. We know you will provide for us, one day, one moment, one meal, one bill at a time. Show us how to prepare our hearts and our home to welcome Baby Girl into this world with all the joy you intend in her new life. Grant Daniel peace and hope in you. I pray you overwhelm him, and me, with the realization that you will provide.

Praise your name.

Amen.

Thursday, September 28, 2017

The first thing I see when I walk in is a small note card sitting on my desk chair. I did not leave that here yesterday. What does it say and who is it from?

I take off my light-weight jacket and hang it on the back of the office door. I really need to ask our maintenance team if they could oil my door hinges because they squeak so loud. I notice every single morning I walk in, yet by the time I sit at my computer long enough to send them an email, I get sucked into the vortex that is my inbox and forget all about the door.

I put my black leather briefcase on the floor under the L-shaped desk, pick up the card and plop on the chair. I cross my legs under my baby bump and a small clump of sand and mud falls off my heels onto the carpet. Ugh. We've got to finish building our patio at home because the mess it's making of my shoes and our house, of everything, is driving me batty.

I text Dan, asking him if he plans on working on the patio tonight when he gets home from work. He's been slaving away at this project for months in the summer heat, and now, amidst the falling leaves. Lately if he's not working, running, or hunting, I can count on finding him out back meticulously placing each patio stone.

He's quite the handyman. I love this about him, among many other things. I really don't think there's anything he can't fix or build, so long as he can find how-to videos on YouTube. It's impressive what he has accomplished so far, not only in our backyard but in our entire home. We bought this 1860's fixer upper when we were engaged, counting on both of our abilities to paint, scrape, fix and redo, pinching pennies at every opportunity. With a little more sweat equity, this house will be very comfortable to raise a young family. It's not the long-term place, but it is the perfect "starter home" as they say.

But then, will we be able to keep the house and still afford to care for our daughter? The question haunts me. I casually joke we will soon live in a cardboard box with all our looming medical bills, but under the mask of humor, I fear we might have to sell our house and live on peanut butter and ramen noodles. Did we work this hard to be financially secure only to lose it all to medical bills? Dan and I keep ourselves busy to avoid thinking about it too hard.

While he's currently laser focused on building this beautiful backyard for our growing family, I had the hair-brained idea to paint the nursery. Oh, and a bathroom and hallway while I'm at it because, hey, I'll already have the sander, ladder and paint brushes out, right? That explains why there's gray and blue paint smears on my knuckles. It's not a terribly professional look. It's a good thing my coworkers are all do-it-yourselfers, too. They get it.

The halls are mostly empty now anyway, with most of them gone executing our biggest event of the year that we've all worked for months to prepare. I am supposed to be with them for our Annual Conference at the Omni Nashville Hotel. I was planning to deliver two presentations to rooms full of attendees, sharing our latest brand research and launching our newest app.

I wish I was with them, seeing our hard work come to fruition and mingling with customers who have become like friends and family. Then again, how could I ever repay my team who pulled together and willingly took on my speaking roles so I could stay close to home for the baby.

I boot up my computer and while waiting, I look down to read the card that's still in my other hand. I can't help but smile.

It says, "*Generous God, you draw us into surprising stories. Use them to disrupt our complacency and remove our fear, that we may follow you into the joy of your kingdom. In the name of the one who taught us not to lose heart, we pray.*"

There's no name on the card, but I know it came from one of my team members who must have dropped it on my chair on their way out the door to Tennessee.

I have the best team anyone could ask for—passionate, professional, incredibly capable, successful, and compassionate men and women. What an honor it is to work among them.

When I didn't return to the office that afternoon after our twenty-week ultrasound, they suspected something was awry. When I still didn't show up the next day, my phone flooded with concerned texts. After mustering the will power to brush my teeth, get dressed, climb in my car and return a couple days later, the love and support whelmed me in the best of ways.

They continue to surprise me. This card is one example of many ways they help me survive these days. They've given me so much hope. My boss told me to cancel any travel plans I need to, so I can be here for all our appointments in Cleveland. I'm used to traveling several times a month all over the country and into Canada. Lately my suitcase collects dust while I spend my days in Wooster, Ohio, at our main office, so I can easily take off and be in Cleveland within an hour.

In between all these appointments, though, coming to work is helpful to fill my time with something meaningful to do. It keeps me busy, and my jam-packed schedule doesn't allow my thoughts or worries to drag me down all day long. While I'm here, I can put my personal life aside for a few hours and focus on something predictable, reliable, known, rather than all the uncertainty of our family's future, which seemed so secure just a few short weeks ago.

The dual monitors blink on and I sip on decaf black coffee while skimming through the latest emails from last night, making sure none are absolutely pressing before I join the remaining crew downstairs to watch the live-streamed Annual Conference opening session. I briefly flip to my Outlook email screen over to the calendar page. There's an appointment titled Baby Whiting Prayer.

At noon a handful of team members will gather in a meeting room, circle up, hold hands, and pray for Baby Girl Whiting. Pray for whatever tests are coming up, pray for healing, pray for strength. This has been going on for about a month now. Every Thursday at lunchtime about ten team members, sometimes more, sometimes fewer, depending on travel and work schedules, voluntarily give the first ten minutes of their lunch hour to pray for our baby, for me, and for Dan. I cry every time.

This is not something I organized, either. It was all organically driven by incredible coworkers I'm also blessed to call my friends. How did I get to work for such a unique company where I not only love what I do, but I love who I do it with, too? I know most people aren't as fortunate as I.

I wish Dan could be here for these weekly prayer circles. I'm sure he would be equally as moved by them as I am. I hope he feels supported by his coworkers, too, though we work in very different industries with vastly different occupations. He is a Welding Engineer

Manager, spending his days building huge energy vessels in a factory with a team of welding engineers. I am an Assistant Director of Brand Research and Marketing, working with a team of brand managers on promoting premium beef. While our end products are worlds different, at the end of the day we both work with people who are husbands, wives, fathers, mothers, sons, and daughters. People who are moved by these crazy fetal diagnoses we've received and who want to help any way they can.

Little notes like this one energize me, refocus me, remind me fear doesn't have to rule me. I am going to give my all to this company and to these people today like they keep giving to me. I hope I can love them as well as they love me.

 ## Financial Fears

The fear of the unknown regarding looming medical bills and all the added cost of medical complexities almost paralyzed us, especially because the world of insurance and billing was foreign. Dan and I were convinced our dreams of ever being financially stable again were dashed with our daughter's diagnoses. But, if I could sit down with myself then, knowing what I know now, I would reassure myself that we would be okay, no cardboard box necessary.

I would tell myself this situation is the reason we have insurance. It's the reason we have an emergency fund. It's the reason we humble ourselves and accept help when offered (more on that later). I would tell myself that there are social workers and financial advisors whose careers are focused on helping families stay afloat in crises like this one. I would reassure myself that with a little diligence and a whole lot of faith, we would be just fine financially, no matter how the story unfolds.

Chapter 10 Identity in Christ

Journal Entry - Tuesday, October 3, 2017

Good morning God,

I can hear the devil's thoughts rattling around in my head.

"You're not qualified to talk about God's design for sex and marriage. You don't know enough about it. You're in over your head. What if they see through you and know you're not trained to speak about these things? You might drive people further away from God rather than closer."

And on and on he goes. Oh Lord, make his noise silence so the only noise I hear is your reassurance and direction. Push the devil aside. Tell him to go to you know where. Lead me, Oh Lord. Guide me with what you want me to say and help me to have the wisdom to say just that, no more and no less. Oh Lord, lead me.

Praise your name,

Amen

Thursday, October 5, 2017

I stare intently into the faces of the young men and women gathered tonight for my sequel talk titled *Five Truths About God & Sex*. I lower my voice and walk confidently into the middle of the group, drawing them in and beckoning them to listen closely.

"Seven years ago, I sat right here in this very church and confessed to Father Larry. After I told him all I'd done between sobs and tears, he extended so much love and compassion to me. Then he said, 'I want you to go home, and I want you to write a letter to God. I want you to tell him everything you've told me.' Then, 'I want you to wait three days and write a letter back to yourself of what you think Jesus would tell you.' I am going to read those letters to you now." I step back to the speaker's stand and pick up two white envelopes. I carefully extract the letters and unfold them. They are wrinkled and worn from the countless times I've read them since that life-changing confession nearly a decade ago.

I take a deep breath, trying to calm my nerves. I'm about to reveal a deeply personal conversation between me and the Lord. My kneecaps are literally shaking. But 25 sets of eyes are looking intently at me, eagerly waiting. I can't let them down now.

The first letter, dated October 24, 2010, is addressed from me to God. I read, *"Dear Lord, I come to you today completely humbled and in awe of your love for me. I have sinned greatly against you and against myself. I have pushed aside the truth and your love for something I knew would come between you and I … I pray that you can forgive me fully and invite me back into your arms with love and understanding …"* I continue reading the page-and-a-half letter to the Catholic Young Professionals Group, a conference room full of 20 and 30-year-olds in various stages of post-graduate degrees and professions.

"Those three days were excruciating, but he did write back to me," I chuckle, recognizing how crazy I must sound. "I mean, I wrote back to me, but I think it's really powerful what he wrote through me … I really think the priest knew what he was saying when he said to ask God to speak to me and write the letter, because these are amazing words that could have only come from him. I would have never had so much grace with myself nor the wisdom."

I begin reading the second letter dated October 26, 2010.

"*To my dearest daughter Emily, you have sinned. You have knowingly pushed me and my love away for a man's who is not committed to you as I am. He does not treasure you as I do, he has not died for you as I have,*" I reread this beginning of the letter again because it holds such important truths, I want the audience to really take them in.

"*He does not treasure you as I do. He has not died for you as I have.*" After a long pause, I resume reading.

"*I have heard your call for me. I have remained with you through the darkness, and you have reached out for me once more. Don't let go of me Emily. I will carry all of your worries and fears, loneliness and dissatisfaction on my shoulders so that you may live for me. You have recognized your wrongdoing and have boldly corrected what was broken. You have come back to me. Your sin is fully forgiven and tomorrow I will not remember its mere existence. So cry no longer, be strong in my arms and be the Emily I have made you to be. Go into the world and serve my people, love my people, but most of all, love me and yourself for who you are in me. Take courage and never lose sight of who I am. I love you. I am proud of you and I feel your sincerity in your cries. Fear not. I still love you more than you can imagine and you are forgiven.*"

I look up from the speaker's stand and put the letter down, scanning the room to make eye contact with my listeners. A young woman's gaze fixes on mine, and I see deep emotion stir behind her knowing eyes. A young man fidgets, staring at his tennis shoes grinding on the carpet.

"I hope as I'm reading you can almost insert yourself into this because I know he didn't just write it for me. He wrote a love letter to all of you in the Bible and he wants this kind of intimacy with you as well …he wants a deeply personal relationship with you and I." The young man looks up with conflict written all over his face. I wonder what's stirring in his heart and mind right now. I make a mental note to catch him at the end and talk one-on-one.

I go on for another thirty minutes recapping the five truths about God and sex we discussed at our last gathering in March, emphasizing the goodness, beauty, and holiness that sex truly is, the power of it, the way it was created as the closest example to the kind of relationship God desires with us. I clarify for those who are confused by this that God is not sexual, but he does desire a relationship with us that can be best likened to the kind of relationship you find in a holy marriage that brings two people together freely, fully, faithfully, and fruitfully. I talk about how he desires a relationship with me and each of them that is figuratively "naked and unashamed."

He desires an intimate relationship with you, I say. Intimacy. In-to-me-see.

Then I dive into answering their questions they submitted at the end of the last session. We get to their third question which is, how do I deal with rejection? The question is about the unavoidable rejection that is part of dating.

I hadn't wanted to bring up the challenges with our baby, though the fact that I'm pregnant is obvious, since not only is my belly expanded to watermelon status, but I also am short of breath every time I give talks these days. But sharing our story is relevant in answering their question. I give them the two-minute version of what's happened over the last ten weeks.

"Here's why I'm telling you this," I say, again walking into the crowd to really capture their attention. "Dan and I were praying the other night and at the end he said, 'You know what Emily, I'm really glad we praise God and not each other.' And I said, 'Why's that?' He said, 'Well, because if we were trying to find 100% comfort in each other this would be really hard'."

"I mean it is hard. Let's be real. It's really hard. But we find support in each other, but we aren't each other's Gods. We can still turn to each other and turn to God and that's a beautiful thing. I share this to let you know that there are going to be lots of bumps in the road, there's going to be lots of challenges in your life, and making sure your identity is in Christ, and your relationship with your significant other is the cherry on top, is going to really help you navigate those bumps as you go along because they are going to happen. That doesn't mean Dan and I aren't in it together. It doesn't mean he's not an incredible support for me and vice versa, I hope, but it does mean God's really the one pulling us through, and we are able to turn to him before we turn to each other." I pause.

"So in answer to the question, how to deal with rejection, I don't have any magical answers and it certainly doesn't take the pain of rejection away, but it makes it a lot easier to navigate when your identity is not in what other people think of you, but that you know you are beautiful, you are loved, you are a child of God, you are the image and likeness of God. That does not replace your pain, but it certainly does help keep it in perspective."

The room is quiet and fixated on me. Is that because I just shared profound wisdom or because everyone sympathizes with me and our situation with our baby? I don't know but sharing the reality of our situation seems to have a sobering effect on everyone and helps get my point across plainly.

Journal Entry - Wednesday, October 25, 2017

Good morning Lord,

I am struggling to maintain my energy. To remain focused and invested in work. To not let the little things bother me. To remember I'm not in this alone.

God, our daughter might not make it. And if she does, she will have a long road of surgeries and therapies. She may be mentally and/or physically handicapped. She needs to be a fighter.

Oh God, I am not strong enough to be her mama through all this. I need your strength. I need your comfort. I need your peace. We may lose her. Or we may have lifelong struggles, or we may have struggles upfront and she'll be okay after that. We have no way of knowing. But we do know we love her with all our hearts.

We know we are so grateful for her life and that we get to be her parents.

God help us be the parents she needs. I can't do this alone, Lord. Father, fill my heart with your love, presence, and peace.

Chapter 11 Showered with Love

Journal Entry - Saturday, October 28, 2017

Good morning Lord,

This week I must admit while I've gotten through, I've been so sad. Sad for our daughter and the struggle that's ahead of her. Sad for the loss we may experience. Sad for the heartache we know is ahead of us. Just sad.

I'm not mad. I don't question why. I'm not anxious (though I have and will continue to struggle with all of those feelings). Right now, I'm just sad.

Oh Lord, I want to be close to you, and yet the only thing keeping us distant is me. I resist you even when I know you're the only one who could make me feel whole and alive and hopeful. God, I need you.

Lord, help me to lean into you with my sadness. Help me to need you through it all and to have the energy to come to you. Don't let me do this alone, even though I'll likely try. Lord, break my independent will and teach me what true trust and faith in you looks like. Lead me, oh Lord.

Sunday, November 5, 2017

Corn husks and pumpkins decorate the entrance of the Medina, Ohio, event center, matching the fall weather. I hike up my cotton form-fitting dress and run for cover under the patio roof, dodging raindrops.

I don't think I dressed appropriately. This ankle-length black maternity dress seems a little grim for the joyous occasion. This morning when I was picking an outfit from my closet I thought my pink pumps and costume jewelry would add enough color to brighten my wardrobe. Now I'm regretting not buying a more festive dress. A more fun dress than this morbid black one, slimming as it may be.

None of my normal clothes fit anymore, so I'm limited to either super baggy clothes or spending money on maternity clothes. Right now, spending money on anything but what's absolutely necessary seems irresponsible, given we don't know how much a birth in the Specialty Care Unit, a Neonatal Intensive Care Unit stay, a possible funeral and/or multiple surgeries and endless therapies are going to cost.

Over the last few weeks, we have spent countless hours painstakingly reviewing our insurance plan, discussing potential costs with my mom's sister who is a pediatrician. She is helping us go over the fine print—just how much cash do we need to pull together to be able to afford this? Thinking about it makes my head hurt.

Dan and I have never hit our out-of-pocket insurance maximum, nor even come close. This is all so new. Our research tells us if Baby Girl survives, we will likely hit that maximum within the first few hours after delivery. Then it's the extra costs of uninsured therapies and any needed medical equipment that leaves a big question mark regarding how much we will rack up.

Thank God Daniel and I have been diligent with our finances ever since we got married, saving for that emergency we never thought we'd actually experience. Even so, the looming expenses weigh heavy on our minds. After we pay all the medical bills, will we be able to afford our mortgage and normal monthly cash flow? I know I need to trust God will provide. *Saying* I trust God is one thing, but this is really putting my trust to the test. Do I *really*?

I get to the covered porch and let my dress drop back down, smoothing it out before entering the party. An extra $60 on a fun dress might have been money well-spent, despite our financial stresses. It would have helped me feel more joyful and less apprehensive walking into this baby shower.

As soon as I get through the double doors I'm met with beautiful, smiling, familiar faces. My worries and apprehension fall to the backdrop of my mind as I hug each aunt, cousin, and friend. I'm wiping tears away as I look around and note the many wonderful women gathered today to celebrate Baby Girl Whiting with me. I see some in the room who came from Illinois, Indiana, Virginia, Southern and Western Ohio.

Do they all know our circumstances? Do they know this sweet babe may not survive? Judging by the pile of gifts, perhaps not. Then again, everyone should have heard by now. I just don't know how far word has reached. Do I tell them? Or will bringing up the diagnoses dampen everyone's cheerful mood?

It all seems just a little fake, celebrating as if this is a baby who will be born crying, pink and healthy. Yet, I'm so grateful my family and friends decided to celebrate this baby, because she is worth celebrating.

Aunt Hannah brings me a virgin mimosa and says, "Here you go, beautiful mama!" I laugh and take a sip before going to check out all the incredible decorations and the delicious spread these ladies pulled together. I feel like royalty. They really went all out. There are tiers of desserts, popcorn, small sandwiches, and finger foods. Each person here contributed in one way or another and it makes my heart overflow with love for them. Whether they know or not, they sure are making this mama feel special.

My own mom is across the room, finalizing the dessert table spread and chatting with a long-time family friend. She's laughing and smiling. Her joyous sound is like balm on my hurting heart. These last few weeks have been so hard on her too, watching me, her baby girl, go through this crazy situation.

She was apprehensive about having this party to begin with, carefully and lovingly suggesting maybe we should wait until after the baby is born. All logic told me she was right. Why have a party and collect nursery items that may never be used? Why complete a nursery only for it to become a painful shrine reminding me of the baby who did not survive?

But logic wasn't on my side. Blame it on raging pregnancy hormones or mama bear resurfacing. Either way, I became indignant at Mom's suggestion to wait for a party until after our daughter's birth. I transferred all my apprehension about how this pregnancy might end, and even my dread of how the world might treat my daughter if she survived and had endless anomalies and complications, to my mother who was trying to spare me from more pain than necessary. My fears were directed inappropriately at Mom, who was trying to help in the most loving way she knew how. Nevertheless, she caught the brunt of my emotion.

"I don't want to wait, Mom," I said through gritted teeth. "I want to set up the nursery and be ready for the baby to come home, and if we don't have a shower until after her birth, how am I going to do that?" My voice shook.

"I just don't want to get ahead of ourselves," she said cautiously. While I couldn't see it in the heat of the moment, seeing Mom today I now recognize the irony—she was trying to protect her baby girl from further pain if we lose this baby, while I was trying to protect my baby girl from possibly not making it.

It's such a dance, this wondering and waiting—a dance between hope and realism. Realistically, Mom was right. We probably shouldn't have this shower for all the reasons that make logical sense. Why gather everyone now to celebrate when we very well may turn around and bring the very same people together at her gravesite in just a few short weeks?

My young nieces bring me gift bag after gift box, eagerly sitting at my feet and helping pull ribbons off each package. Their mother, my sister-in-law, gently reminds them to "Let Aunt Emily open the gifts." I hope my daughter is pulling ribbons off packages at someone else's shower someday. What a gift that would be.

They bring over one of the last gifts and I recognize the wrapping. Mom's. She's been working on making a baby quilt and I have a sneaking suspicion that's what's inside. I helped pick out the pattern and fabric but have not seen the final product. Mom has also thoughtfully sourced fabric for a burial cloth, if needed, which I have not seen and I hope never to.

My niece's chubby sweet fingers rip the ribbon off and pull tissue paper out of the bag, revealing a gorgeous soft pink and sage green floral hand-quilted blanket. I pull it out and unfold it, taking in the intricate, beautiful, and meticulously crafted blanket. On the back bottom corner there is a note sewn into the fabric that reads "Made with love by Claire Foley Kuhn, Sponsored by Phil Kuhn, November 2017 (aka Grandma and Grandpa)."

Mom's dancing this dance with me, too, between hope and realism, trying to figure out the next steps. I look across the room at her and see we both have tears running down our cheeks. We exchange knowing smiles of love and support through the pain.

 Family Dynamics and Mourning

When facing devastating diagnoses, it's not only the child's parents who mourn, but the family and friends, too. This may seem obvious, but parents on the front lines caring for their child often have little energy to recognize and empathize with their support system's grief. A simple awareness that they too are grieving can help parents have grace with family and friends, knowing everyone deals with loss and pain differently.

Chapter 12 Elephant in the Room

Thursday, November 9, 2017

"Where do you want the crib?" Dan asks as he piles the Pampers and Huggies diaper boxes in a corner of the room, trying to clear some space. The circles under his eyes are prominent tonight in the dim light. He moves slowly, giving away his weariness.

"I was thinking along this inside wall, so she doesn't get too cold on an outside wall, and so she's away from the heater vent and doesn't get hot air blown on her all winter," Dan says, pointing to the longest wall in this cozy little bedroom, now turned nursery.

"I agree, that sounds good," I nod. "Check out this sticker decoration I found. I think it'll be perfect beside the crib." I eagerly show him my latest Hobby Lobby find.

Once assembled, the package shows it will read, "You are Fearfully & Wonderfully Made." The scripture verse is in a soft, feminine font surrounded by a wreath of pink flowers and sage green leaves, matching Mom's quilt. I can't think of a more fitting decoration for our daughter's bedroom.

I hope she internalizes this truth, that she is fearfully and wonderfully made. But why would God fearfully and wonderfully make a child who is destined for pain and suffering? He had the power to make her healthy, yet he didn't.

Why?

I brush the question aside. I may never know the answer and I'll go crazy if I fixate on trying. What I do know is God loves this child more than I can even imagine. More than I love her. Which is astounding. So, if he loves her that much and he made her develop the way she did in utero, he must have some kind of plan much greater than my feeble mind can comprehend. While all I see is suffering, pain and heartache ahead, he must see something beautiful. I hope I can stay strong and patient enough to see what he sees.

 ## Why Would a Good God Let Kids Suffer?

This question—why would a good God let a child suffer—is one I do not have an answer for, but every parent faced with their suffering child wrestles with.

Sure, I can give theological answers like, God gave us freedom and in that freedom humanity chose sin and with sin comes suffering. Like, God never causes pain and suffering but rather allows it. Like, his ways are not our ways, and his ways always lead to the good of those who love him even when we don't understand.

While these answers are true, they hardly satisfy when you're the parent watching your child suffer unspeakable pain. These answers simply don't cut it. They don't begin to adequately answer the parent's heart cry for justice.

One thing I do know is there is no shame in asking the question and pressing for answers in humble, earnest prayer, recognizing his ways truly are not ours and we may never know the answer (or at least be satisfied with it) on this side of heaven.

I push a laundry basket of newborn baby clothes, tags still attached, aside so we can start carrying in the various crib parts. Dan looks briefly over the assembly instructions and says, "I'm going to get a screwdriver and hammer." I reach out and touch his shoulder as he walks past me toward the stairs. He stops and turns toward me, pulling me in for a surprisingly strong and tender embrace. I melt into him and hold on tight, hold on for dear life. I need his steady, quiet strength.

I take a deep breath and my nose fills with the smell of fresh paint. Mom and I just cleaned up our paint supplies last week before moving in all the baby shower "loot" as I jokingly call it. Who knew so much stuff came with a tiny human?

Petey whines and circles us as Dan pulls back. Dan checks out the wall sticker I'm still holding, then looks me in the eye as if about to say something. Instead, he pulls me in for a kiss, and another, before turning and starting down the stairs to get the required tools.

Petey eagerly follows Dan, happy to have something to do with his nervous energy. I put down the decoration so I can return to the mission at hand. I walk to the hallway and grab an armful of white and gray painted wood and silver screws. Heading back into the nursery, I accidentally kick something soft. I look down around my awkward load and protruding belly to see a stuffed elephant that fell out of one of the many boxes holding baby supplies and gifts. I gently sweep it out of the way with my bare foot. I really need to sort through everything, but step one is building this crib.

The boys return with the necessary tools and Dan sits on the floor to start construction. Petey follows suit, plopping right in the middle of my wood pile, tongue hanging out the corner of his mouth, panting.

"Do you mind, Petey?" Dan chuckles and ruffles his black floppy ears. Petey licks Dan's hand as if begging to be comforted. He has always been a nervous dog but tonight he seems extra anxious, picking up on Dan and my apprehension. While Dan starts assembling the backboard and railings, I help him sort through the parts and hold pieces while he screws them together. I used to pride myself on being super handy, wielding a hammer and nail with confidence. Then I met Dan and decided he can accomplish tasks like this one in half the time it takes me. So, I gladly step aside so he can run the show.

We both try to focus on the task at hand but the real elephant in the room is suffocating. This should be joyful, preparing for our first baby, together. This should be exciting. It's anything but.

I'm surprised we assemble the crib fairly quickly. I lower the new mattress in and lay Mom's quilt over the back rail.

"It's really hard to build a crib we both know our baby may never sleep in," Dan cuts the silence and finally voices what's running through both our minds. Dan's eyes fill with tears. We've become accustomed to crying often, growing comfortable with frequent outbursts of emotion. There's not been a day since the 20-week ultrasound that at least one of us has not cried.

I hoped maybe if I didn't say it out loud, it wouldn't be something Dan was thinking too, and we could try to enjoy this big milestone. I was hoping his weariness and silence tonight was just due to a long work week. I thought maybe if I kept quiet the prognosis of our child wouldn't overshadow this project, like every other aspect of the second half of our pregnancy has been overshadowed.

I take a deep breath and sigh, releasing tension I didn't realize I was carrying. Now that Dan put words to what we both feel, I am relieved. Thank God I don't have to act like everything is fine around Dan. I should have known better than to have tried.

Chapter 13 While I'm Waiting

Saturday, November 18, 2017

"How do we pursue God in the meantime? How do we ensure we are becoming the person God created us to be while we are in the waiting, so that when we have the opportunity to be intimate with someone else we are ready to welcome that kind of intimacy and we are truly going to be able to accept the incredible beauty God designed it to be?" I look through bright stage lights out into a room full of more than 100 high school kids at their fall *LifeTeen* retreat.

I continue, "Trusting God in the area of intimacy and sex is hard and it is rare." Or really in any area of life, especially the most challenging ones, I think to myself.

"I don't want to paint this picture that now that we've had this talk it's going to be super easy to just wait for your deep desires for intimacy to be fulfilled. It's not! It's hard! And that's why I've tripped up so many times in my life. But anything worthwhile is worth waiting for. Is there anything you've wanted so badly but you couldn't get it until you reached X milestone?," I ask. I try to quickly think of relevant examples for this age group. "Like you have to wait until Christmas Day? Or until football season starts? Whatever it is, anything worthwhile is worth waiting for."

Am I speaking to these kids or to myself? I'm speaking truth into my own weary, impatient bones, waiting to see what God's going to do with our baby, if he's going to answer my prayer for her life. Waiting to see if he's going to pull our family through this devastating situation.

"Galatians says, *Let us not grow _tired_ of doing good, for in due time we shall _reap_ our harvest, if we do not give up.* And Romans reiterates and says, *but if we hope for what we do not see, we wait for it with _endurance_.*" I elaborate, "Another word for endurance is patience. But patience is my least favorite thing ... so the really cool thing I've learned is that waiting is not a passive act," I pace the stage with my now beach-ball-sized belly. I share a few examples of my mishaps with patience in the arena of relationships.

I talk about how waiting is not an idle act of surrender but an active decision to pursue God fervently and pursue the person God created each of us to be. "Do not mistake waiting as giving up or simply letting life happen to you. It's a time of preparation for what God has in store," I say, letting this truth sink deep into my aching soul.

"It can feel very confusing, like God's holding out on you or like he's telling you you can't have this thing that you really want. But he's not holding out on you or me. He's holding something so much better for you and he wants to shape and mold you into the person

92

that's ready to accept it," I say with conviction.

I give the most relevant example I can for this group of 13 to 18-year-olds, "So, going back to this boy I told you I broke up with my junior year of college, I called him back, like a crazy person, two years later. We hadn't talked once … I left him a voicemail and I'm pretty sure I sounded like I was dying because I needed him to call me back," I laugh at myself and the audience chuckles. "He did call me back. And the call lasted for four minutes and four seconds and here's how it went." I lift my hand to my ear as if it's a phone, "'Hi, this is Emily. I'm the girl that broke your heart two years ago. I broke up with you and I'm really sorry, and I've never gotten over you and I just needed to tell you that.' Really long silence … painful. He finally responds, 'Uh, can I call you back?' Long story short, he did call me back and we ended up getting married."

The whole room erupts with "awwww" and they start clapping.

"He's in the back of the room, not to make him blush but …" I laugh as everyone turns to see Dan standing in the back of the room.

"God's not holding out on you, he's holding something so much better for you," I repeat, smiling. If God could write such an incredible love story for Dan and me, surely he's going to do the same for our daughter. I must hold on to this truth when the waiting and wondering wears me thin.

Chapter 14 Melt Down

Monday, November 20, 2017

I've heard so many good things about this place and have wanted to try it for years. My coworkers say it is delicious and has some funky menu items. Any other day, maybe I'd be excited to try a gourmet grilled cheese sandwich and thick cut french fries. I look over the Melt Bar menu several times but can't seem to make sense of it, my thoughts hard to rein in and focus.

"Have you decided what you'd like to order?" the waitress asks. I wish that was the only decision I needed to make.

My brain feels like marbles bouncing in a glass jar. Garbled and loud, unorderly. "What's your favorite thing here?" I hear myself ask the question I always ask at restaurants.

"The Chorizo and Potato Sandwich is delicious, I just ate one myself," she replies.

My stomach lurches at the thought of trying to down anything, let alone all those carbs. But that's probably how I'll feel regardless of what I order, even if it's a green salad. "I'll take that," I say.

The waitress writes down our order, collects our menus and walks back to the kitchen. Dan reaches across the table and grabs my hand.

"We need to consider your health and survival. If your life comes into question, your health has to come first," Dan says with conviction. He adds, "Without you, there is no baby." Underneath his comment, I hear his fear of raising a medically complex child by himself.

I pull my hand away, annoyed. "My health isn't in question, Dan. I'm going to be fine." If only my health *was* in question and not our daughter's. If I could take our daughter's place, I would a million times over. Why does my daughter have to face all these challenges while I'm perfectly healthy? My heart feels like it's ripping out of my chest.

"I'm just saying if your health ever *becomes* a question, we need to take care of you first," Dan clarifies.

"I don't care what happens to me. I want our baby to *live*," I hiss. Dan goes quiet. I stare at the swinging kitchen door where the waitress disappeared, willing her to return with our food so we can be distracted from this conversation.

When she doesn't come, I get up. "I'll be back," I say as I walk to the ladies room. I need to collect myself before I say something I regret. Dan is scared. So am I. I love him. I love our daughter. He loves me. He loves our daughter. We are in this together. Remember that. I look at myself in the mirror above the bathroom sink and try to blend my makeup to cover the tear streaks on my cheeks. It's no use.

I take a deep breath, put my hands on my belly reassuring myself she's still there. I pray she can't hear our conversation. I don't want her to ever question her value, my life versus hers, though I know that's not what Dan meant.

When I can no longer linger in the bathroom to pass the time, I reluctantly return to our table. Sitting there are two heaping plates of sandwiches. I sit down and watch the steam curl up and disappear. How am I going to fit any of this cheese and bread in between the dread that fills my stomach? It feels like a stone is blocking my throat.

"Dr. Carvalho says to enjoy our time together this week as best we can, rest and prepare for what's ahead. He says you and I need to decide how far we will go with intervention before we opt for comfort care," I figure maybe if I say what's really the problem at hand, get it out of our heads and onto the table, this dread will come out too and make room for me to eat. I need to eat. We left our respective workplaces this morning and met to drive the hour North to Cleveland for our seventh fetal echo in four months. Then we drove a half-an-hour South to Dr. Carvalho's office in Independence for a maternal-fetal check-up. It's 4:00 p.m. and we haven't had lunch.

"How does any parent make that decision? How would we know how far to go?" I ask through a fresh stream of tears. These blasted tears. I'm sick of them. I've cried more in the last few months than maybe my whole life combined. I take a long drink of water to replenish my seemingly bottomless well.

Dan is pale. His eyes red-rimmed. "Well, let's hope it never comes to that, but I don't want to keep her alive just for our sake. If she's going to basically be on life support for the rest of her life, then I don't want to do that to her. But, if it's a matter of surgeries, wheelchairs, and therapies, then of course we are going to do all we can."

"I guess as long as there is a next step to take in her healing, then we are going to take that next step," I say hesitantly, saying out loud what's in my head to see if it sounds right once given airtime. Yes, that's right.

Then with resolve, "As long as God shows us the next step, we will just keep putting one foot in front of the other. And if it comes down to deciding comfort care versus intervention ... well let's pray it never does. If God wants to take her home to him, then I pray he just does it and doesn't ask us to make that decision."

Dan nods. He stares at one of the many TVs behind the bar, but he doesn't really see the basketball game that's on.

"What are you thinking?" I ask.

"At what point is medical intervention selfish? I mean, at what point is keeping her alive for our sake and not for hers?" Dan asks.

I shake my head back and forth slowly. "I don't know," I admit. He's asking the question that keeps swirling around in my head. What parent knows the answer to this? How far will we go to save her? My mama bear response is a defensive, "To the ends of the earth!" Yet, I don't know if the end of the earth is truly the best for our daughter.

"And what if we put her through all these surgeries and interventions only for her to die later, having only known pain and suffering and struggle?" I add, overwhelmed by the enormity of this responsibility. It's as if the weight presses me so low to the ground I think I might become the dirt itself.

Mom often says, if heaven is as great as we believe it is, then why hold on here any longer than necessary? She's right.

Yet, life is precious. Our daughter's life is precious. I don't have the heart to let her slip away if it's in my power to help her live. But why would I keep her here if she's better off with him?

Oh God, please let that never be in my control. Oh God, please. Oh God. Don't let me ever have to decide whether she lives or dies. Just take her home with you if you must. I'll deal with the aftermath here. But I don't think I could survive having to decide for you. For her.

"I'm going to bring my cot," Dan interrupts my internal plea to God. I look at him and squint, trying to comprehend. "What?"

"I'm going to take my hunting cot and set it up in the delivery room. Carvalho said the first night of induction is just ripening the cervix. You won't be in labor yet, so we need to try and get good sleep. Plus, when we toured the Special Delivery Unit the room was huge. There's plenty of space for my cot and the nurses said the couch in there is not comfortable. I'm going to get a good night's sleep before she's born, and no one sleeps again for weeks."

I picture the Special Delivery nurses and the Gynecologist tiptoeing around Dan snoring in a cot, trying to get my vitals and check the epidural. I picture our dingy cot sitting in a pristine sterile white walled room. That cot has been in much less clean environments, that's for sure.

"I'll clean it and sterilize it, of course," Dan adds, as if reading my mind.

A laugh boils up from my diaphragm and rolls out in waves, providing sweet humorous relief. I can't stop. Now I'm crying and laughing. This is the man I've married. Logical to the core and totally dismissive of what others might think. I imagine him walking through the halls of Cleveland Clinic, lugging his big green cotton and aluminum cot. What will the hospital staff think? It doesn't matter. He's going to get a good night's sleep.

He grins victoriously, like this is the most brilliant idea.

He leans over the table toward me. "We have a week before induction now," Dan says. "I think we should go on a date. It might be our last one for a long time." He pauses, then adds, "and I think we need to pray it never comes down to us deciding whether she lives or dies. And if it does, let's pray God gives us the wisdom to know what to do."

I fall in love with him just a little bit more. I knew there was a reason God brought us together. His fierce love for me, for our baby and for our God is beyond what I could have hoped. If what they said in our pre-cana class when we were engaged is true, that the goal of marriage is to help each other get to heaven, then he's doing a darn good job doing his part.

"Are you going to eat?" he asks, looking from his empty plate to my full one. "You need to eat something, Emily."

Journal Entry - Wednesday, November 22, 2017

Good morning Lord,

You are so faithful. I needed an ear to hear. I needed a shoulder to cry on. I needed someone who wouldn't try to make me feel better or who wouldn't lead me into deeper depression. The only one who truly knows how to console is you and you were there for me despite my resistance.

Thank you for letting me wail and for letting me get my emotions off my chest. Lord, you are so faithful. Forgive me for my resistance to your love. Help me to lean into your love more each and every day. Prepare me for the challenges ahead. Teach me trust and hope.

Praise your name, Lord.

Amen.

Chapter 15 Delivery Day

Journal Entry - Monday, November 27, 2017

"For God did not give us a spirit of cowardice, but rather a spirit of power and of love and of self-discipline." (2 Timothy 1:7)

Today is the day, Lord. Today we go to the hospital to "ripen the cervix" so that tomorrow we can be induced. Lord, praise your name for giving our daughter life for all nine months of pregnancy. Praise your name for all of our family and friends who are fervently praying for our daughter. Praise your name for our date night last night and the quality time you gave us. Praise your name for your response to my prayer for peace in my heart. You answered beyond what I could have hoped.

Lord, calm Dan and my fears. Help us not to have a spirit of fear and timidity but of power, love, and self-discipline. Lead us today and every day this week. Help us to discern your will and have confidence in your direction.

Tuesday, November 28, 2017, 2:00 a.m.

"Why can't you stay awake with me?" I demand in between moans.

"Huh?" Dan sleepily lifts his head and looks up at me in a daze. He is sitting on his freshly sanitized cot, leaning on my hospital bed with his head in his hands. He's useless for helping me through this labor. With each new contraction I call his name and reach for him. He stirs, weakly grabs my hand, but remains slumped and mostly unresponsive.

Another wave of contraction comes, and I can't catch my breath enough to elaborate. "Breathe in through your nose and out through your mouth," Dan coaches me groggily.

I'll give you breath in and out, Daniel! How dare he advise me how to labor while he's mostly sleeping through it.

The contraction subsides and I repeat through gritted teeth, "Why are you so sleepy? I know it's 2:00 a.m. but you are acting like you can't physically stay awake to help me."

A look of embarrassment washes over his face and he doesn't say anything for a minute. Then he finally admits, "I took a pill to help me sleep."

"You did what?"

"The doctor said tonight would just be ripening the cervix and we needed to get a good night's sleep before induction tomorrow. So, I took Benadryl. How else am I supposed to get a good night's sleep in a loud hospital with all these monitors beeping?" he retorts defensively.

I can't believe what I'm hearing. His logic is sound, but I feel betrayed. Someday this will be funny. Not today.

My abdomen starts to tighten. I might vomit. I curl into the fetal position, grip the bed rail and groan through another contraction. I guess I'll labor by myself.

He is right. I am not *supposed* to start laboring until the morning when they give me Pitocin, an intravenous synthetic version of Oxytocin. Apparently my body decided one cervix ripening pill, Prostaglandin, and it was time to get this baby out into the world. They said it normally would take two Prostaglandin pills and then the IV Pitocin before any action would begin.

"Let's hope this baby holds on long enough for the Benadryl to wear off before she's born," I say angrily. Will he sleep through the few moments we have with our daughter before she either passes away or is passed to hospital staff for intervention? I feel my abdomen climbing the wave of another contraction, dismissing my concern about Dan, and refocusing me on delivering this child. I can't worry about him right now.

Instead of reaching for Dan, I grip the red stuffed bear Dan packed for me. The one I squeezed to death during the amniocentesis months ago. I try to remember what they taught us in birthing class. Something about saying "He He Ho" with each exhale, but all I can muster is a deep moan through the pain. It's inescapable.

"When are you going to get the epidural?" Dan asks.

"I wasn't planning on it until tomorrow. Probably soon though, this is getting unbearable," I say, breathless.

The delivery nurse comes in and adjusts the electronic fetal monitors strapped around my large belly. Each time I move, the two uncomfortable elastic and velcro belts and transducers shift around my dome of an abdomen, making it hard to pick up the contraction pattern and fetal heart rate. Because Baby Girl needs to be so closely monitored, many of the different labor positions we were taught in birthing class are irrelevant. I cannot go anywhere without these monitors and the IV.

"Wow Emily, that didn't take any time at all! Especially for a first-time mom. It usually takes much longer to induce when this is your first," comments the nurse.

I shouldn't be surprised. Nothing about this first-time mom experience is going as expected.

We arrived at Main Campus Cleveland Clinic last night at 7:00 p.m., valeted the car and we slugged our luggage through the main entry, down the long sleepy halls that are usually bustling with activity during daylight hours, and up the elevators to the second floor Specialty Delivery Unit.

It was such a strange feeling, packing our bags for the unknown. The hours, days and weeks ahead could go many different ways. What do you pack when you don't know how long you'll be gone or what you'll be doing? Will we be holding a dead baby soon, or will we be sitting in the hospital waiting for her to come out of surgery? Will we stay for a week, a month, a year? No one knows.

As of today, Baby Girl is 37-weeks-gestation. Just three weeks shy of being the full 40-week term. Praise God she made it this far!

After dancing around induction for the past several weeks, Dr. Carvalho deemed it time to get the baby out. At last week's ultrasound, it became apparent the kidneys were blocked and no longer draining. Her amniotic fluid was decreasing while her kidneys swelled, telling us she continued to drink the amniotic fluid like a baby should, but she did not urinate it back out like she should. The fluid was stuck in the kidneys and causing irreparable damage.

Dr. Carvalho had the tough job of letting the baby grow as big and strong as possible in utero, to give her the best chance at survival outside the womb, while also monitoring her kidneys and deciding when to induce so as to cause the least amount of kidney damage.

Would she be strong enough to handle the outside world? Would her heart be able to handle it? Yet, he reassured us that leaving her in the womb any longer would have minimal benefits compared to the resulting damage to the kidneys which could lead to dialysis or even kidney transplants.

While the nurses suited me up in a green and white hospital gown, grippy socks and an IV, and asked a million questions to check me in to Labor and Delivery, Dan set up his cot and got comfortable. Apparently he got *really* comfortable. Since he'll get a good night's sleep tonight, maybe he will have energy tomorrow when I'm drained from labor. This might actually work out okay.

9:00 a.m.

"It's go time!" says the doctor as she pulls off her purple surgical gloves and throws them away, reaching for new ones. "I just checked, and you are ten centimeters dilated, Emily. The baby is transitioned. How are you feeling?"

"Ready to do this!" I say, swallowing down the waning nausea. It is finally time to meet our sweet babe. Ever since 4:00 a.m. when I broke down and got the epidural, labor has been peaceful and almost even fun. I joined Dan for a little cat nap for a couple hours before labor kicked into high gear. I've been able to ride out each contraction with minimal discomfort besides the recent urge to vomit.

Thank God for strong drugs!

I reach for Dan, "Where are our parents? Are they on their way?"

"They are driving here now. I texted them a little while ago when you were four centimeters dilated. They should be here in the next hour or so, by the time they get parked, through security and to the second floor," Dan explains. Our parents were hoping to be here and in the waiting room during delivery. No one expected delivery to be this early, barely 12 hours after arriving at the hospital.

The room door swings open, and a flood of strange faces fill the space. I am laying with my legs spread wide for the world to see. No one seems phased except me.

We were warned there would be a lot of medical personnel here when it was time for delivery—thus the large room—but nothing could have prepared me for what it is like sharing this very private and intimate occasion with a room full of strangers. Some are here for me. Most are here for the baby. I haven't met any of them. I'm about to push out my baby, only to hand her to a bunch of strangers and hope for the best. But this is the situation we find ourselves in, so, here goes.

They fade to the background as the delivery nurse and doctor refocus my attention on their voices and coach me through what's going to happen next. The nurse holds my knees up to help with the pressure and to make way for the baby. I feel eerily calm and focused. I have one goal—get this baby out, alive.

"I'm Dr. Rick Rodriguez, it's a pleasure to meet you two, Dan and Emily," an Argentinian man walks up and leans over the hospital bed, interrupting my laser focus to shake my hand. "I am the Neonatologist on staff, and I will be taking care of your baby girl. Does she have a name?"

Dan and I look at each other. "Not yet," Dan says. "We need to see her before we decide. We have a couple options in mind."

Dr. Rick chuckles, "Very well. We will call her Baby Girl Whiting for now. She is very lucky to have you two. And we are going to do everything we can for her. I've read over all of Dr. Carvalho's notes as well as all the tests and prenatal appointments she's had. We've prepared for her in the Neonatal Intensive Care Unit, and we have all the necessary surgeons and medications ready bedside, depending on what's needed right away. You can rest assured she will get the best care. Do you have any questions?"

I feel pressure and look to the monitor to see it display the sharp incline of a contraction. With this epidural, I am able to still hold a conversation while laboring. How strange.

"I just have one question. If after she's born, you think her heart is viable, can I hold her for a minute before you whisk her off?"

107

This is *the* question I've wondered, the hope I've held onto for the last few weeks. She may not live long, but I want to hold her. I want to hold her *alive*.

Dr. Rick smiles knowingly and looks at Dan and I with such deep compassion. "If after she's born, I check her heart and she's strong, you may hold her for 30 seconds before we take her for care." A rush of gratitude and excitement courses through my veins. I'm going to hold my baby, alive, even if only for half a minute.

For as unhelpful as Dan was through the night, he's by my side eager to contribute now. The Benadryl must have worn off. He has one hand behind my head and the other under the opposite thigh as the delivery nurse, talking me through each push. He occasionally wipes sweat off my forehead. "You're doing great, Babe. She's almost here!" he encourages.

"She's going to crown soon, Emily. Do you want to be able to see in a mirror?" asks the OBGYN.

I did not meet her before this morning, either. If I had the energy or the time, I might worry about having a stranger deliver my child. What are her credentials? Does she know what she's doing?

She must because she's in the Special Delivery Unit. I just have to trust Cleveland Clinic knows what they are doing in their hiring process. Don't most parents know the doctor who delivers their child? This one seems capable enough.

"Yes, please!" I say, excited. I had no idea that was an option, to watch my baby be born. They wheel over a small rectangular mirror about the size of an 8.5x11" sheet of paper. They adjust it until the angle is just right for me to see.

Meanwhile, a nurse starts fanning my face as sweat drips down my temples.

"Okay now, when I say push I want you to bear down and push hard for ten seconds," says the doctor. "Okay here comes another contraction, take a deep breath and start pushing Emily. I'll count ... One, two, three ..."

I bear down with all my might but only make it to six before breaking the push.

Dan laughs, "That wasn't ten, Emily!"

"Maybe I should have done some aerobics before this. There is no way I can make it to ten," I say.

"Okay Emily here we go again. Push!" says the doctor. "Here's the head. She's coming. Dan, do you want to see?" The doctor ushers Dan near her to see his daughter's head crown. We both watch with wonder. "I'm holding her head now, Emily. One more push and you'll have your girl!" she announces.

"One, two, three, four, five, and here she is!" announces the doctor as she scoops the tiny little cheese ball of a baby up, catching her in a blue and white striped hospital blanket. I strain to see her as I catch my breath. I can't quite get a good glimpse yet, but I hear her crying. The sound is so beautiful. Tears of joy and relief flow down my cheeks, matching her cries.

Dan looks over us both, grinning from ear to ear. The pride and joy on his face matches what I'm feeling. "You did great, Babe!" Dan says and kisses my sweaty temple.

The doctor lays her on my lower abdomen and waits for the blood in the umbilical cord to stop pulsating. I can see the top of the baby's head. It's cone shaped with spots of blood and a thick covering of cheese-looking substance.

"Do you want to cut the cord?" the doctor asks Dan.

"No, thank you," Dan says. He wants the doctor to do it so it was sure to be done right. As soon as the cord is cut, she scooches the baby up to my chest so I can get a better look.

"Give her a kiss, Mama! Here's your babe," the doctor encourages. Should I kiss her while she's still covered in vernix caseosa and blood? Yes. I do not care. I close my eyes and kiss the top of her head, breathing in her newborn scent. My heart beats wildly.

"Hello sweet girl," I softly whisper. I open my eyes, knowing I need to take her in with all the senses before she is whisked away. I take a good look at her and notice right away that her ears are folded in half and her upper lip looks twisted as if the tongue and lip are tangled.

I'm caught off guard. I knew she had cleft lip, but in the midst of all the diagnoses, it never occurred to me to look up what a newborn looks like with cleft lip. I was so laser focused on the life-threatening diagnoses that I nearly forgot she even had a cleft. Now I'm shocked at what I see. As soon as the shock hits, a wave of embarrassment takes its place. How could I not have known what to expect? Fear soon follows—is the cleft more severe than we thought? Then guilt—how could I focus on her cleft lip and her bent ears when right now I should just be soaking up every minute with her in all her beauty?

I kiss her little cone head again and she is carried off to Dr. Rick and the NICU staff who are watching and waiting on the other side of the room by what they call the Giraffe, a big white bassinet that measures the baby and is set to temperature to keep her warm while the Neonatologist does his initial assessment. Dan leaves my side and follows the crowd of medical personnel with the baby. While the delivery doctor cleans me up and starts stitching my three tears, thank God I cannot feel any of it due to the epidural still pumping in my veins, I watch Dan and Dr. Rick across the room.

They exchange a few comments and a few laughs. I can't hear what they're saying but Dan's glowing with pride. That's a good sign. I follow their every move, watching to see if there is anything urgent to deal with, if her heart is stable.

It's like an out of body experience. This child who was with me for the last nine months, is now twelve feet away. Her heartbeat used to be just below mine, and now others are listening to her heart via a tiny stethoscope. I put my hands on my belly which feels like a deflated balloon. She's no longer part of me.

"Two point five nine kilograms and 47 centimeters long. That's 5 pounds 11.4 ounces and 18.5 inches long," Dr. Rick announces over my thoughts and the baby's cries. He crosses the room and lays her back on my chest. "She's stable, you can hold her for a little while longer," he grins like a proud Papa himself. The nurses swoop in and fuss over us, to make sure we are comfortable for our short snuggle session.

"Kangaroo care is best right now, skin-on-skin with mama,"

says one nurse as she pulls blankets out of the way and creates a little nest for us both. The baby quiets and opens her eyes the minute our skin contacts. She looks around and meets my eyes with hers, then continues to scan the room, taking in her new surroundings.

She looks like she knows what is going on. I had no idea a newborn could be so aware and alert from the start. She appears to be very intelligent. Though I don't really know why I think that.

It strikes me then. She's a tiny human being. She's separate from me, her own identity, and her own entity. I knew this intellectually, but laying here watching my baby look around, I internalize this truth, mourn it, and celebrate it all at once. She's her own person. Beautiful. Unique. Treasured. Wanted.

The room is humming with activity, but all I see is this child. My world is quiet amidst the buzz. It's as if the world stops, if only for a moment. Dan stands over us, his arm around us both, watching. I can't take my eyes off her.

"She's perfect," I whisper.

"Yes, she is," Dan agrees.

Realizing I'm not the only one in the room, I remember Dan might want some time with our daughter, too. "Do you want to hold her, Babe? I don't want to hog her in our short time with her."

"No, you keep holding her," Dan reassures. "She's comfortable."

Good, I didn't want to give her up anyway.

Dr. Rick pops his head around Dan's shoulders and says, "I'm so sorry but I'm going to need her back."

112

My heart sinks and I wrap her back up in the blanket before reluctantly handing her over. Who knows when I'll hold her again.

"We'll take great care of her, Emily. We are going to thoroughly check her heart and do a full assessment. We won't make any big decisions or do any intervention until we speak with you, unless absolutely necessary." The nurse swaddles her warmly and places her in the Giraffe. She wheels the baby back over to me to wave goodbye.

"I'll be back with you as soon as I can," I tell her. Then Dr. Rick, the mobile bassinet, the baby, and the swarm of staff shuffle out of the room, leaving Dan, the delivery doctor and two delivery nurses in their wake.

Still on the high of having just given birth, the shakes set in from losing so much body heat and blood. Naturally, I exclaim enthusiastically, "Let's do it again, Babe! That was amazing!"

Dan looks at me in horror and responds, "Let's dry this one off first before we think about having another one."

The hospital staff chuckle as they finish stitching me up and fetch me warm blankets to bring my body temperature back up.

"You did great, Babe," Dan grasps both my hands and smiles down at me.

"There's two sets of grandparents outside eagerly waiting to see you," announces a delivery nurse. "Do you want me to let them in, Emily?"

I look to Dan to see what he thinks. He nods.

"Yes, maybe just our moms first since I'm still kind of exposed," I say wearily, suddenly feeling the effects of the marathon my body just ran, pushing a human being out into the world.

Once the doctor finishes suturing, she leaves and the nurse goes to fetch our mothers, giving Dan and I a few minutes alone.

"What are we going to name her?" I ask. "Do you think she looks like a Gwenevieve or a Charlotte?" These are the two names we've waffled between.

Dan hems and haws for a few minutes. "I don't think she looks like a Gwenevieve or a Gwen. She seems like a Charlotte to me. Or a Charlie."

"Charlotte it is!" I agree, "Charlotte Jo Whiting. Charlie Jo for short." Baby Girl Whiting has a name.

Grandma Claire and Grammy Nancy enter the room, and both come to hug and kiss and congratulate Dan and me. Before saying a word my mom's eyes meet mine and tears stream down both of our faces. Tears of joy, pride, exhaustion, fear, and a whole host of other unidentifiable emotions break free. There's something about seeing a familiar and loving face that lets all the emotions surface in a sigh of knowing relief.

Both moms reach for my hands, and we hold tight to each other, sharing our deepest thoughts without saying a word.

My mother's hands. They are the 30-years-older version of mine. Long and slender, worn from years of changing diapers, raising kids, quilting, baking, gardening, laboring.

Dan's mom's hands. They are smaller than mine, but somehow tougher at the same time. They, too, are worn from years of caring for her children, putting band aids on booboos, picking strawberries and apples, and hauling crates of eggs to sell at their farm market to support her family, laboring.

Both women laboring for their families—that's what our moms do. I'm so grateful they are here by my side while I learn how to labor for mine.

"You did it!" Grammy Nancy exclaims, adding some levity to the room.

I feel like I've climbed a mountain and am finally at the peak. The satisfaction of having delivered a breathing baby fills my lungs and heart like a stunning view from a mountaintop after a long grueling hike.

"*We* did it," I whisper in awe and gratitude, agreeing with Grammy and knowing it took these two wonderful women and a whole host of others to get Dan, me, and Charlotte to this day.

Chapter 16 Visitor

Wednesday, November 29, 2017

"Come in!" I raise my voice to ensure whoever is at the door can hear me from the bathroom. Who is it now? My hospital room door seems to revolve with doctors, nurses and staff coming in for one reason or another—blood pressure checks, admission paperwork, asking me how my bleeding is, asking on a scale from 1-10 how I rate my pain, flushing my unhooked IV to make sure the lines are still clear, and who knows what other reasons they've come. Between all the interruptions, pumping every two hours, the discomfort from delivery and the pressure point hospital bed that moves every twenty minutes, I might have slept a total of three hours last night. Then there is the separation anxiety.

For nine months my baby has been nestled right under my heart, never distant from me. She went to work with me. She went to bed with me. She got up with me in the mornings. All I had to do was look down at my expanding belly to be reassured of her presence. I look down at my deflated abdomen now and put my hand on the then stretched, now sagging skin. My loss is palpable. I miss my baby.

Now, since I delivered her nearly 24 hours ago, she's been in an isolette in the NICU, on a separate floor, in an entirely separate building from me.

Isolette. What a fitting name, since in it, she is isolated from me.

Apparently, they didn't take into consideration that mothers would want to be with their babies when they designed the NICU, Special Delivery Unit and Postpartum Recovery Floor placement. Obviously, a mother was not involved in the hospital layout planning committee.

Last night, after I was pushed in a wheelchair through what felt like miles of white-walled hallways, going up and down several elevators and finally arriving at my recovery room ten minutes later, I expressed my frustration and confusion to the innocent night shift nurse. Who in their right mind thought this was a good idea, putting postpartum mothers up in a hospital room that might as well be lightyears away from their sick babies, and in a unit that doesn't even specialize in delivery recovery?

This clearly wasn't the first time this nurse was confronted with a baffled and hormonal mother.

"The buildings are old and the way they are laid out, there simply isn't any room near the NICU to keep moms," she explained. "And we don't have enough deliveries here to warrant a postpartum unit of its own, so this is a women's care floor. Typically, you're only inpatient for a day or two to recover from delivery before being discharged anyway," she justified as if that made it all okay. Then her tone softened with empathy, "I know it's inconvenient."

Inconvenient? This isn't just inconvenient. It's inhumane for both me and my daughter who is fighting for her life all on her own while I supposedly 'recover' here. As if reading my mind she added, "You can go visit the NICU anytime, we just ask that you come back to your room every four to six hours for vitals and pain meds until you're discharged."

There's that word again, visit. I can 'visit.' Last night when I was finally able to be with Charlotte, after her NICU admittance and all the testing that ensued—an echo of her heart, an ultrasound of her kidneys and abdominal cyst, a cranio-facial plastic surgeon consultation and taping of her face—I was given a visitor's pass to let me in.

VISITOR.

The big bold all-caps word typed in black ink on the sticker pass left a dry feeling in my mouth. I am not my daughter's visitor. I am her mother. I feel like the hospital took possession of my daughter, meanwhile I am on the sidelines watching helplessly.

Yet, what options do I have? I can't rightly take her out of the hospital. She wouldn't survive a day without this institution's help.

Oh God, help me. I don't want to be her visitor. I want to be her mother.

I hear the door swing open and something bang through the door frame, snapping me out of reliving last night's "visit" and reminding me I just told someone to come into my room. I peek my head out of the bathroom and see a short, cheerful woman waving around a broom and dustpan, pushing a trash can on wheels through the large door frame.

"I'm here to clean your room," she says. Then she does a double take and looks at me curiously. "Girl, you just had a baby, right?" she asks.

"Yes, yesterday," I confirm.

"Well, I never," she chuckles.

"You never what?"

"I've been cleaning rooms for years at this hospital and I've never seen a mama get up and get dressed and put on makeup the day after having a baby," she shakes her head and chuckles some more, starting to sweep. "You're something, Missy."

I look in the mirror and see my black maternity tights awkwardly pulled over my huge postpartum briefs and thick pad, my nursing tank top and long gray button-down sweater hanging over my shoulders. My straight blonde hair is freshly washed and dried. My left eyelashes have black mascara on them and the mascara wand is in my hand, ready to finish the right eye. It is kind of funny.

"Well, I figured if I get up, take a shower and get dressed as if the day is going to go well, then maybe it will," I justify while laughing with her. Now that I see the situation through her eyes, it seems a little ludicrous. But if I show up at Charlotte's bedside this morning ready to fight the good fight, "dressed for success" as we say at work, then maybe, just maybe, success will come our way today and we will be that much closer to going home with our baby girl, alive.

Dan's up now too, sitting on his cot that he lugged through the hospital halls last night, following my wheelchair. He rubs his eyes and peers over at me curiously. He smiles and joins us chuckling too. This is the headstrong, stubborn woman he married. For better or for worse.

"Good morning, Babe," I say. "I don't think I can quite walk all the way to the NICU yet. Would you mind wheeling me over there? I want to be there in time for rounds this morning to hear what the doctors have to say."

Poor guy. He just woke up from what was an equally sleepless night. It's only 7 a.m. He spent most of yesterday and a lot of last night at Charlotte's bedside while I was unable to be with her. And now, without a moment to collect his thoughts, I pounce on him with a request. He's used to this though, me rearing to go in the mornings and hitting the ground running. He groans and stands up to put on sweatpants and a hoodie. He runs his hands through his disheveled hair, slips his glasses over his nose and goes to get the wheelchair ready. I feel like such a burden, needing to be pushed around. But I must get to my baby.

Before I plop into the chair Dan unfolds for me, he pulls me in for a hug. We stand there embracing for a few minutes.

"How are you feeling this morning?" Dan asks.

"I'm fine," I say, "I just really want to be with her." Tears roll down my cheeks like I've become accustomed to. They don't surprise me anymore. Dan pulls me in harder and holds me there. I melt into him. He has a way of stopping my crazy and recentering me.

"She's doing great so far, Babe," Dan reassures. "She's a fighter and God is with us."

I nod silently as he helps me lower slowly into the chair and begins pushing me down the hall.

Chapter 17 Cheated

Journal Entry - Wednesday, November 29, 2017

Charlotte Jo Whiting was born yesterday at 9:37 a.m.! Praise your name, Lord. Praise your name. She has many challenges ahead of her, but she has made it so far, too!

Lord, you gave her life. You formed her in my womb into a beautiful baby girl. She has sass and spunk and a great heart, too. We are so in love.

Lord, these days are long and hard. Doctors poke and prod her all day. They deliver news constantly, some good and some not good. Some new news and complications, some known issues. But Lord, you know all. You have knit her together perfectly and you knew her by name long before we did. Lord, if it is your will, help her to heal. Heal her and give her a heart after yours. Grant her your peace, your blessing, your hope, your life and your light.

Lord, you love her more than we do. So, Lord, care for her in every way possible. Provide for her and provide for her parents so we may be your hands and feet for her. Lord help us. Strengthen us in your love and hope. Lead us Lord. Lead us. Let your will be done.   Amen.

Wednesday, November 29, 2017

"Small babies' skin is very thin and sensitive, so rather than rubbing her arm, try gentle but firm pressure," instructs Candace, Charlotte's nurse today. Candace cups her left hand around Charlotte's apple-sized head and her right hand around Charlotte's tiny feet. "I know it's heartbreaking to not hold her, so here's a good way to help her feel held even while she's lying in the isolette," Candace demonstrates to Dan and me. We are sitting on either side of Charlotte's bed.

Candace steps back to give Dan room to try. He very gingerly folds his calloused hands around either end of Charlotte. His bear paws make her look like a tiny rag doll, enveloping her. My heart throbs. Watching him as a father is a whole new level of love I didn't expect. I always suspected he'd be an amazing dad but seeing his commitment to this little girl is beyond anything I could have imagined.

I reach in too and touch the palm of her tiny hand. Her long, skinny fingers quickly wrap around my index finger and squeeze tight.

"That's a very natural reflex for babies, to grasp what touches their hands. That's great!" Candace encourages. Candace looks to be in her early fifties and her eyes are filled with compassion and care. She's nursed hundreds of babies before, and apparently their parents, too. She's teaching us how to interact with our sick baby and adjust to NICU living.

The NICU. It's a place like none I've been before. The fragrances of sterilizing chemicals, plastic, baby formula and lotion intermingle. Wood paneling gives away that the unit hasn't had a facelift in years. It's warm, like shorts and t-shirt weather warm. Fluorescent lights buzz along the ceiling adding to the rhythm that resembles an *a cappella* group using hushed vocal instruments—the squeak of nurse shoes, the faint cries of tiny babies, the pulse of the monitors, the sliding of drawers and running of water, the quiet chatter among medical staff, the rocking of moms, dads and babies, the ring of the receptionist's phone, the hospital codes announced over the loudspeaker. It's like a world of its own, rocking to its own beat and existing on a quieter, slower, more methodical yet simultaneously more intense plain.

Thankfully, Charlotte seems peaceful. Dan's eyes mist, staring at Charlotte, reveling in this small moment of connection. Her eyes are closed, and her chest joins the NICU rhythm, quietly going up and down with each relaxed breath. She's wrapped up in Daddy's hands and in a NICU version of a swaddle, cloth that wraps around the outer edges of her little body but leaves her front fully exposed to room air. The "swaddle" has two pieces of fabric that lay over her chest and lower abdomen, which when pulled around her, help resemble the small cozy feeling of the womb.

"We work on a three-hour cycle here," Candace continues teaching. "Every three hours we do what we call Hands on Care. We check vitals, change diapers, adjust Baby's position, check all the lines to make sure they are clear and working, and when she's ready to start eating, we will feed her every three hours, too. Charlotte also has blood pressures ordered Q3, meaning every three hours, or eight times in 24 hours, so we will do those when we do vitals. It's almost been three hours since our last vital check," she says, looking at her watch. "We will let her rest and snuggle in Daddy's hands for a bit longer, and then you can help me change her diaper if you'd like."

We both nod in agreement, not taking our eyes off Charlotte. It's healing for our hurting hearts, seeing her peacefully resting here in our hands. We are so grateful for Candace's guidance. I've held and changed a handful of babies' diapers before, but never a baby who cannot be picked up. Never a baby who has fragile IV lines and monitors. Never a baby who is this tiny. As much as I'd love to take her home soon, I would have no idea how to care for this little peanut without the nurses to guide my every move. The thought of caring for her on my own terrifies me.

"While we wait, I'll explain some of the equipment you see and help you get acquainted with Charlotte's bedspace," Candace continues. She points out each monitor, line, lead, drawer, and supply in a five-foot radius, explaining how everything works and what it's for, what every beep signifies. As she shows us the monitors, Dan nods knowingly. He's been studying Charlotte's heart rate, pulse and blood oxidation numbers obsessively. They are displayed on a large black screen right above Charlotte's isolette. His engineering mind has already quietly observed and investigated how the monitors work. He anxiously watches to make sure the numbers stay where they are supposed to.

"And this little camera is for NICUview. It's an app you can download on your phone so you can see Charlotte at any time, whenever you aren't able to be here," Candace points. "So, when you wake up at 2 a.m. to pump Mom, you can log onto the app and watch Charlotte. Or Dad, if you have to return to work soon, you can see her throughout the workday. Of course, you can call anytime too, but this way you can see her, day or night."

The reality that I have to leave my baby here each night while I sleep elsewhere hits me afresh. I look around the room, trying to assess if rolling a bed in here for me is feasible. The room is a fairly large rectangle, and each corner has a baby. With four babies, two nurses managing their care, doctors and hospital staff coming in and out of the room constantly, plus all the equipment each baby needs, there is just enough room for two chairs for visitors at each bedside. There is no way a bed could fit too.

This is not natural. I don't want to view my baby on a camera. I want to be with her at all times. I am her mother. I dream of rolling over in my bed to find my baby right there in a bassinet beside me. I dream of picking her up and changing her diaper, nursing her and swaddling her tight to go back to sleep, with a real swaddle, not this one that leaves her half exposed. And certainly not watching her on a webcam as nurses do all these things. Yet, I'm grateful someone was thoughtful enough to install this camera. I'll probably use it often to lick my wounded mama heart in the middle of many nights to come, when I should be rocking her to a blissful newborn sleep, rather than sitting at a cold hard desk listening to the 'whir whir, whir whir' of my pump extracting milk for my baby who cannot even eat it yet.

"Charlotte has a visitor. She says she is your aunt. Should I let her in?" the NICU receptionist pokes her head into the room and interrupts my depressing thoughts.

"Oh, yes please," I say.

"Okay, but I can only allow two visitors at Charlotte's bedside at a time due to fire code and a limit on people in the room, so one of you will have to step out," she says, looking from me to Dan.

"I can go," I say. I need some coffee and I want my aunt to come in and lay eyes on Charlotte. I want her to speak with our nurse and neonatologist to make sure Charlotte is getting the best care possible.

As a pediatrician herself, she is someone I know and highly trust, among a slew of medical professionals I've only met yesterday. I'm eager for her input. And God bless her for being here. She lives out of state with five kids of her own. Yet, she drove eight hours north to Cleveland, Ohio, to spend an indefinite amount of time here with us. After she helped us work through insurance plans a few months ago, in preparation of Charlotte's expensive arrival, she asked how she could best help once Charlotte was born. I thought about it for a while and finally concluded I wanted her by our side at the hospital, if at all possible. I knew this was a lot to ask, but without hesitation she agreed. I cannot fathom doing this without her now. In a world of so many unknowns, new faces and a slew of diagnoses, having her here helps me feel like I can breathe in a situation that seems to otherwise suck the oxygen right out of my lungs. She keeps saying she's not doing much but moral support, but even if that's all, her presence is vital.

I lean over and give Charlotte a kiss on the forehead, then

slowly get up and walk to Dan's side of the bed to give him a kiss goodbye. "Do you want me to wheel you out?" Dan asks.

"No, I'm only going to the Ronald McDonald Family Room right down the hall and it'll do me some good to stretch my legs," I say, turning slowly and doing the I-just-gave-birth Mom waddle out of the NICU and into the hall. I carefully make my way to the Family Room at the end of the hallway.

We discovered this room yesterday afternoon. It's a warm and inviting space with bathrooms and a kitchenette where families can catch a little reprieve from the chaos of their children's hospital beds, escape the insanity-inducing never-ending beeping bedside, and the sterile mind-numbing white-walled hospital environment.

I find both my parents and Dan's sitting there with coffees. Nancy, Dan's mom, jumps up to get me a cup. She knows my obsession with black coffee. "How are you holding up, honey?" she asks as she pours from the community carafe.

"I'm okay," I reply wearily. "I wish we could all be in there with her now. Taking turns with only two at a time seems cruel." I know I need to stop thinking this way, thinking about how everything in this situation is not natural. Not normal. Not at all what I want.

It's unhealthy and unhelpful to obsess over things I cannot change. But I can't help it. If we were home, Dan and I would be the ones deciding who came to visit and when, and how many at any given time. We would be sharing the joy of our little girl with family and friends, obsessively squirting Purelle in everyone's hands. Not taking turns visiting her two-by-two. Not watching her on a webcam. Not sitting in a hospital 'family room' while our family is divided in separate parts of the hospital.

I feel cheated of the newborn experience I envisioned before her diagnoses came to light at that 20-week ultrasound. Familiar guilt tugs at my consciousness, too. How dare I lament the situation when I should be celebrating that my daughter is stable? This roller coaster of emotion is maddening.

Chapter 18 Life Goes On

Thursday, November 30, 2017

"Happy birthday to you. Happy birthday to you. Happy birthday dear Mom, Claire, Grandma … Grams, Grammy. Happy birthday to you," we all laugh after listing the names we collectively call her, Grandma being the newest name added to the list, plus a few nicknames we've tossed around as potential titles.

Mom smiles, "What great voices you have," she says with a sarcastic chuckle before blowing out the singular candle. Dan and I are here, along with two of my three siblings, Dave and Alan, Mom and Dad, Alan's girlfriend Annie, Dan's parents and my aunt. We've basically taken over the Family Room with our large group.

Dave baked a chocolate cake for the occasion. Frosting drips off like I drip with gratitude for his efforts to make Mom feel special amidst all focus being on Charlotte. I battle feelings of guilt for my lack of attention to anyone or anything besides my daughter. I know no one holds this against me, least of all my mother. Yet, she's here for me for every up and down. She's an incredible shoulder to lean on and

I've leaned on her hard throughout this situation. I want her to know how much she's appreciated. But I don't have the energy to think about how to do so.

Dave asked me how he could help a couple days ago. My response was, please get a gift for Mom and come up with a plan to celebrate her birthday for me. Given the circumstances, he knocked it out of the park.

"What did we get her?" I lean over and whisper in Dave's ear, who's sitting beside me on the big brown well-worn leather couch.

"A book about the science of cooking she mentioned she wanted," he responds. Awesome. She opens the gift and makes the appropriate oos and awes. For a brief moment, we forget we are in the battle of our lives, of Charlotte's life.

Charlotte continues to have a myriad of tests including a Magnetic Resonance Imaging (MRI) today of her brain and abdomen, for which she had to be put under light anesthesia. Doctors are working to determine the extent of brain malformation and identify what the cyst is in her abdomen. We await the MRI results among many other test results.

As we wait, the timing for this little party works well despite Charlotte just returning from the radiology department. None of us can be with Charlotte right now anyway. It's shift change.

Apparently due to the Health Insurance Portability and Accountability Act (HIPAA), no visitors are allowed in the NICU during shift change while the nurses pass private patient health information from the current shift staff to the next. This pesky policy means we have to leave the NICU at 3 p.m. and 7 p.m. for roughly 45 minutes every day. It drives me crazy to have to leave Charlotte. But I suppose shift change does provide forced time to do other things, like celebrate Mom's birthday.

It's strange how life goes on, birthdays still happen, even though it seems like our own life has come to a screeching halt. It's like the world continues spinning around me at a dizzying pace, a pace I used to keep up with no problem, while I watch it from a distance, knowing I should participate but not having a clue how anymore.

Life goes on, even as my own is stopped, frozen in the slow-motion space of a tiny isolette, holding a tiny sick baby whose hours and days may be numbered. This is a new vantage point I've never viewed the world from before, and it is shifting my perspective on just about everything. Especially on what really matters, and what really doesn't.

Chapter 19 Pinned

Friday, December 1, 2017

"I'd like to come help," I say with conviction to the nurse, Neonatologist, and fleet of NICU staff gathered around our daughter's isolette. I look right in the eyes of Dr. Rick with what I hope is a confident, yet kind, expression of stating, not asking. I don't want to be abrasive, but I want to go with my daughter. After all, Dr. Rick is the one who told me to be my daughter's best advocate. He told me to express concerns, ask questions and not let 'white coat syndrome' hold me back from ensuring the best care for her.

I am currently looking at what seems like a sea of white coats and scrubs peering at me, Dan, and Charlotte, who is lying in her isolette beside us. She is the constant subject of discussion. This is the first time since Charlotte's birth I've had a passionate opinion of how things should be handled, or at least the first time I've firmly expressed it.

"Are you sure?" Dr. Rick asks with concern. "It's a long test to stand there and watch and I assure you she will be well cared for by

Roberta," he nods to the nurse assigned to Charlotte for today's shift, indicating she will take Charlotte for her hepatobiliary iminodiacetic acid (HIDA) scan this morning. Suellen, the nurse practitioner everyone calls Sue, looks up from her white, five-foot Computer On Wheels, what I hear referred to as the COW, where she's charting. She pulls her glasses up and props them behind her ears like a headband, looking at me curiously, clearly showing her reservations to the idea of me accompanying Charlotte to her scan. Sue's expression makes me waiver only for a moment.

"I am her mother. I want to be there to comfort her and from my understanding this is a test I can go to, so I would like to," I say firmly. I don't voice the fact that I want to see what happens at all these tests, when she's wheeled away time and time again in her isolette and doesn't come back for hours. Where do they take her? I don't voice the fact that sitting and waiting for her to return is agonizing and I'd rather spend the time with her than wandering the hospital halls, sipping burnt coffee and wondering what's happening. I don't say I feel like it's my duty as her mother to be with her in her pain and discomfort, even if it's painful for me to watch. I feel I owe her that. If she has to endure it, then I should be able to handle being there with her and for her. I don't voice I want to see how she is treated during these tests and if they are doing all they can to make her as comfortable as possible, like they say they do. They've given me no reason to doubt, but as her mother, it's my duty to protect her. I'm tired of watching her being wheeled away for test after test. I want to go with her.

"Okay, you may go," Dr. Rick permits, seeing my

determination. "So long as you're okay with helping out, which means you'll need to hold her still for the gamma camera to get good images. Only so many people can fit in the room so that'll be your job. We would normally send a nurse's aide to help."

I breathe a sigh of relief. I didn't realize I was holding my breath, waiting for his response to my assertion. A small sense of victory washes over me.

He looks at the clock on the wall, "As soon as we are done rounding on Charlotte, let's get her ready for the scan," he tells Roberta, who nods in agreement.

It's 9:00 a.m., the start of rounds, and they chose Charlotte first among the 16 or so babies in the unit. Someone told me they choose the sickest baby first to round on, to make sure his or her care and next steps are addressed right away. I'm grateful Charlotte is getting the time and attention she needs, but if this is true, it means she's the one in most dire need of their attention. Somehow this makes me feel simultaneously sick and satisfied. Sick that my child is the worst off among those who are all bad off in a level four NICU, the most acute NICU there is. Satisfied that we are getting the ball rolling fast today. My efficiency-oriented mind reasons this might mean we can address issues faster and get that much closer to going home soon. Plus, it's Friday and we have a lot of questions that need answered before the weekend when I'm told many key staff go home.

"We are working with Urology to assess next steps," Sue pulls her glasses back down to rest on her nose and resumes updating Dr. Rick for today's rounds. "Assessment: Prenatal MRI concerning renal pelviectasis, bilateral hydroureter. An abdominal ultrasound on 11/28 demonstrated severe bilateral urinary tract dilation of both kidneys and both ureters, abnormal renal parenchyma bilaterally. Urine output wnl for first 24 hours, elevated creatinine. On 11/29 VCUG showed ectopic insertion of ureters, reflux into dilated distal left ureter …" she goes on for five minutes, updating Dr. Rick and all the gathered staff on lab numbers, test results, known diagnoses, undiagnosed symptoms and the plan of care as it currently stands.

Dan and I listen intently but comprehend a fraction of what's said. I am out of my league, knowing enough of what's going on to be dangerously misinformed.

Dr. Rick sees me trying to wrap my head around what all this means as I take feverish notes. As soon as they are done discussing among themselves in complex medical terms, Dr. Rick turns to us.

"So basically, Emily and Dan, Charlotte is stable and doing well, but we need to address her kidney blockage soon. Urology is working on reviewing all lab and test results to determine next steps. Today is Friday … we likely will surgically intervene on Monday to provide some relief for her kidneys."

"What about her heart?" Dan asks. We thought her heart would be the first thing to need surgical intervention after birth.

"The most recent echocardiogram on 11/30 shows the ductus arteriosus is closing beautifully. Each day lowers our concern for patent ductus arteriosus, or PDA, which we were concerned about at birth. That's good news, but we still need to monitor closely because the echo also confirmed suspicions of tricuspid valve regurgitation, non-compaction of the heart muscle in the left ventricle and a possible dilated ascending aorta," Dr. Rick explains. "Only time will tell if intervention will be needed, but the heart is stable. It appears we have time to address cardiac concerns later and the kidneys are priority surgically."

"Any other questions, Dan and Emily?" Dr. Rick asks, pausing for a long time to ensure we really think about anything we might want to ask.

We look at each other and both shake our heads no, though the reality is we have more questions than we can verbalize. "Thank you for your thorough care of our daughter," Dan says to everyone huddled around. They nod and shuffle to the next baby's bed.

"Excuse us," Roberta says as the elevator dings and the B button lights up, indicating we've reached the basement of the hospital. She and I wheel Charlotte's isolette past two others standing in the elevator, out onto the cold cement floor. She's at the helm of the big plastic mobile infant bed, steering it through the maze of halls while I push from behind and hold the blanket over the plastic top, blocking the hallway lights from disturbing Charlotte. She squirms in the nest of blankets we made for her, her naked body staying warm by the heated enclosure.

She has yet to wear any clothes since birth. Between the three-heart monitor leads stickered to her chest, the pulse ox wrapped around her big toe and the umbilical venous and arterial catheters going into her belly button, there is no room to maneuver clothes on her. Plus, doctors say they need clear visual access to the umbilical lines at all times, because if they are disturbed, she could bleed out. How's that for terrifying.

Even if we managed to wrestle clothes on around all the protruding lines, we'd have to take them off seemingly every five minutes for the various tests being run—the ultrasounds, MRI, heart echoes, blood draws, and now the HIDA scan.

She might not be able to wear clothes, but one thing she can have is a pacifier. Thank God. She goes to town munching on that thing, hoping to get a drop of milk. It has yet to produce anything.

She hasn't had her first meal and she's four days old. Between the heart and the kidneys, doctors keep evaluating when to take her to the OR and on the chance that it could be at any moment, they've kept her NPO, meaning "nothing by mouth" from the Latin *nil per os*. Terms I did not know until we were plunged into the neonatal intensive care world just a few short days ago. Another reason for keeping her NPO is because they aren't sure if her digestive system will be able to handle food. Given the large unidentified mass in her abdomen and her urinary complications, are there other things malformed with the gut that we don't know about yet? This HIDA scan will help us get closer to that answer. Closer to Charlotte's first meal.

We brought a small bottle of my colostrum with us for this HIDA scan, knowing that despite her having an NPO order, maybe just a drop of milk dipped on the pacifier will help her stay calm during this hour-and-a-half long procedure.

I cock my head to the side to walk under large ductwork in the basement ceiling as we roll Charlotte's isolette down a ramp to another long white hall. This basement wasn't designed for six-foot people. In front of us there is an intersection of halls and a red stop light flashes. Roberta halts the isolette in time for a short stainless-steel robot to drive by, delivering supplies to another unit in the basement. My sense of dread rises as we continue down into the bowels of the hospital, finally arriving at the Nuclear Medicine department. The nuclear medicine technologist begins prepping Charlotte right away and injects something into her umbilical line.

"What is that?" I ask.

Roberta says, "A radiopharmaceutical. Once it's fully administered, we will start imaging, watching the radioactive molecules go through the bile ducts, gallbladder, and liver. Come over here by Charlotte's head and help me hold her still for the imaging."

The technologist and nurse move Charlotte to lay on a cold exam table and the large gamma camera looms over top of Charlotte's small body. She squirms and squawks but generally cooperates. We cup our hands around her as best as we can, helping her feel safe and warm. Eventually she drifts off to sleep. Thank God.

Please let her sleep through this whole thing, Lord. Please.

I'm so anxious to keep her asleep. It's like an obsession. Every little sound and bump worries me she will wake. Despite my worry, about a half an hour into the process, her eyes open.

As the test drags on, she begins to protest. Her small whimpers grow to full on screams. Her arms start flailing and her long skinny legs kick violently. This tiny five-pound human is very effective at letting us know her disdain.

"Is it hurting her?" I ask loudly, to ensure I'm heard over Charlotte's cries. This little girl has such a deep authoritative and sassy voice, especially when she's ticked. Her whole body flushes red with anger with each aggressive flail.

"No," says Roberta, "but it's cold and uncomfortable for a baby to lie flat on her back in the wide open. She's used to being in the uterus where it's warm and cozy. Plus, she's probably hungry. But, we have to keep her as still as possible, or the camera won't get clear images. I'll hold her legs down, you hold her arms by her face so she feels as if she's swaddled."

This was not at all what I envisioned when I signed up to help 'hold her still.' I muster the courage to pin my infant daughter down, which elicits even more vehement cries. Her eyes are wild with fear and anger. When they catch mine, I feel ashamed and horrified.

My daughter sees me. She knows I'm pinning her down on this cold, unforgiving table. I look for a clock. How long must we do this? I think this might be hell on earth, forcing my child to lay still against her four-day-old will. All for the cause of her health.

This is for her own good. We need the results of this test to evaluate her gastrointestinal system and determine next steps in her healing. But right now it doesn't seem like it's for her own good at all. It's torture. I want to scoop her up and run away with her. Far far away.

My hands are supposed to provide comfort, love, warmth and safety. Instead in this moment they are forcing her to hold still on a hard cold table.

The nurse holds Charlotte's legs with one hand and reaches for the pacifier with the other. She dips it in the milk and offers it to a spitting mad Charlotte, who momentarily silences her screams to investigate what has been inserted into her mouth and nose, which are all one large cavity without the palate to separate them. She munches angrily, "Umph umph numph," before rejecting the pacifier, pushing it out with her tongue and resuming her screams.

"Emily, you're going to have to hold her down tighter. She's moving too much for the camera," Roberta says. Maybe I should have heeded Dr. Rick' warnings. Sue's apprehensive look should have been enough to tell me this was a bad idea. The minutes drag on as Charlotte's screams remain full force. Maybe she'll tire herself out and fall back asleep.

Please Lord. Please.

I shift my weight from one foot to the other and notice how much I ache. Just as she is only four days old, I am only four days postpartum and I'm feeling the effects of labor and delivery. The Advil and Tylenol combo barely seems to take the edge off the discomfort. Then again, I'm probably not supposed to be standing on my feet, on hard cement, bent over an examination table for this long, this soon after birthing a child. I feel hot liquid and I know I'm bleeding heavily. I hope my pad is thick enough to handle the volume for the duration of this. Yet, who cares about my discomfort. My baby is fighting for her life and currently fear-filled and uncomfortable. Does she feel betrayed by me, her mother, who is seemingly imposing this on her?

"She's a feisty one," comments the technician.

"Good," I say defiantly. "She needs to be with all she has to overcome." But I wish she'd just fall asleep.

Please Lord let this be over soon.

I now see why nurse aides come to these tests and not parents. As I will the time to pass and the nuclear medicine to work through Charlotte's system quickly, my mind wanders to Jesus' mother Mary. I've never given her much thought, but in this moment I wonder if this resembles how she felt as she watched Jesus carry the cross to his death. As she watched her child in agony and pain, struggling, like my child is struggling. Her mama heart must have shattered into pieces, like mine is now. It seems a little dramatic to compare the two very different situations, but a mama watching her baby suffer is hell, no matter the circumstance.

My resolve to withstand the pain renews. If Mary could do this, I can too. If Charlotte has to go through this, I need to, too. But after this test, I vow I will never hold my child down like this again.

Never again.

 Embracing the Pain

At this moment, I feared my child would identify me as yet another set of hands that inflicted pain. Because of this, I vowed I'd never hold her down for a medical procedure again. I took it so far as to leave the room whenever she was having pain inflicted upon her while in the NICU (think blood draws, IV placements, retaping her face for the cleft, etc.). Yet, as time went on it became apparent that avoiding her when she was in pain was in fact a selfish thing to do on my part. She needs me to be present with her in the pain, and she needs to know I won't leave her when things get tough. I've come to learn that honesty is the best policy, being painfully (literally) clear with her about what's going to happen, and then being there with her every step of the way.

I learned this most poignantly from our occupational therapist who helped me think about "holding Charlotte down" in a whole new light. There are and will be endless examples of when Charlotte needs me to be there for her in the hardships of life and avoiding them is not helping her identify my hands as gentle and loving. It's in fact teaching her that I abandon her when things get tough. So now, I try to be there when things are uncomfortable, talking her through it and providing as much comfort as possible, even amidst the pain and yes, even if it requires me to hold her down.

Chapter 20 Clownfish

Friday, December 1, 2017

"Who's going to scrub in for Huddle? Mom or Dad?" the operating room (OR) nurse gestures a neatly folded and stacked extra-large white gown, blue bootie covers and a matching hair net toward Dan and I. Dan is ghost white. I probably look the same.

"You go. Be with your baby," Dan says. He senses my need to see her. To touch her. To reassure her everything will be alright. But will it? She's only five days old. Is she strong enough to be put under anesthesia? Will her heart handle it? Are we making the right decision here, to send her to the OR with complete strangers and hope for the best? Yet, we don't have much of an option, really.

Without delay, the nurse starts unbuttoning the large disposable paper gown and ushers me to step in. I feel like I'm having an out of body experience. I watch as Dan steadies my arm and I balance on one foot, then the other, as the nurse puts the bootie covers over my tennis shoes. The nurse stands up and finishes buttoning the front of the gown as I shove my three-day-unwashed greasy strands under a hair net. To think I was so focused on dressing for success the first day after Charlotte's birth. Now it's a good day if I comb my hair or brush my teeth by noon. Doing both is a huge win.

"We provide nothing but the best style. Introducing the marshmallow gown," chuckles the nurse, breaking the tension with a little humor. I look like one of those blow-up Halloween costumes with a built in fan. The scrubs swallow me.

Charlotte is lying in her isolette right beside us as we make final preparations for surgery. She squirms, wanting to sleep after the traumatic HIDA scan this morning, but catching no rest with all this hubbub. I wonder if she senses the tension. The overwhelming and now-familiar urge to scoop her up and run away rushes through my veins. I envision myself running through the hospital halls carrying a tiny infant like a football, wires dragging behind us and my oversized white and blue garb swishing with every hurried step. I doubt I'd get very far before security would tackle me and confiscate my baby.

But this all happened so fast. We knew surgery was looming, but today? Right now? Didn't we just discuss in rounds this morning that surgery would likely be Monday? Was that just this morning? It feels like weeks ago. I'm so tired.

Apparently a space opened in the OR schedule and the surgeon was able to squeeze us in before the weekend, so here we are. Charlotte and I had just returned from the HIDA scan, and I left to pump, grab a sandwich and take a deep breath. I needed to calm my shaken nerves after the stress of this morning's test. After pinning my child down. I had no idea I'd return from lunch to see her packed up and ready for the OR this afternoon. How much can one little body take in a day? Or her mother, for that matter. Yet, I'm grateful we are getting this show on the road. No more standing around, testing and wondering who will make the first surgical move. It's go time.

We are all gathered in the second-floor hallway, one level below the NICU. The OR doors are ahead of us to our right. To our left is the Special Delivery Unit where I gave birth just a few short days ago. Was that merely a few days ago? It feels like a lifetime ago, yet my groaning body begs to differ. It keeps trying to heal while I keep putting it through hell. I hurt so bad and my body cries to sit down. I silently reprimand it, willing it to obey. There is no room to deal with my body right now. It'll just have to wait.

A couple of doctors in scrubs wheel a COW just like the ones from the NICU up next to us and begin reviewing plans for surgery. "I am the anesthesiologist from the cardiac anesthesiology team," says a man with a very thick accent. I can't place what country or nationality he is. I strain to understand him. We've worked with so many doctors from all over the world already. I've gotten used to having to really focus to understand the many heavy accents. The melting pot here at Cleveland Clinic is amazing. I love that doctors from Lebanon, India, Portugal and countless other countries have come here to practice medicine. This reassures me Cleveland Clinic must be a sought-after hospital where the best of the best medical professionals come to work.

To be honest, I never researched Cleveland Clinic or any other hospital to determine which would be best suited to care for our daughter. With all the various diagnoses and no one syndrome or diagnosis to explain Charlotte's anomalies, it was entirely too overwhelming to even think about researching. Where would I start?

Would I look for the best cardiology team? The best cranio-facial for her cleft? And the abdominal cyst was still unidentified so what specialty would I research for that? How about the brain malformations with neurology? Then there are the kidneys and urinary system. Would I research the best pediatric urology hospital? I decided to just trust the countless people who told me Cleveland Clinic was an excellent hospital and leave it at that. Was that bad of me? Was I a bad mom for not vetting out these people before I delivered Charlotte here? Too late now.

"I've reviewed all the notes and tests and I will take all the precautions possible, knowing her heart conditions," says the anesthesiologist.

Dan and I nod, hearing him but not really processing. Our heads spinning. It's all too much to take in.

"Sign your consent here," he hands an e-sign pen to Dan.

"I'm Doctor Apple, a Urologist who works with Dr. Fuhrman. He's the Urologist you've worked with thus far," she steps forward and extends her hand to shake ours. "Dr. Fuhrman and I work closely together and this afternoon I will be performing Charlotte's surgery. I have young kids of my own and I treat every patient as if they were mine." She has an air of authority about her, and though her words should be comforting, I find myself feeling angst toward her. Where is Dr. Fuhrman? I don't know him well but at least I've spoken with him once or twice and I know he's personally reviewed Charlotte's charts and test results.

"We are going to place two nephrostomy tubes through

Charlotte's back directly into both kidneys, allowing them to drain into nephrostomy bags," she continues. "As you know, Charlotte's ureters are blocked and while she has had some urine output since birth, it's not nearly the volume it should be."

Okay, so she must have done her homework. That is comforting.

"Her kidneys are enlarged and creatinine numbers are climbing, indicating the kidneys need pressure relief before further damage is done. We are hoping we can save the majority of the kidney function by inserting these tubes. The nephrostomy tubes are a temporary measure, until she can grow a little bigger and we can surgically implant the ureters into the bladder, which are not currently connected. Now of course this comes with risks …"

 Targeting Emotions to Others

Emotions are obviously running high in situations like this and it is easy to target our emotions at the medical staff—the very people working to help us. It's common to feel angry, bitter, anxious or annoyed by doctors and nurses, like I was feeling toward Dr. Apple, though my emotions really had nothing to do with her and everything to do with the situation at hand.

Similarly, it's easy to subconsciously target our emotions toward well-meaning family and friends who are there to help. Sometimes simply an awareness of this helps us understand what we are really feeling and why, and how to avoid taking our emotions out on them.

She goes on to list all the possible complications that could result from this intervention, like at the end of a pharmaceutical commercial where the voice-over speaks in triple speed about how you could have chest pain, vomit, diarrhea, or possible death. Just like that. It's enough to make us think we are making the worst decision for our child, taking on all these risks.

"But all of these outcomes are very unlikely. I just have to tell you all possible risks," she pauses, noticing our fear-stricken expressions. "This is a simple procedure, really. In no time, you'll have your girl back and her kidneys will be draining," she comforts like a pat on the head.

"We will also conduct a cystoscopy to better assess the cyst on Charlotte's biliary tree and liver while she's under anesthesia. The gastroenterology team will be there for that portion of the procedure. The whole operation should take us a few hours," she concludes. "Do you have any questions?"

So many. Yet, none. Dan and I both shake our heads no. "Okay, then please sign your consent here." Dan and I look at each other for confirmation. We both nod and he signs.

The OR nurse hands Dan an old-school black pager on a lanyard. "I'll be with Charlotte through the entire procedure and will provide you updates on this pager. You'll probably hear from me halfway through to tell you how everything's going and then again at the end. When it's all said and done, Dr. Apple will come out and speak with you while we get her settled back in the NICU for post-op care. Then you can come be with her, bedside. Dad, you can give your baby girl a kiss goodbye now. Mom, you'll go with us into the OR for Huddle. It's where we will again go over the procedure, confirm your child's birthdate and name, and make sure everyone is on the same page before we begin. Then you can come back out to wait with Dad."

Daniel turns to Charlotte and opens the two small oval side doors of the isolette, designed for arms to fit through. He cups Charlotte's head and feet like Candace showed us. His eyes fill with tears and despite his best efforts to hold them back, I see one slip down his cheek and splash on the clear plastic isolette before rolling off to the floor.

"I love you sweet girl. Daddy loves you," he quietly whispers. His gaze lingers for a few seconds before withdrawing his hands and closing the two doors again. Without hesitating, the OR nurse begins wheeling Charlotte into the OR room and the surgeon ushers me after.

It's just like in the shows and movies—the whitewash walls, the bright lights, the army of scrubs, each person with their specialized role in the whole operation, tools and equipment lining the walls and one tiny little table in the middle of the room for the infant patient. They transfer Charlotte from the isolette to the operating table which has a blue air mattress pumping warm air to keep her temperature up in the exposed and otherwise cold room. I step around the mass of wires still connecting her to the isolette and slip my index finger into her tiny little hand. She grasps on.

The surgeon runs through all the details again. I hear Dr. Apple's questions. "Mom, can you please state the full name of our patient? What's her birthday? And in your own words, what are we going to do today?" I'm struggling for words. My brain is foggy and it takes me a moment to generate her name and birthday in my head. Like the filing cabinet of my brain is dumped and scrambled and I cannot find the most important file. After I finally spit out my answers the room goes silent and all eyes land on me.

"You can give her a kiss Mom and then our OR nurse will walk you back to Dad," Dr. Apple says.

Now it's my turn to cry. I can't help it. Like a rush of damned water that was building, building, building, it comes. Until now it's been all business. All focus on getting to the OR. Now we're here and it's time for me to leave. Swiftly and silently the tears stream down my face. I try to hold them back. What if they are not sterile? What if I splash them on Charlotte and screw things up? How absurd a thought. I don't want to look like I can't keep my act together in front of all these professionals. But what's the use of trying to seem tough. I'm not. I wipe my cheeks with the back of my sweater sleeve. I watch through blurred vision as they place a mask over Charlotte's mouth and nose. She starts crying, but the sound is muffled in the mask and eventually fades as the gas from the mask puts her to sleep. Her grip loosens on my finger and her long skinny arm gently falls to the table. I watch, horrified.

"We will take great care of her. She is comfortable now," I feel the OR nurse's hand on my arm, ushering me out of the room. I lean over and give Charlotte's forehead a kiss and mumble, "*Lord, help us,*" before following him through the large double doors, leaving my baby girl splayed on the operating table.

"Did you see Nemo?" Dr. Apple gestures toward the eight-foot-long aquarium that's beside us in the hallway of the pediatric floor, right outside the NICU and PICU. "He's a hit among our pediatric patients. He's an anemonefish, a clownfish. Did you know all clownfish are protandrous sequential hermaphrodites, meaning they're born male and the largest most dominant one becomes female?"

I stare at Dr. Apple, confused. Why are we talking about fish?

"I can see you are both really stressed," she says to Dan and me, who are clinging to each other for dear life again, an all-too-familiar position. We are holding our breath to hear how the surgery went and how our daughter is doing. I don't give a flying fig about a white and orange striped fish's reproductive tendencies.

"I sometimes tell parents that fun fish fact to help break up the tension and divert your attention for a minute. Your brains need a break from the stress, even if only for a minute," she looks at us with concern. "These days must be very stressful for you both."

I think I might jump out of my skin. Get on with it! Tell us what's going on! The well-intended diversion has caused my anxiety to skyrocket.

"Your daughter is doing very well. She's in the NICU recovering now," she gestures toward the secured NICU door. "As soon as the nurses are ready, they'll come get you to be with her. We successfully inserted the nephrostomy tubes and they are draining. She had a lot of buildup in the kidneys. This weekend will be telling, to see urine output, measure volumes and follow labs. The GI team will come speak with you separately about the cystoscopy."

She pauses and lets us process this news before resuming. "Emily and Dan, this is a marathon, not a sprint. We are going to be working with you over the next few years to correct Charlotte's urinary system and I know that's only one system of multiple that needs repairs. But she is a tough girl, and we will take it one step at a time. Today was a big step."

Chapter 21 Mourning

Sunday, December 3, 2017

"Alleluia, Alleluia, Alleluia," everyone around me is singing. I can't find my voice. Every time I open my mouth to join the congregation, squeaks are all that come out. The tears won't stop flowing and they only amplify every time I try to say or sing something. I've given up trying to contain them. It's like someone left the hydrant on. My eyes are a leaky hose and my nose is dripping too. The soggy kleenex smashed in my right hand is useless at this point, shredded and leaving little white wet balls of tissue residue all over my palm.

I've never been a pretty crier. I remember one time in elementary school I was sitting in the school office waiting for my mom to come pick me up because I had strep throat. I was crying and my face was all red and blotchy, an annoying trait of my fair complexion. The principal walked in and looked at me with shock. "Are you having an allergic reaction?" he asked with urgency.

"No," I whimpered. "I'm just crying."

Dan is standing next to me with his right hand on my back, unsure how to help. There's nothing he can do to help. All I want is my baby. I look down and try to focus on the hymnal balanced in my cold and shaky left hand. My arms should be full, holding my newborn right now. I should be holding Charlotte. My memory flashes to the few minutes after she was born when they laid her on my chest, skin-to-skin. When I could feel her breath against me, her heart beating next to mine. When I could smell the top of her head. She smelled like me.

I want to rock her to the songs and the prayers. I want to teach her about her loving God. I want to comfort her and sing to her. But she's lying on her back in a hospital infant bed, two days post-op, while I am sitting on this hard wooden pew and I'm falling apart.

This is the first time I've left the hospital to go anywhere besides my own bed, which is now three blocks away from the NICU. When I was discharged a few days ago, the Ronald McDonald House down the street (not to be confused with the Ronald McDonald Family Room that's inside the hospital) opened their doors and gave Dan and I a bedroom to stay in for the indefinite future. I'm so grateful for the opportunity to be near the hospital, rather than commuting an hour each day from home. I cannot fathom being 60 miles away from my daughter every night, fighting to get through rush hour to get to my child's bedside each morning. I don't want to be ungrateful, yet 60 miles, 3 blocks or one building, any distance farther than in my arms is too much. I haven't even held her since the day she was born, besides pinning her down for that horrific HIDA scan.

I close my red-rimmed eyes and imagine what it will be like to hold her again.

For our first public outing, this is going horribly. But we had to rip the band aid off sometime. We knew we couldn't stay in the NICU forever without losing our minds. We were starting to go batty in there. Patty Clewell fondly and wisely put a term to what we were feeling—NICUitis—that feeling you get when all you've heard for a week straight is the beeping, bumping, pumping, squeaking of the NICU.

Patty is Charlotte's nurse today and she found herself nursing Dan and me, too. Apparently, we looked pretty ashen and sickly, because after fetching us both water and asking us if we'd eaten anything recently, she lovingly but firmly said we needed to leave.

"I have everything under control here. You two need to go," she said. "You're going to be no use to Charlotte if you don't take care of yourselves. Go get some dinner, take a long shower, go on a date, do whatever you want. But you need to get out of here. I will take care of her like she's my own daughter." And I believed her. Watching her care for Charlotte today was evidence that she takes her job very seriously. She moved calmly and methodically as she performed the same duties she must have done a thousand times before on previous patients. Every motion was gentle and confident, checking Charlotte's temperature, taking her blood pressure, moving her pulse ox, changing her diaper, adjusting her position, swaddling her, checking her lines, making sure the unsterile nephrostomy tubes didn't cross with the sterile IV lines, carefully adjusting the tape on Charlotte's face that held her divided lips together. She even referenced Charlotte as Little

Peanut throughout the day. The endearing nickname made me feel so grateful this is more than a job to Patty. It's clearly her vocation.

But how could I leave my child? Moms don't leave their newborns. Anywhere. Ever. Not at least for the first few weeks, and even then I've heard of moms who really struggle to leave their babies with babysitters or even with the child's dad. It's not natural. It's not normal. I have got to stop thinking about what is normal. This situation is far from normal and if I continue down this path of comparing what is normal I will go absolutely crazy. I've been doing it all day.

This morning during rounds Dr. Rick decided today was the day they'd introduce a small amount of breastmilk to Charlotte's digestive system and see how she handled it. I was elated. Charlotte's first meal! I insisted Patty make sure I was there when Charlotte received her first feed because that's what a mom does—moms feed their babies. Patty promised that when it came time to administer the feed, she would wait for me. I rushed to the pump room and came back twenty minutes later with a 65mL (a little more than two ounces) bottle of fresh, warm breast milk. I handed the bottle to Patty, proud of how much I had made, and Patty sucked 15mLs (a half of an ounce) into a syringe. She then proceeded to attach the syringe to an orange nasogastric (NG) tube that went through Charlotte's right nostril and down her esophagus. She placed the syringe in a machine and programmed it to slowly administer the feed. A speech therapist, ironically also named Patty, was there to help teach Charlotte to suck even though the milk was being automatically emptied into her stomach. She dipped a small blue rubber pacifier in the bottle of remaining breastmilk and gently inserted it into Charlotte's mouth, using her free hand to rub Charlotte's chin.

"The goal is to teach her that a full stomach comes after sucking. Rubbing her chin stimulates the sucking reflex," explained Patty, the speech therapist. "We are starting with the NG tube and a pacifier, before we introduce a bottle, to make sure her digestive system can handle feeds. Then we can progress to a bottle and see how she does with eating in light of her cleft lip and palate. She should be able to handle a specialty bottle no problem, but we want to only introduce one variable at a time. So for now, the variable is the milk, not the feeding method."

Charlotte munched on the pacifier aggressively. "Good job, Charlie Jo!" I encouraged, not knowing what else to do with myself. I was here for the feed as Patty promised, but I was watching on the sidelines. It was such a shockingly unfamiliar way to feed a baby. I was elated that her belly was going to finally feel the satisfaction of having some food in it, albeit a miniscule amount, but I was simultaneously fighting off disappointment that her first meal was administered by a machine and a therapist. Then came that familiar rush of guilt. Why was I worried about how she gets fed, so long as she *is* fed? Yet, this approach was so unnatural. I longed to hold her to my breast and let her suckle like she was programmed to do. Like babies are meant to do. There's that comparison to normal again.

"When do you think I can try to breastfeed her?" I asked. I knew full well Charlotte may never be capable of breastfeeding, even if given the chance. Medical reasons aside, her cleft likely would limit her ability to form a full seal that is necessary to create suction. Before she was born, Dan and I dutifully, or perhaps defiantly, attended a breastfeeding class for first-time parents because we were told there was a small percentage of cleft babies who *can* indeed form suction. It just depended on the severity of the cleft, said the breastfeeding consultant. Charlotte's is a complete cleft lip and palate on the right side, meaning there is no lip extending all the way into the nose and there is no roof of her mouth on the right side, all the way to the back of her throat. She also has a partial cleft lip and palate on the left, meaning there is a notch missing in the lip and the first half of the palate is missing on the left side. So, pretty severe. The Plastics team refers to her diagnosis as bilateral, meaning on both sides of the mouth.

"We will certainly give it a try, once she's able to be held, proves she can handle breast milk from the NG and then can also transition well to the bottle," Patty the speech therapist said. "Keep up with pumping in the meantime. Breast milk is the best source of nutrition for her right now." So, it's going to be a while. I've never enjoyed running, but the image of a long-distance runner jumping hurdles popped into my mind. I hear Dr. Apple's comment on repeat, "This is a marathon, not a sprint."

I absently watch the priest go through the motions of the mass while I replay all the conversations and hurdles of the day, riding this tidal wave of grief. It's winter in Northern Ohio, and the sun is already set for the Sunday evening service. The church is warmly lit with Christmas tree lights and the first purple candle on the Advent wreath is lit by the altar. But my heart matches the dark stained-glass windows, once filled with bright vibrant color, now shadowed, cold, black.

When Patty shooed us out of the NICU, we didn't know where to go. So, we landed here with plans to get dinner after the service. I hoped coming here would provide respite for my hurting heart. Yet my sorrow is so deep it seems to have seeped into my very bones.

People keep telling me it's okay to cry. That it's okay to not be okay. While well intended, this comment is infuriating. I nod and smile but I want to say, "Do I really look okay to you?" I must be putting on a tough face because I am *not* okay. Do I need to prove it to people that I'm not okay, to help them feel better about my current emotional state? I don't have the capacity to worry about their emotional needs. I can hardly meet my own. What do they want from me? It's like they need validation that I am hurting. Like my tough exterior scares them.

There's hardly any time to cry in the NICU anyway. There is a steady stream of specialists, doctors and nurses who come to meet with Dan and me. They tell us the latest diagnosis for this or that. They review test results, examine Charlotte for the millionth time and run through the litany of if-this-then-that's. I don't have time to cry. I feel like I'm Charlotte's medical manager who is booked all day long with consultations. This is the most intense job I've ever had with minimal opportunity to even take a restroom break. Who has the time to break down in tears when every fifteen minutes there's a new person standing by our daughter's isolette, waiting to speak with me as soon as the person in front of them is done? They literally line up to meet with me and Dan. In between all these meetings I am pumping every two hours from the beginning of the last pump, round the clock, and each pump takes twenty minutes. So that leaves only 1 hour and 40 minutes to squeeze as many doctor consults in as possible before I have to sneak to the pump room again.

Plus, there is no space to cry. Ironically, at the back of many Catholic churches is a room labeled the Cry Room. It's intended for parents to take little kids when they need space to let their kid make a bunch of noise, as kids do. The NICU needs one of these rooms, but for parents. A safe space to close the door and let out all the bottled emotions. And there should be coffee, water and wine available in this room, along with a comfy couch and soft tissues, not the sandpaper that is mislabeled as tissues offered by the hospital sanitation department.

I suppose I feel safe in this space, here in God's house, because the emotions are spilling out at an alarming rate. And hey, there's wine here, too! I'd love to take the entire chalice and chug it. The irony of the fleeting joke, and the resulting image in my head, makes me chuckle to myself and snort in the midst of my silent tears.

Oh Lord, I need you. I'm falling apart at the seams.

"Go in peace, to love and serve the Lord," concludes the priest.

"Thanks be to God!" replies the congregation before they spill into the aisle toward the doors to head home.

Dan and I make it to our car before he breaks the silence and asks, "Do you still want to go to dinner?" He's wise enough not to ask if I'm alright. Clearly I'm not.

"I don't think I can face being in public anymore tonight," I say.

He looks at me with empathy and concern and says, "It's about time for the hormone shift they warned us about in birthing class. I'm sure that's not helping."

He's right. My milk just came in full force yesterday and my hormones are whacked. My body's adjusting from growing a baby inside of me to feeding a baby outside of me. I'm grateful he really paid attention at birthing class and his knowledge about hormone shift makes me feel loved and supported, even if he can't do anything about it, besides maybe find us some take out.

He pulls out his phone and researches the nearest restaurant. Even on a good day I'm terrible at picking out good places to get food. I've always left this task to him. "What are you in the mood for," he asks. "Mexican or Chinese?"

"I don't care," I say. "I'm not sure I'm going to be able to eat anyway, so get what you want."

He looks at me disapprovingly.

I feel guilty for being so weepy, like I'm letting him down on our big night out. "I'm sorry I'm not much fun to be around tonight," I say.

He doesn't respond right away as he continues searching Trip Advisor for the best reviews of local joints.

"I found a place one block away. Let's order there," he says. Then he looks up from his phone and adds, "It's okay Emily. I just wish I could make it better."

I wish he could, too.

"She's doing great though," he adds.

I nod absently.

He places the order, and we drive to pick it up before going back to our Ronald McDonald House room. It's much like a hotel room. Simple, yet effective. There's a double bed, a mini refrigerator, a television, dresser, and bathroom. It's a handicap room with extra wide doors and a walk-in shower. I'm grateful for the extra space since we will likely be here for a long while. Will we be reserving handicap-accessible rooms for the rest of our lives as Charlotte gets older? Will she be wheelchair bound? The question rolls through my mind as we spread our Chinese take-out on the bed and sit Indian style to choke down the already cold food.

Journal Entry - Monday, December 4, 2017

Good morning God,

We have a beautiful baby girl! She's seven days old and absolutely perfect. You formed her in the womb, and she is an image of you. God, we are so thankful for her. But God, you know all her health challenges. You know the struggles we are facing.

God, I feel broken.

When people ask me how I am I say "good" but think "broken." I haven't held my daughter since she was born, she has had a surgery and so many countless tests. She got to eat for the first time yesterday.

We went to church last night and I just cried the whole time because I wanted her with us. God, I want to be up all night with my baby. I want to be sleep deprived from feeding her and soothing her, not from doctors visits and surgeries. I know I'm pouting right now. I know I'm being a big baby myself. I know she's in the best care possible and I'll get my time to take care of her. But God, I'm still so sad and angry about it.

She's a beautiful newborn who doesn't get to do any of the typical newborn things. And she will have so many countless surgeries and appointments for the rest of her childhood. And God, the last couple days I've been mad at you. So darn pissed I could scream. But I need you now more than ever. Please don't shy away from me in my anger. Don't leave because I push you. Lean into my pain like I need to lean into Charlotte's pain.

God, I am sorry for my frailty and anger. Help me, God. I've never needed you more than now. I know we are blessed to be her parents. Help me to embrace that blessing and not to dwell on the 'what if's' and the 'it's not normals.'

Oh God, help me.

 ## It's Okay to Have all the Feelings

There is no need to be sorry about feeling angry or frail or any other emotion we experience. Emotions are valid and okay to experience. Here's the amazing thing—it's in our emotion and inner thoughts and experiences that God wants to meet us.

Remember, God desires intimacy with you—in-to-me-see. That means he wants to be let in to your true feelings and what's really going on in your heart. He will meet you right there in your anger, hurt and any other emotion you experience, if you let him. There is no shame in your emotions. In fact, they are an invitation to grow intimate with the Lord.

"Blessed are the poor in spirit, for theirs is the kingdom of heaven. Blessed are those who mourn, for they will be comforted. Blessed are the meek, for they will inherit the earth." (Matthew 5:3-5)

Why? Because it is when we are poor in spirit, when we mourn, when we are meek that we have the opportunity to let our Lord into our hearts at an even deeper level than maybe we realized or were open to before. It is here we have the opportunity to be intimately close with our Lord, and that closeness is what our hearts deeply desire.

Chapter 22 Broken

Monday, December 4, 2017

I can't take my eyes off her. Her little head fits perfectly in my cradling left hand and her tiny body is lost in the tangle of blanket, wires and leads as she rests in my right arm. The nurse hovers over us working diligently to place each line so it's not kinked or tugging on Charlotte's skin. She uses two hemostats, scissor-looking tools that do not cut but clamp, to secure the yellow nephrostomy bags to the pillow that's laying on my lap under Charlotte, supporting both her body and my arm.

"Are you comfortable?" asks the nurse as she fusses.

I nod but barely register what she's asking. I'm so engrossed in my daughter. This is the moment I was dreaming about last night and every other minute since Charlotte's birth. She's finally back in my arms.

I gently rock back and forth out of maternal instinct, then stop and look up with fear, "It's okay to rock, right?" I ask urgently, snapping out of my euphoria, worrying I'm going to screw up the IV or otherwise harm my child from rocking her.

"Yes, of course," she reassures.

I sigh in relief and resume gentle motion back and forth. Back and forth. Charlotte is sound asleep. Peaceful. I thought I'd cry happy tears when I finally got to hold her again. But no tears come. Maybe I emptied them all out last night. Let's hope so. I'm so tired of crying. Now I just have an overwhelming sense of relief. A sense of rightness. I keep rocking, back and forth, back and forth, staring at her.

She scrunches her face in her sleep like she's having a bad dream. "It's okay, Sweet Girl," I whisper. "Mama has you." Her face relaxes again. My own mother is sitting with me, watching me hold her granddaughter. She's snapping picture after picture, smiling, and sniffling back her own tears.

I feel a little woozy, like my head is in the clouds and my throat hurts. I will the signs of illness to go away. I don't have time to get sick. I am busy holding my daughter.

Dan came with me to the NICU this morning but left after twenty minutes because he wasn't feeling well. He said he felt feverish, and his throat hurt. We know better than to bring any illness into the NICU. These babies don't need to get even the common cold, on top of all they are dealing with already. I thought I felt fine so I stayed. I do feel bad for Dan, though, that he's missing this opportunity to hold Charlotte.

Am I just paranoid now and feeling symptoms because I'm afraid I'm getting sick, too? Or am I really starting to feel ill? It's hard to tell the difference when I just generally don't feel well all the time anyway. Blame it on just giving birth a week ago, on the average of four hours of interrupted sleep every night, on the crazy stress of this situation or on hormone shift. There are about a million reasons why I might not feel good, so surely I'm not actually sick.

"She looks content," comments the nurse, smiling at us from her computer on the other side of Charlotte's isolette, where she is now charting, giving us space to snuggle.

Charlotte looks just like Dan. I'm told that's nature's way of helping father's bond with their children, because most newborns look just like their dads.

Charlotte has his wrinkly forehead that's super expressive. I thought I didn't want her to inherit this trait, but now I find it endearing. Every time her eyebrows go up or down the nasal elevator, which is basically a tiny plastic rounded hook in her nostril that's taped to her forehead, bobs up and down with each expression. The hook is meant to help her nose stay in place, since due to the cleft it lays flat like it's been smushed. Our craniofacial plastic surgeon says if we are diligent about keeping the elevator in place it will help her nose gain shape and might even alleviate a rhinoplasty surgery in the future. It also helps her breath currently by holding the nostril up where it should be.

She's so beautiful.

There is all the normal commotion of the NICU surrounding us as doctors and nurses and parents come in and out, attending to the other three babies in our room. But my world falls silent and all I see is my baby. It's as if the rest of the room blurs into a haze of background motion while me and my baby are crystal clear. Like time slows and I observe every second in great detail.

Her breathing. In. Then out. Her head covered with fuzzy, dark, baby fine hair. Her hair line like an adorable old mans, starting halfway back on her head. The soft warmth of her head in my hand. Her little, white-socked foot sticking out of the blanket bundle as if to defy being contained. Her beautiful lips, albeit with a great portion missing and currently taped together, are relaxed. Her ears so cute, tiny and perfect, taped back to her head because they still fold in half just like at birth. When pulled back to their intended position, they are shaped just like Dan's.

Again, Plastics says using the tape regularly will hopefully alleviate having to do anything surgical to fix the ears and will optimize the success of the lip adhesion surgery which is slated for when she is three months old. Apparently babies' skin and cartilage will grow in whatever position you put them. The goal is over time, so long as we keep the nose, lips and ears in the right positions with tape and an elevator, they'll grow to stay that way on their own. Amazing.

Before we arrived this morning at our usual 9 a.m., the NICU staff pulled one of Charlotte's two umbilical lines, the one that was the most fragile, and started transitioning her to a regular IV. That means holding her is now possible because the threat of bleeding out is lowered. Hallelujah for that.

My mind wanders to all Charlotte has and will face in her life. While my focus up until very recently was on the question "Will she survive?" I have subconsciously transitioned to the question, "What will life look like for her?" It's hard to imagine because all I see is hurdle after hurdle after hurdle. We know she will need countless surgeries to correct everything … we don't know how many, but it will surely be in the double-digits.

And every specialist has their own commentary of all the possible outcomes. One example: Neurology read the MRI results to us a couple days ago and confirmed she has Agenesis of the Corpus Callosum, meaning the bundle of nerves that connects the right and left lobes of the brain is missing. We knew this before her birth, and we also knew the implications of this are all over the map. She may never walk or talk. Or she may be able to run marathons. She may have learning delays or she may be a straight A student. No one knows. Her nervous system is only one of the many bodily systems in question.

My head spins with all that needs to be accomplished in the next week, month and year(s) just to keep her alive and help her possibly even eventually thrive, if I dare let myself dream that to be the case. But if her own mother can't dream of her thriving, then who can? I must hold on to that hope, while still living the daily reality of these diagnoses. She's counting on me to hold on to that hope.

Then the startling question: did we make the right decision to go through with this pregnancy and keep her here with us, only to face all these horribly painful and seemingly inhumane interventions? This question keeps popping in my head and I keep shoving it away like an unwelcome visitor. I don't want to even acknowledge the idea that we could have ended her life long ago. I cannot fathom it. Yet, are we selfish expecting her to fight for her life now? For the first time, I allow this question some headspace and really think about it.

No. I know we absolutely without a doubt made the right decision to not abort. If God gave her breath and a heartbeat, I am not going to take that away based on my idea of what life *should* look like or my preconceived notions of what 'quality of life' means. I cringe at the reality of what a late-term abortion would have looked like for Charlotte, had we chosen it.

They would have dismembered her body, limb by limb, while she was still in the supposed protective care of my womb. They would have pulled her out, arm by arm, leg by leg, removing the head last. The procedure is called a D&E, dilation & evacuation. With no use of anesthetics or numbing agents for the baby, she would have felt the unimaginable pain of literally being pulled apart, just like she feels pain now. And I would have been left with an empty uterus, empty arms, and the sickening subpar reassurance that I spared her a lot of pain later in life. Or worse yet, that I spared her from a life of disability. As if we even know what ability she could have or which abilities are worth living for.

The thought makes me feel like I'm going to wretch—that sickening feeling like something is so grotesque that I have to get away from it lest the evil of it consume me. I feel guilty for even thinking about the reality of what aborting Charlotte would have been like. I pull her in closer to me in a position of protection as I rock—protection from the world and also protection from my wandering mind.

Yet, should we have ceased intervention to keep her here, and simply let her pass after birth? Comfort care, as Dr. Carvalho referred to it. Living in today's age, we have so many medical advances that are amazing, yet do we prolong a life that should be allowed the mercy to pass?

The irony hits me. One moment, we human beings are willing to end our babies' lives in horrific fashion, literally ripping their limbs apart and their heads off under the guise of women's rights, and the next moment we are performing radical intervention to save babies' lives. The same babies who, once born, are illegal to kill, but so long as they are invisible to the naked eye inside a woman's body, it's accepted by culture to kill them. It's mind boggling.

I could have legally ended Charlotte's life up to 22-weeks-gestation based on current 2017 Ohio law. Yet, looking around me here in this NICU, there are 24-week-old babies fighting for their lives and the chances of them surviving are high. How twisted and confused and ugly are we! We are so blind to the gift of life.

 ## Value of Life

This situation—having a child with major medical complexities with a very unknown future—it was inconvenient to say the least, it was beyond scary, it was not what I signed up for when I wanted to become a parent and it was certainly unexpected. Yes, the situation was unwanted, but it's important to distinguish the situation from the child.

The child remains a gift even in light of the situation. Therefore, we as parents are invited to open to this gift and receive, as hard and painful as it might be, trusting the Father gives good gifts to his children (Matthew 7:11), even when we don't understand.

If you're reading this and you have terminated a pregnancy or been involved in an abortion, oh how I wish I could wrap you in the biggest hug of love. While I will never pretend to understand your specific circumstances and what led to your decision to terminate, I have experienced how these situations can make you feel like your only option, and the most responsible/loving option is to abort. But oh, how untrue that is.

After further reflection, I've come to realize too that I had all the resources to help me choose life for my daughter including financial stability, a committed partner, supportive family, a knowledge of the value of every life from the moment of conception, and so much more. Many parents don't find themselves in such an environment that makes the decision as easy as it was for me and Dan. This realization has made my empathy for parents who have chosen abortion skyrocket and any trace of judgement squelched. Simultaneously, it's made me passionate about supporting parents at the point of diagnosis and beyond, so they feel empowered as capable parents who can do hard things for their children.

Our materialistic culture has shaped our ideas about children to subconsciously think of them as commodities, things we can have or do away with as we think is in the best interest of ourselves, our futures, our children and our families. So, out of good intentions we make a misguided choice to terminate our child's life. There are very rare occasions when a mother's life is in danger and treatment for the mother has the unwanted and unavoidable result of the loss of the baby's life (for example some forms of cancer or an ectopic pregnancy). That is different, when treatment is a life-saving act for the mother, not an intentional killing of the baby, and all possible avenues of saving the baby's life are considered. The bottom line is this: intentional termination of a fetus is a direct rejection of the gift that child is.

Oh, but please don't hear these words as condemnation or judgment. Please, please, please, hear them as only love and mercy. I wish you can hear my tone and see my face as I say them, so you can see the compassion in my eyes as I speak.

If you've been involved in an abortion, you can be sure that sweet precious babe remains alive and well with Jesus and Jesus is eager to extend forgiveness and love and mercy to you whenever you're ready to humbly ask him for it.

Oh, how very deeply he loves you. And if I, a sinful, broken human being can look at you with deep compassion, love and mercy, imagine how much more our Lord looks at you in this way. His mercy knows no end and it's offered to you, his beloved.

My anxiety spikes and I start to sweat as I mull these thoughts over. I don't want to dwell on abortion or on humanity at large because there is nothing I can do about it right here and now. However, I need to really wrestle with this question—the question of whether we should have opted for comfort care. If I don't, the stress of leaving it unaddressed is going to eat me from the inside out.

Staring at my daughter, rocking back and forth, I roll the question around in my mind.

Thus far, there has always been a next step. There has always been something to do to help her live. There has never been a "should we pull the plug" moment, so-to-speak. Our prayer before her birth was that if God wanted her to come home to him, that he just do it. And if he wanted her to stay with us, then please give us the next step to help her live.

And that is exactly what he's done. Always the next step. Not the next two, five or ten. But always the next one. I feel a sense of peace wash over me, reassuring me that we of course made the right decision to keep the pregnancy and we continue to make the right decisions to help her heal.

But it comes with a cost. A very hefty price. And I'm not referring to money. The hundreds of thousands of dollars racking up in medical expenses pale in comparison to the price of suffering. Great suffering for both her and me and her dad and everyone emotionally and physically involved in this wild ride of ups and downs.

I wish so badly I could take her suffering upon myself. I wish I could be the one hooked up to a bunch of monitors with tubes sticking out of my back and tape all over my face. My inability to intervene makes me feel helpless. And angry. So angry. Like a cornered animal. Like my hands are tied and there's nothing I can do but observe as painful experience after painful experience is inflicted on my child.

But that's not the way suffering works. I don't get to choose who is dealt suffering, and I don't get to take it away from my daughter. I only can be here for her. Love her through it. Hold her hand and give her as much support and encouragement and strength as possible. I don't get to control hardly anything about the situation, besides the way I show up to be here for her. This is one giant lesson in letting go of my control issues.

Perhaps that's parenthood in a nutshell—loving your child no matter what and helping them as best you can to navigate the struggles of this life, learning to let go of the fact that you cannot control them nor what happens to them. I hope my parenting can lead Charlotte to God, to take all her suffering to him and give it over to him. He may not take the suffering away, he didn't even take it away from Jesus, his one and only Son, but I know he will work all things for the good of those who love him. If Jesus' great suffering led to the salvation of all who believe in him, then surely Charlotte's suffering will lead to something good and beautiful, too. After all, she is made in his image and likeness.

While I am confident in this truth, I don't pretend to

understand it. Yet, my hope for Charlotte is that she grows to love him above all else and she leans on him as her perfect parent, more so than me, her imperfect mother who has a whole lot of questions and not a whole lot of answers.

I don't know what God is up to in this story as it's unfolding before me. But I have a sneaking suspicion it's something much bigger than I'll ever know, at least on this side of heaven. I have a feeling Charlotte's journey is going to have a profound impact of some kind, in some way, on countless people. I can't put my finger on it, but it's like I'm looking at this tiny little baby and at the same time looking at the face of someone who is actively changing the world for the better, starting with stretching her mama's capacity for love to a whole new level. Starting with teaching me how to suffer well. I never even knew suffering well was a thing, before her. Starting with teaching me about Love Himself.

Here I thought I'd be teaching her, but I'm quickly realizing it's quite the opposite. She is the teacher, and I am the pupil. She brings the light of God's love to earth in a very real, tangible, profound way. In her tiny, feisty, five-pound body that's resting on my lap right now.

I don't understand it. I may never understand it. But when I look at her face, I see the reflection of God.

"She handled her EBM trophic feeds through the night well, 1mL Q6," Dr. Rick says. EBM is short for Expressed Breast Milk. Trophic means a tiny amount to test the gastrointestinal system. Q6 means every six hours. So, basically, a drop of milk in her cheek every six hours. I'm getting the hang of this medical jargon.

"I think it's time we let her try the bottle and see how she does. Today we are going to increase her feeds to Q3 to match our NICU schedule and start at 15mLs per. If she does well we can slowly increase her feeds and decrease TPN." TPN means total parenteral nutrition, aka, the nutrition she's receiving from her IV fluids.

Dr. Rick is standing in front of me with his entourage of rounding NICU staff, looking at me holding Charlotte. He's smiling knowing what a momentous occasion this is for us both—Charlotte and me.

"You're doing great, Emily. Parental involvement is so critical to a baby's success here in the NICU," he says. Then he gets a little reflective for a moment. "You know, I've cared for hundreds of babies, all with varying levels of needs and family situations. There was one baby boy who stayed with us for seven months due to chronic issues. Every morning I'd come into the NICU and go straight to his bed to tell him good morning. He'd respond with a little wiggle and some excitement. He and I would talk about his night and we'd play for a minute before I started my shift. I loved that little boy. Shortly after I came in, his parents would come and greet him, too. It was as if I was chopped liver compared to them. He'd start wiggling like crazy and babbling for them. He'd light up with so much joy," Dr. Rick looks off in the distance as he relives this scene. Then refocusing on me he says, "You know something Emily, no matter how much I loved that boy, he always knew who his parents were, and he lived for when they came.

So, Charlotte is very blessed to have you. Very blessed. Your involvement, and Dan's too, and both your parents' who I see here every day with you, will help Charlotte more than any medical intervention we have. Together, with your love and our medicine, we are going to take good, good care of her."

Thank you, God, for Dr. Rick.

He's more of a physician than I could have hoped for.

"And fair warning," he adds. "Once I get to know a patient and their families, they become my family. So you're not getting rid of me anytime soon." He smiles mischievously and winks. Are all Neonatologists this amazing, or did we just strike gold?

They finish rounds on Charlotte and all-in-all, it sounds like it's going to be a day focused on feeding, resting, and healing for Charlotte. They move on to the next baby and I realize I desperately need to pee and pump lest my bladder and chest explode. I do not want to put Charlotte down, but I can't sit here forever. The nurse helps me move Charlotte and all her equipment back to her bed and she begins to wake.

"This is good," the nurse says. "Why don't you go pump while I check vitals and change her diaper. Then when you get back she'll be fully awake, and we can feed her your freshly pumped milk." I hurry to the bathroom and pump room, excited for this momentous occasion—Charlotte's first bottle!

When I return 20 minutes later Charlotte is wide awake and starting to fuss. She's hungry and annoyed with all the poking of the thermometer and blood pressure cuff. It turns out she *hates* having her temperature taken. I love how opinionated she is. She clearly has enough brain activity to get appropriately mad.

I pick up the pacifier and try to comfort her while the nurse preps the bottle. It's a Dr. Brown's Specialty bottle which is designed for babies who can't form a seal and suction.

"All she has to do is make the motions of sucking and the pressure from her tongue will express milk from the bottle," she explains as she pours 15 mLs in. "Now, for this first feed, I'm going to give it to her. I'm sure you really want to give it to her and you can once we've established she can swallow without trouble. But for the first one, it's best if I do it and am ready to help her if needed." While that disappoints me, I find comfort in knowing if anything goes south, Charlotte is in the hands of a very capable nurse.

She props Charlotte up on her bottom in the isolette and angles her body sideline. She supports Charlotte's head and shoulders with one hand while she offers the bottle with the other. "Here you go, Charlotte, you're first bottle," she says encouragingly. Charlotte curiously opens her mouth and feels this new rubbery material, rolling her tongue around the nipple. After getting a small taste of what is inside, she begins eagerly chomping. Before we know it, the bottle is empty and making a bubbly sound as she beckons every last drop out. Her body relaxes as the nurse sits her upright and begins burping her.

"Well, that was a success!" the nurse says.

Charlotte falls sound asleep in the sitting up position, her chin cradled in the nurse's hand, tuckered out from the effort of the tiny meal.

Mom and I are sitting beside the isolette, observing. I swell with pride and gratitude. Another hurdle jumped.

"Way to go, Charlie Jo," I whisper. The nurse lays Charlotte down and begins rearranging her bedding and wires again.

"It's Charlotte's web in here!" she jokes. "Do you want to hold her again, Mom?" she asks me.

I want to say yes, but I feel my temperature rising and my stomach hurts. "I think I might need to leave," I say. "I don't feel so good. I hope I'm not coming down with whatever Dan has."

She looks at me with concern and gets the thermometer. She waves it over my forehead. 100.7 degrees Fahrenheit. "Yeah, your temperature is elevated," she confirms.

This is the second time today that I'm rocking. But this time, I'm at home. My arms are empty and a cold pump is extracting milk as it rhythmically "whir whir, whir whirs" in the dark night. My dog circles anxiously around the rocking chair, sniffing this new contraption that is hooked up to me. Petey doesn't like it. He whines and flops on my feet as if exacerbated he can't take it away from me.

I'm so grateful both our dogs Petey and Gracie are home with us, providing some much-needed pet therapy. Mom's sister, Aunt Mandy, has kept them at her house since we left to give birth and she graciously dropped them off right before we got home today so we could have them with us. We figured we might as well come home to wait this virus out rather than stay cooped up in our Ronald McDonald House room, since we can't be with Charlotte anyway.

Dan's downstairs mindlessly watching YouTube while snuggling on the floor with Gracie. The Christmas tree is set up in its usual corner spot, standing bare. We never got around to putting lights on it or decorating it before Charlotte's birth. I wonder if we will even decorate it this year. Any other year I'd be stressed about getting it decorated ASAP. This year, my priorities are reshuffled. I couldn't care less about ornaments and twinkly lights.

I'm upstairs sitting in the hallway landing, pumping for what feels like the millionth time. As I rock back and forth I can see into the nursery we so diligently prepared for our baby. The nursery she has yet to be in. The nursery that sits empty.

Her crib is all set up, her stuffed animals neatly stacked in a basket, her clothes washed and folded, bows ready to adorn her head, diapers arranged with wipes at the ready. The room looks frozen in time, like it's patiently waiting for its owner who may not show for a long, long time.

When we got home this evening the house was all stuffy just like when you return from a long vacation and the air is stale. We were greeted by Oscar our cat howling as if he was dying, and the stench of feces. We found piles of his poop littered around the house. Welcome home.

At first, we thought something was wrong with him. But after investigating, we realized he was just rebelling against being left in a house for a week without his family. Mom's other sister, Aunt Gail, has been coming to check on him regularly and feed him, but apparently that was not enough to satisfy his need for our presence.

Dan got to work cleaning up the mess and opening windows despite the cold, while I came upstairs to pump.

Both of our fevers climbed all afternoon, mine currently at 101.5 degrees Fahrenheit and his at 102. As soon as the nurse took my temperature late this morning, I knew I had to leave. I felt so torn, not wanting to leave my baby girl but not wanting to get her sick either. My mom graciously volunteered that she and Dan's mom, Nancy, would take shifts staying with Charlotte in Dan's and my absence, until we were well enough to return. Thank God. I don't think I could have ripped myself away from the hospital if not for knowing Charlotte's loving grandmas would be with her.

As the pump drones on, I try to pinpoint what it is that I'm feeling. I don't seem to be feeling much of anything. I realize I'm feeling … empty. Empty like this nursery. Empty like my arms. Empty like I have nothing left in me. Empty like this pump is methodically working to drain me. Like my soul matches our Christmas tree branches … empty. And not just empty, but … broken.

Broken like my tear ducts don't work anymore. Broken like my body and immune system doesn't work anymore. Broken like my heart was left beating in Cleveland on the third floor in room one of the acute care NICU. Broken like I'm alive but barely breathing. Like I have nothing left in me but the next feverish breath. And the next one. And the next one. Like I'm going through the motions, but I am emotionless.

No tears. Just broken.

Chapter 23 My God, My God, Why Have You Abandoned Me?

Journal Entry - Thursday, December 7, 2017, 8:00 a.m.

Good morning Lord,

I don't know where to start praying this morning, so I guess I'll start by praising your name.

Praise your name for my milk supply. Praise your name for our home and our animals and our family and our neighbors and our work. Praise your name for Charlotte and the good couple of days she's had in a row. Praise your name for her creatinine numbers coming down and her kidneys functioning well with the nephrostomy tubes. Praise your name for an incredible NICU team and all the doctors and nurses who have cared for Charlotte. Praise your name for Dr. Rick and his incredible talent and people skills. Praise your name for our moms and Charlotte's grandmas and their constant care for Charlotte and us.

Most of all, praise your name for your constant love in the midst of my fear, worry, anxiety, sadness and anger. Praise your name for my husband's steadfast love and commitment to us. I clearly have so much to be thankful for, Lord. Help me to focus on these things in the days to come. Help me to focus on your goodness and not on the evil of this world.

Lord, if I'm honest, I'm still so angry and sad. Charlotte doesn't get to have a carefree childhood but instead will be in and out of surgeries for most of her young life. I'm sad and angry we don't get to enjoy the basics of having a newborn like bringing her home right away, snuggling with her at home, taking her to church, etc. I'm sad and angry that she has to be on pain meds. I'm sad and angry for her and for me and for Dan. But I know I have to remember we could have easily lost her completely and these are the tradeoffs to saving her life.

And Lord, her life is precious. She is so treasured. She is yours and she is loved. She is mine and I'll do what it takes to help her grow up to be the woman you created her to be.

Help me, Oh Lord. Help me.

Help Dan too, God. Continue to lead his heart to you and help him to process the hurt and lean into the pain. Thank you for his steadfast faith, God. Thank you.

Please draw my mom and Dan's mom closer to you too, Lord. We need them to be strong in the faith with us. Help them to share their worries and fears and anger with you too so you may help them heal.

Amen

Thanking God When You're at a Loss for Words

When you're at a loss for words or feeling hopeless and empty, prayer can feel impossible. A great place to start is by thanking God for all he has provided you. You'll be surprised how long the list is, no matter how dire your situation, and rather than simply focusing on the struggles you're facing, this will help you simultaneously appreciate the graces and gifts he's poured over you during your suffering and struggle. Gratitude doesn't replace pain and struggle, but it does adjust your perspective and renew your hope.

Thursday, December 7, 2017

"I see the NICU view camera is off. Is Charlotte okay?" I whisper, pressing the phone hard to my ear to hear Charlotte's night-shift nurse's response over the drone of my pump.

"She's a little fussy tonight. I think she's missing you," the nurse says.

I hear Charlotte crying in the background. She sounds hoarse, like she's been crying a lot. I recognize Charlotte's voice through the phone, knowing it's not one of the other three babies in her room because her cry is so unusually deep and forceful. The strength of her voice reminds me she is tough and full of spirit. Piss and vinegar as my mother would say.

My soul crushes listening to her wails, not being able to do anything for her. My ear aches from how hard I push my phone to my head, as if I can reach her through it.

"Dan and I just got back to Cleveland. We are at the Ronald McDonald House for tonight. Our fevers broke this morning so hopefully by tomorrow we will be 24-hours fever-free. We plan on coming in tomorrow morning," I quietly explain why we aren't there now, as much to help the nurse understand as to verbally remind myself why I cannot be with Charlotte tonight. We've made it three grueling days staying away from the NICU, to keep our germs at a safe distance. We just have to make it through one more night.

"I'll take good care of her, Mom. Grammy Nancy left at shift change and I turned on some Disney orchestra music which she seems to like. Especially the *Beauty & the Beast* soundtrack. I'll try turning it on again. It's bath night, too, so hopefully that soothes her," the nurse reassures. "You get some rest," she sounds distracted now.

I know she needs to hang up so she can get back to dealing with Charlotte. "Okay, thank you," I try to control my voice so it doesn't go up three octaves and reflect the shattered fragments of my heart. I hear her hang up on the other end of the line, but I keep holding the phone to my ear, wishing I could still hear my sweet baby's voice.

Charlotte likes Disney orchestra music? Why does a nurse know that about my daughter and I don't? I haven't even met this nurse before, and she knows more about my child than I do. Hot jealousy courses through my veins. I should be the one discovering my daughter's likes and dislikes. I should be the one trying to figure out how to comfort her best. She's been growing for nine months to the music of my beating heart. I want to lay her on my chest when she's crying and soothe her to that familiar rhythm.

And bath night … bathing her with all those lines attached to her scares me, yet I want to be the one gently wiping her down and rinsing the suds off. I want to be the one rubbing lotion on her sweet little legs and singing softly to her. Instead, I stare at the black screen on the NICUview app waiting for the nurse to turn the camera back on so I can watch her sterile-gloved hands do all these things in my place.

"Enjoy it while it lasts," said a well-meaning family friend when I lamented this weekend about not being my daughter's primary caregiver. "Because when you do take her home it'll be up to you 24/7. You'll miss the nurses and being able to get a full night's sleep by yourself. It won't happen again for years." He chuckled as he said it, like he just enlightened me with such infinite wisdom. I want to be furious at him for saying something so senseless. But he doesn't get it. He just doesn't get it.

I'm sure he means well. Everyone means well. Yet this comment is one of many that make it painfully obvious even people who love and care for us so deeply have no way of understanding what we are going through. They have no grasp of the realities of this situation. Try as they might, they just don't get it. And anyone who says they understand doesn't. Because if they truly understand, they'd never actually say that they understand.

 No One Understands

It becomes easier to have grace with others—family, friends, medical staff and even strangers—when we recognize they simply do not understand our situation. And quite frankly, thank God they don't understand because if they did, they too would have lived something so painful.

A familiar sense of loneliness creeps up on me and fills me in this dark room. I look out our window toward Cleveland Clinic and see city streetlights and traffic headlights buzzing below in the night. White flurries drift past our third-floor window and settle on the frozen December ground.

God, I'm so lonely.

Dan is sound asleep in the bed behind me. The pulse of the pump keeps beat with his snoring. How does he get to sleep so soundly, meanwhile I'm up, again, pumping milk to feed our daughter and worrying about her as I obsess over this NICUview app? Must be nice to sleep peacefully, uninterrupted. I wish he could help me with all this pumping so we could share the burden a little more. I am tempted to wake him, but for what? What would he do besides sit next to me and watch as the milk pools in the bottles? Loneliness sets deep in my bones, and I pull my sweater tight around my shoulders as if it's presence could comfort me.

God, why do I feel so alone? Where are you? Why have you abandoned me in this? I used to sense your presence with me day in and day out. I used to know you were with me, even amidst all the hardship, because I felt you. But now? I don't feel you at all. Where did you go?

The honest and earnest impromptu prayer bubbles out of me like a spring of water before I can catch and silence it.

My God, my God, why have you abandoned me?

As soon as this last question crosses my mind in a silent, desperate plea, Jesus' last words on the cross ring in my head. "*Eli, Eli, lama sabachthani?*" that is, "*My God, my God, why have you forsaken me?*"

(Matthew 27:46). I might not be nailed to a cross and left hanging to die, but I sure feel like I'm stuck in an unimaginable situation with no one to rescue me. No way out.

Burning tears stream down my face as I stare at the black NICUview screen. I don't know what to do, so I do the only thing I can think of. The thing that comes so naturally to me because I've been doing it for years now. I reach for my prayer journal and a pen. I have to get these thoughts on paper before they consume me. I start writing, but to my surprise, this time the words are not my own. My pen flies and before I know it I've filled an entire page.

Journal Entry - Thursday, December 7, 2017, 11:00 p.m.

Emily, my beloved,

I love you. I have not left you. I will not abandon you. I have not forsaken you. I am with you through these hard times. I have sent literally hundreds of people to be my hands and feet for you, Daniel, and Charlotte. I brought you and Daniel together for a reason and with great purpose I have formed Charlotte between you.

Love her. Love Dan. And most of all, love me. Do not shut me out in your hurt. For I Am the great healer. Come to me, you who are weary, and I will give you rest. I am strong enough to bear your pain, your hurt and even your anger. My love is so much bigger than any of those things.

Don't try to control the situation. Trust me and your only job is to love me and to love your family. Follow me. I will heal you—all three of you. Trust me.

Your loving Father, Abba

I put my pen down and sit mesmerized by what is written in front of me.

"*I will not abandon you,*" he says.

"*I have sent literally hundreds of people to be my hands and feet for you, Daniel, and Charlotte,*" he says.

"*With great purpose I have formed Charlotte between you,*" he says.

"*I will heal you—all three of you,*" he says.

Somehow, deep inside my being, in a way I simply cannot adequately comprehend nor explain, I know these things to be true. Like the fresh winter air fills my starving lungs every night after being in the stuffy hospital all day, for the first time since Charlotte's birth I feel like I can breathe again. I know without a doubt these words are of God and from God. I would have never been so bold as to have promised myself such lofty ideas. I never would have had such profound love and grace and compassion with myself or with the situation. I certainly would never have promised myself that he would heal us, all three of us. That would only set myself up for too much pain, if it didn't turn out to be true.

But my God, my Father, Abba. He has not left me. He's surrounded me.

I look over to the dresser on my right and see the falling-over stacks of cards that fill and overflow our Ronald McDonald House mailbox each day from family, friends and strangers who want to share an encouraging word. We can't even keep up with opening the letters and gifts before more pour in. Literally hundreds.

I think of the strangers who seem to come out of the woodwork with calls, texts and social media messages filled with comments like, "We are praying for you," and "Our hearts are with you."

I recall how Dan's uncle who lives in Brazil has churches throughout the South American country praying for Charlotte and the Whiting family. Brazil! People who've never met us before are gathering in public places and in private homes around the country and world to pray for us.

I look to my left and see a stack of clothes our sister-in-law drove twenty minutes to come pick up yesterday, in between her two kid's school schedules and her own work schedule. She returned them today, clean, folded and with an encouraging note and a hot meal.

I look down at the desk my pump sits on and see a sizable check from a distant family friend who "wanted to share what God has given us and help a family in need." Beside the check lay stacks of Starbucks and gas station gift cards sent by family and friends who are dying to help in any way they can. Literally hundreds.

In the corner of the bedroom lay a pile of baby gifts from acquaintances and strangers, all wanting to make a positive difference for us in an otherwise unimaginable situation.

I look at my phone screen and see the nurse has finally turned on the camera. I watch her hands carefully and lovingly change my daughter's diaper as she wails. This woman whom I've never met before, giving her night, her heart, talent, and expertise to our child. She reminds me of all the medical staff who have carried us through from the moment of the devastating 20-week-gestation anatomy scan to today. Each top-rated and globally sought-after specialist and medical professional who seems to appear the moment we learn of a new diagnosis. Literally hundreds.

Any need we've had up to this point has been met and exceeded in over-abundant fashion. Our daughter may not be miraculously healed yet, but she sure is miraculously cared for by literally hundreds.

God has not forsaken me, he's surrounded me. I close my eyes and breathe deeply in this truth. I may feel lonely at this moment, but I am so far from alone.

 Not Feeling God's Presence

Sometimes in our greatest time of trial, suffering and need, God feels distant. Yet it is precisely at this time that he draws so very near.

The scene of Jesus' final hour comes to mind when he cries out, "my God, my God, why have You forsaken me." (Matthew 27:46 and Mark 15:34) Did Jesus really feel abandoned? Did he really wonder where his loving Father went in the midst of his crushing pain?

Maybe in the midst of Jesus' pain and anguish he knew God was present though he didn't feel God. Maybe Jesus was giving us an example to live by, trusting in faith and not feelings. Though not remotely comparable in magnitude, this reminds me of a lesson from Dan and my marriage preparation class. The teaching couple warned my husband and me there would be days we would feel incredibly close and madly in love. There would also be days when we honestly wouldn't like each other.

That is when real love begins, they said. When, despite the lack of butterflies, we roll up our sleeves and choose to love each other anyway. That kind of love is an action, a verb, a choice. It's about leaning into each other and choosing each other even when the easier answer, and the one that may feel better in the moment, is to simply walk away. Maybe God's presence is just like love—an action, a verb, a choice. How fitting ... since God is love.

Sometimes we distinctly feel him close. Sometimes our hearts burn and our souls sing with the joy of his presence. But sometimes we feel empty and all-poured-out, broken and alone.

Maybe the true test of faith is when we don't feel his presence but are asked to lean into him anyway. When we don't sense his love but believe in him despite it all.

It was in this time of great trial and pain that I learned first-hand—feelings and faith don't always go hand-in-hand.

I think about the countless people raising their hearts, minds and prayers to God for our sake. I chuckle to myself thinking he must be tired of hearing about this baby named Charlotte. We've taken heaven by storm with all our pleas! I don't pretend to understand how the after-life works, but I am told there is a cloud of witnesses, and I imagine all the beautiful people and angels surrounding God saying, "Please, for heaven's sake would you just heal this kid already! We're tired of hearing about her!" The image makes me laugh out loud, making a weird snorting sound as I try to stay quiet and not wake Dan. Though it makes me laugh, I also wonder if there is some truth to it.

"*I will heal you—all three of you. Trust me,*" he says.

I've been praying to God for our daughter's healing since the beginning of this crazy journey and never once have I heard him directly answer me like he did tonight. I also never even dared expect an answer. What a promise he just gave. He says he'll heal us. Dare I believe? I'm afraid to believe, because what if it doesn't end up being true? What if it's all just a figment of my imagination?

Lord, I believe. Help my unbelief.

I now realize, though, God's definition of healing may look very different than my own. My definition of healing is that Charlotte's ailments simply disappear, and she is suddenly a perfectly healthy newborn, like the miracles I read about in the New Testament. That I will walk into the hospital tomorrow morning to find Charlotte unhooked from every monitor and line, with her bags packed and the doctors saying, "We don't know how or why, but she's totally healed! She can go home now. She doesn't need us anymore."

I'm realizing perhaps that's not the kind of healing God has in mind for Charlotte. Perhaps his version of healing will be more drawn out, more grueling and ultimately more glorious than anything I envision. Perhaps, even, his version of healing will mean taking Charlotte home to him before I think it's time. Maybe healing actually looks like dying to me, while it looks like rising to him. Strangely enough, I am now at peace with this thought.

Whatever healing needs to look like, Lord, let it be done and grant me the grace and the strength to deal with it. Or maybe better yet, grant me the humility and brokenness enough to let you deal with it.

Perhaps being broken is exactly how he needs me to be in order to receive his promises in this very moment. In this letter. Perhaps there's a reason he waited until now to speak so plainly to me.

Maybe he needs me to reach the bottom of my own strength and self-reliance so he can become my strength and total dependence. Like a farmer breaks the soil with a plow in the Spring, preparing it for planting, maybe God is tilling my heart so it's fertile to receive him.

Regardless of what God is up to, there's one thing I now know for sure. He will heal us—all three of us—and he's doing so through Charlotte's army of caregivers and supporters. Literally hundreds.

Chapter 24 Want To Take Her Home

Friday, December 8, 2017

"Welcome back!" Dr. Rick says with a smile. "Charlotte really missed you but I'm glad you took a few days to recover. I'm sure it was hard to stay away."

I'm rocking Charlotte in my lap while they round on all the babies, once again starting at our bedspace this morning. I don't see many other parents with their babies right now, so maybe they are just starting with Charlotte because Dan and I are here? I hope that's why and not because she's still the sickest among them.

"I'm glad you two are feeling better. Your parents were here taking turns with Charlotte in your absence. You're truly blessed to have such wonderful and supportive family."

I couldn't agree more. I don't know how we would have survived the last several days if not for knowing our daughter was still with her grandparents, even if she wasn't with us.

Sue smiles at Dan and me and then starts listing all the latest lab results and measurements from the night before for Dr. Rick. He stares at his feet and listens intently, processing and computing all that Sue shares. The pharmacist, dietician, speech therapist, social worker, nurse, resident fellow, and a few other new faces gather round and lean in to hear. Once Sue finishes her report, Rick turns to Dorie, the pharmacist, to hear her updates on medications.

My eyes bug. There are new medications in this list that Charlotte wasn't receiving before we left with our fevers. Dr. Rick sees my reaction and gives me a reassuring look.

"We routinely check all newborns' hormone levels to ensure their thyroid and pituitary glands are doing what they're supposed to. For Charlotte this is even more important because these two organs are in the midline of her body, which is where most of her anomalies lie. So, it's no surprise that Charlotte's thyroid hormone level is a little low, called congenital hypothyroidism. Now, this is only based on the latest bloodwork, and she may be able to correct her levels all on her own, but we aren't willing to risk it and wait to see, because if left untreated, low thyroid hormone can affect brain development. Thyroid hormone is critical in the first few years of life."

I'm trying to really focus and take in this new information.

Dr. Rick goes on, "The only trouble is, once you start treating hypothyroidism in an infant, you cannot stop to find out if it's truly needed until she is about three years old because she can't afford the missed doses in case her body truly does need it. It's great we caught this early, but it does mean she will be on Synthroid, a synthetic thyroid hormone, for at least the next three years."

"Now that you've caught it, will this affect her growing at all?" Dan asks.

"No, we will maintain daily treatment and she'll be just fine," Dr. Rick assures us.

"If her levels have been low since birth will the last week of low thyroid hormone have a lasting effect on her growth?" Dan presses.

"No," Dr Rick responds confidently. "We've caught it early enough that she shouldn't experience any effects."

"What about the other drug I heard you say," I direct my question to Dorie. "Gabbo- something?"

Dorie chuckles at my attempt to say the name. "Gabapentin." she confirms. "It's an anti-epileptic medication, meaning it is typically prescribed to manage seizure activity. Charlotte doesn't have seizures, but she's presenting signs of neurological discomfort and distress so Gabapentin will help manage her discomfort while in the NICU."

That familiar mama-bear protective feeling boils up inside my gut. I left the NICU for three days and came back to find my baby on new medications I've never heard of before. "What do you mean she has neurological discomfort? She seems at peace right now," I say, bewildered, looking down at my daughter sleeping peacefully in my arms. Is she truly comfortable or just drugged? Dr. Rick calmly steps in to help explain.

"While you and Dan were home recovering, Charlotte showed signs of distress. And it's not surprising for several reasons. One, she's in the NICU which is a highly stimulative environment that can cause any baby to be on edge. Neurotin, the brand name for Gabapentin, will help put her at ease for the duration of her stay. Two, she has two tubes going into her back and she's laying on her back most of the time. That is not comfortable. A third reason is that while she is at ease when she's held by her family, that's not possible at all times and we want to help her remain comfortable as best we can. Her being comfortable is going to help her save her energy for healing and ultimately help her get better."

I wish I could hold her 24 hours a day so she doesn't have to be on drugs. A pang of guilt hits me, as illogical as I know that is. I know it's unreasonable and impossible to expect myself to be here round the clock, but my bodily limitations in caring for her in this unnatural situation make me feel like I'm failing her as her mother.

Is my child being poisoned with drugs that have long weird titles, in the name of helping put her at ease? I recall friends who, as new moms, hesitate to even use over-the-counter Tylenol for their fevering infant children. And here my daughter is being pumped full of unfamiliar meds for reasons far beyond anything Tylenol can treat. Dorie sees my panic rising.

"I know you don't want your daughter on any more medications than absolutely necessary. I am happy to answer any questions you have and help you feel comfortable with our treatment plan. It truly is what's best for Charlotte and it's not for forever. She can wean off Gabo as soon as she doesn't need it anymore," Dorie reassures.

Wean? She has to wean off of it? So it's addictive in nature, and/or strong enough to need to slowly come out of her system once it's in? I'm mortified. I look down at my tiny child and see the IV line, knowing it's full of TPN and also now administering periodic neurological treatment.

"Neurotin is necessary for her right now, Mom, and we will let you know as soon as it's possible to stop using it," Dorie adds softly, with great compassion and understanding. I remind myself to breathe. These people have Charlotte's best interest at heart, and I have to trust them. What else can I do? But I now have a new mission—get Charlotte off Gabapentin as soon as possible.

"We are working on scheduling a family meeting with both of you," Dr. Rick gestures to Dan and me, changing the subject. "I'm coordinating as many specialist teams as possible who are involved in Charlotte's care. We will try to meet sometime next week. It'll be like a roundtable of sorts, where each specialist team will go over their portion of care and you'll have the opportunity to ask questions. The specialists will use the time to collaborate on next steps and the most effective way to order treatment plans and surgical interventions, considering all the systems involved. It should be a very good meeting for everyone involved to get the big picture care plan."

"In that meeting will we discuss a target date to go home?" I ask, and then immediately feel bad, like maybe I'm insinuating we don't like our care team, which is the furthest thing from the truth. They are fabulous. But I want out of here, stat. I backpedal, "Not that we don't think you all are doing amazing work, I just really want my baby home." I hope I haven't offended anyone.

"Of course, you want her home. What parent wouldn't?" Sue pipes in, validating my question.

A look of understanding washes over Dr. Rick' face. "After rounds Emily, I'm going to come back and speak with you more on this," he says compassionately.

He and the herd of rounding attendants shuffle to the next bed and on her way by, Dorie puts her hand on my shoulder and squeezes, "Charlotte's doing great and she's truly in the best care possible. You can come to me with any questions at all, at any time."

"I'm sorry Emily and Dan but soon it'll be shift change," the nurse says. I look at the clock. How does time seem to fly by here in the NICU? It's already 2:45 p.m. Shift change is at 3:00. By now we know what this means, we must step out of the NICU for 45 minutes while nurses share private medical information with the incoming second-shift nurses.

I dread shift change, being forced to leave my child. I can't hear what nurses are saying about other babies anyway. Not to mention, I probably can learn more about other babies and their families by sitting in the room during rounds than I would by being here during shift change. But hospital policies are hospital policies no matter how illogical and frustrating they sometimes seem. Anyway, I could use a stretch and snack, and I wouldn't permit myself to leave Charlotte's side until now, so I guess it's okay.

"Why don't you go ahead and finish giving Charlotte her

bottle, Dad, and then I'll burp her while I catch the next nurse up to speed," the nurse suggests. Dan nods but doesn't take his eyes off his daughter. He's sitting on the right side of her isolette, propping her up with his right hand under her head and holding the bottle in his left.

Charlotte's eyes are cracked open, quietly watching us as she slowly and intently sucks down the milk. She's so observant. It's shocking, really. I had no idea infants, and especially medicated ones, could be so aware of their surroundings. She must not be too heavily drugged.

She seems very intelligent, though I have no way of knowing whether this is true or not. I watch as Dan very carefully and gingerly feeds her. She's content and I realize how satisfying it is for me to see her eat. It's such a simple pleasure, watching my child eat. It's like a deep satisfying drink to my dehydrated mama soul.

A family friend's comment from a couple days ago pops into my head. "Our job as parents of an infant is basically to keep them comfortable." She was referencing the normal newborn experience—feeding, burping, changing diapers, swaddling, rocking, etc. That's far from my mothering experience thus far. If my primary job is to keep Charlotte comfortable I'm doing a horrible job of it. Of course she didn't mean this was our experience. But watching Charlotte eat now makes me realize how satisfying it is to help her feel comfortable. It's an innate drive in us parents and I feel at peace when Charlotte is at peace. Like all is well in the world, even if it's not.

The nurse had offered to help Dan hold Charlotte on his lap for this feed, which is his first time ever feeding his 11-day-old child, whom he's not held since her birth either. When he declined the offer and said he'd feed her from the isolette I couldn't help but be annoyed.

Why wouldn't he hold his daughter? Was he not interested in holding her? The question worried me for Dan and for Charlotte, both. They need each other. Couldn't he see that? As if reading my mind, Dan explained to the nurse and me, "I'd rather wait until the umbilical IV line is gone."

Oh, okay, that makes sense.

Dr. Rick told us this morning during rounds that the final umbilical cord IV would be pulled soon and transitioned to a regular IV in her arm or leg, wherever they find the best vein to access. Dan wants to wait until the umbilical cord IV is removed to hold Charlotte because it makes him too nervous he'll accidentally bump it or otherwise damage it in the process of holding her.

I chastise myself for thinking negatively about Dan and letting myself get carried away with unnecessary worry. I've got to get better at that. Why do I seem to trust positive intent from everyone else, but when it comes to my husband, the man I'm supposed to love and cherish and trust the most, I'm far less gracious? It's like I'm suspicious that he's going to let Charlotte and me down. Yet, I have no reason to doubt him and his dedication to us. Does he ever let us down? Sure. He's human. I let him down all the time, too. But his heart is always in the right place, and he always has good reason for doing whatever it is he does.

Whether I ever voice my negative thoughts or not, I know they come across in my body language and interactions with him. I make a mental note to try and focus on assuming Dan has the best of intentions, rather than always jumping to conclusions prematurely. It's an old habit that I need to kick.

Watching him feed her now, I honestly struggle to understand his fear—my drive to hold my baby is so strong that I easily dismissed the fear of hurting the IV when the doctor gave me the okay. As Charlotte slowly drains each mL out of her bottle, my frustration with Dan turns to respect and admiration. He is protecting his daughter even at the cost of depriving himself the joy of holding her. I don't have that kind of self-control.

"You did it, Charlie Jo!" Dan says proudly as he lifts up the empty bottle to show us.

"Hungry girl!" I say, smiling at her.

"At this rate she'll be fully bottle fed by the end of the weekend," says the nurse excitedly. With each feed they've increased milk volume by 5mLs and equally decreased TPN in hopes that once she gets up to a full bottle, they can turn off the IV fluids and Charlotte can be 100% bottle and NG tube fed.

Dan lays Charlotte down and the nurse steps in to burp her. We both blow Charlotte kisses. Dan walks around the isolette toward me, reaches for my hand, and we walk out of the NICU for shift change. We make a beeline straight to the coffee pot in the Ronald McDonald Family Room at the end of the hall, where other patient parents have the same idea, everyone in shared rooms banished from their child's bedside for the next ¾ of an hour.

Dan pours two steaming cups and hands me one, black, just

the way I like it. I close my eyes and inhale the fresh aroma, basking in this small moment of calm. I'm learning to treasure these glimpses of peace. I need them to sustain me. As I'm in my own little coffee world, the Family Room door opens, and Dr. Rick pops his head in.

"Hey Emily and Dan," he says, "do you have a moment to talk?" He doesn't come in. This is sacred space for families. Doctors try to stay out as much as possible.

"Sure," Dan says and I nod. We follow him out of the Family Room, down the hall and into the empty waiting room. Dr. Rick gestures for us to take seats and pulls up a chair in front of us.

"I'm working on getting this family meeting scheduled, and I'm curious what days or times work best for you two next week?" I'm blown away that we even get a say in when this meeting takes place. There are so many doctors involved in the meeting, I just assumed they'd find the time that works best for them and then we'd accommodate it.

"Ideally, you'd both be there." he continues. "I know that may be tough with work schedules. Remind me what you both do? When do you plan to return to work?" He looks from me to Dan and back to me.

I'm caught off guard. It's like I've totally forgotten about work and the life I used to lead just eleven days ago. Work? I don't know. My child is fighting for her life. It's a little hard to think about schedules and when I'll be going back to team leadership, brand research and market analyses.

This mindset surprises me. Before Charlotte, I was so focused on work. My team members were like my children, though they are all as old or older than me. I was solely focused on helping them succeed in their roles. That was my job, and I took it very seriously. I put my heart and soul into every day at the office and in the field with customers. Now that life seems so distant, like a long-ago memory of the old Emily.

"I'm an Assistant Director of Brand Research and Marketing for a beef brand," I say.

Dan pipes in, "I'm a Welding Engineer Unit Manager. We build energy vessels."

"Wow, very interesting," nods Dr. Rick. "And do you have maternity and paternity leave?"

"I have 6-weeks maternity leave plus I'll be taking 6-weeks of FMLA," I say. FMLA stands for Family and Medical Leave Act, which is unpaid job-protected leave.

"I do not have any paternity leave so once I run out of vacation time, I'll be using FMLA when necessary," Dan says. "I was thinking of going back to work next week, but I can take time off to be here for the meeting," he adds.

The thought of being left at the NICU managing all the specialists and conversations each day by myself reminds me of what it felt like when the relentless strength of the Atlantic Ocean undertow submerged me, dragged me to the sandy bottom of the South Carolina seafloor, and pummeled me over and over when I was a kid.

But I know our mothers, Dan's and mine, will be my life rafts. They will step in and help out as much as they can. I try not to focus on next week. I just need to get through the next minute. And then the next. And then the next. I've learned by now that if I try to think through details beyond the current minute I'm in, I will succumb to the undertow of the unknown and the fear.

"Okay, then I'll aim to schedule our meeting with the specialists for next Wednesday after rounds. That seems to be the best time for most of the specialists involved," Dr. Rick concludes.

"Now Emily, I said I'd address your question from this morning." He leans in like he's about to say something of great importance. "You've asked about going home almost every day since Charlotte's birth and that's understandable. No one wants to be in the hospital with their kid for longer than necessary. While I cannot predict when you'll get to go home, I do know it will not be for a long time. There are many hurdles she needs to overcome before she can leave."

My heart is racing as I listen closely. I reach for Dan's hand— a subconscious habit I've formed whenever a doctor is delivering more news.

"Certain things can be done outpatient, but there are several that need doing before she leaves the watchful skilled eyes of our nurses and doctors. We need to address the cyst in her abdomen. We need to monitor her liver and her heart. She needs to be able to feed all on her own and start growing. The cleft is no problem, that can be addressed outpatient. She could even potentially be sent home with nephrostomy tubes still in."

That thought terrifies me. How would I care for an infant with two tubes coming out of her back?

Dr. Rick doesn't bat an eye. "But if I send you home too early, you will just end up being readmitted. And that is worse for Charlotte and for you. We are going to do all that is necessary to prevent you being readmitted for any reason other than future pre-planned surgeries. So, instead of asking 'When can we go home?' the better question is 'What are the next steps to help Charlotte heal?'"

Dr. Rick has a way of delivering hard news and redirecting me that neither feels chastising nor rude. I don't know how he does this, but instead of feeling deflated or angry, his words make me feel energized. Like he is inviting me to be on Team Charlotte, not just to get her home sooner, but to help her heal the best.

I let this sink in for a moment and then ask, "I know you don't have a crystal ball, but if you were to predict how long we will be here, what do you think?" I need to wrap my head around how long we are talking about. "And you can give me a big range because I know there is no way of truly knowing," I add.

He shakes his head, "I wish I knew that answer. Now you can't hold me to this, because a lot of factors can change, and on a daily basis too, but if I were to guess, I imagine you'll be here for three months or so."

Wow. Okay. This is a whole new reality I simply wasn't planning on. Three months. Okay. I sit back and let this sink in. I do quick math. That puts us in the middle of February next year. "We are going to take great care of her, and we are going to help her heal," Dr. Rick reassures.

I muster the courage to finally ask what's really pressing in my mind. "Please shoot me straight. I want to know the real answer. In your professional opinion, knowing what you know now about Charlotte's diagnoses, do you really think she can heal? Do you think she'll survive all this and be okay?" There, I asked it. Point blank. I asked it.

His answer surprises me.

"Oh yeah, I think she'll survive," he says confidently.

"Really?" I ask, not sure whether I should be excited or skeptical. Is he just feeding me a line of hope or is he giving me his true medical prognosis?

"Oh yeah, so long as we do our job well and with you both showing up for your daughter, she's going to heal. Barring any unforeseen complications, of course. The good news is almost all the complex anomalies we see with Charlotte are mechanical. We can fix mechanical issues with patience, time and skilled surgical intervention. We have all of that here. The only thing in question is neurological. We cannot fix brain malformations. We know she's missing her Corpus Callosum, but plenty of people have Agenesis and are walking around functioning just fine. It will take time and her growth before we ever know the effects of that."

He thinks for a minute, then adds, "If we had a chromosomal defect to explain Charlotte's anomalies, an overarching diagnosis to explain it all, I might think differently. But as it stands, we have no way of knowing why she developed the way she did and we have no way of knowing what her future looks like. I think that's a good thing because she will show us what she's capable of over time."

"She has Charlotte's Syndrome!" I attempt a joke.

"Yes," Dr. Rick humors me with a laugh. "According to the Genetics' Team they have no explanation for Charlotte and there is no other person in the world, recorded anyway, with the same combination of anomalies. So, she'll show us what she's capable of. But as far as I'm concerned, she's going to be just fine."

I'm blown away. I look at Dan, and I can see he's drinking this information in and processing what it means for our family.

"You two are doing great and Charlotte is, too. She has a fighting spirit. We are going to do our best to help her heal and I want you both to feel comfortable to ask questions and even question what we are doing at any time. You are her best advocates. You are her parents, and you know her best. With you and us working together, we will get you home, eventually." Dr. Rick stands up. "Now I'm going to go get this family meeting scheduled."

When Dr. Rick leaves the room, Dan and I are left holding onto each other, stunned. Rick says he thinks Charlotte will heal. It's as if he is confirming what God told me last night.

"I will heal you—all three of you."

Thank you, God for Dr. Rick.

Just as my eyes were opened last night to a new reality of what healing may look like, Dr. Rick reoriented my focus. No longer is my greatest concern going home. I am renewed with resolve to focus on Charlotte's healing, one day, one hour, one moment at a time. We will go home when Charlotte is good and ready to go home.

Until then, God please give me the strength and endurance to run this race and to run it well.

I take a sip of my now cold coffee. "Are you ready to go back in there?" Dan asks, looking at the clock. It's 3:45.

"Yes," I say.

Chapter 25 Hiccups

Sunday, December 10, 2017

"As you know, Mrs. Whiting, Charlotte's conjugated bilirubin numbers have not come down since birth. Basically, what this tells us is the abdominal cyst is interfering with proper function of the biliary tree and liver," explains a tall blonde man in a white coat with a name badge that says "Dr. Carter." He looks like a man who on the weekends collects wine bottles for their interesting labels. He's the fourth doctor who's come by to speak with us today. Or is he the fifth? I can't remember. My head is spinning from all the conversations of this organ and that organ, this potential surgery and that potential intervention.

Today is reminiscent of those busy days in the office when I'd hop from one meeting to another, one phone call to another, one impromptu hallway discussion about XYZ project while I was on my way to the coffee pot for my fourth cup of the day. That feeling like I'm powering through full speed ahead with little time to breath. Like

I'll probably crash soon but there is no time to think about it now. Except, here in the NICU we are addressing life and death topics and instead of bouncing from meeting to phone call, I'm bouncing from consultation to pump room.

After such a quiet and calm Saturday with Charlotte, apparently every specialist decided Sunday is the day to come talk to the Whiting family.

Dr. Carter seems like a new face. He doesn't look familiar. But that doesn't mean much. I've seen so many faces parade by Charlotte's bedspace and explain their involvement in her care that I could have met him three times by now and I still wouldn't remember. Heck, some people seem to come by just to gawk at my daughter in amazement. I suppose maybe that's the nature of a teaching hospital—you end up having a lot of spectators coming by in the name of learning.

I can't help but feel like she's an exhibit at a zoo sometimes. I often want to say, "She's not a giraffe, now please, unless you have something critical to share for her care, move along." Of course, I never say a word. I don't have the energy to worry about unnecessary confrontation. But Dr. Carter seems critical to her care, or so I'm learning.

I try to focus on what he's saying, realizing he may be the most important person I talk to all day, or even all week. After all, he's here to tell me we may be facing the operating room (OR) again sooner than later, and for life-threatening reasons. I wish Dan was here now to hear this news himself. He stepped away to get us some lunch, which is long overdue seeing as it's already 2:00 p.m.

"We are going to wait until tomorrow and see what her bilirubin numbers do in the morning labs. That will indicate our course of action. We were hoping to make it a few more weeks before having to surgically intervene and remove the cyst, so she can heal from the last operation and so she can grow bigger and stronger. That just might not be an option at this time ..." He goes on with further explanations of what each lab number means and then offers to draw me a picture of the liver, biliary tree, and gastroenterology tract so I can understand what we are talking about.

"Yes, please do. Pictures always help," I say, ripping out a piece of paper from my notebook the NICU social worker gave me. He pulls a pen from his chest pocket. As he begins to draw I notice a faint but familiar sound. I look over toward Charlotte who is comfortably snoozing in her isolette and confirm the source of the noise. She's hiccupping. I smile.

"So, as you can see here, Mrs. Whiting," Dr. Carter points to his freehand drawing.

I interrupt him, "You know what Dr. Carter, I'm so grateful for your time and your input and I really want to hear what you have to say. I love your drawing and your helping me understand what we are facing. But could you please step out for just a few minutes? My daughter is hiccupping, and I want to sit with her and listen."

He must think I'm crazy. Maybe I am. I am dismissing the Director of Fetal Surgery, a Pediatric General and Thoracic Surgeon, whose time and attention is very valuable, and he's telling me we might be walking back into the OR this week.

But my daughter is hiccupping. I want to listen.

He looks at me, bewildered. I can tell he's trying to understand what I just said.

"Just, like, ten minutes. Could you come back in ten minutes?" I ask.

He nods, "No problem, take your time. I'll go speak with the attending Neonatologist and then I'll come back." He graciously walks away, and I get the sense he truly does understand, as much as he possibly can anyway. I sit down next to Charlotte and open the little side doors to her isolette so I can better hear her hiccups, which are muffled inside her little clear plastic cocoon. I cup my hands around her head and feet like I've grown accustomed to doing, and I listen.

Charlotte's nurse watches me curiously. "Could you help me have just ten minutes with Charlotte? If anyone else comes to talk with me, can you ask them to wait and come back in ten minutes?" I ask the nurse.

She nods with a surprised smile on her face, "Absolutely."

I feel empowered. This is the first time I've ever dictated when I will speak with specialists, surgeons, or any other medical staff member for that matter. I feel emboldened. Like maybe I'm not just the puppet on a string like I've felt for so long, being pulled this way and that way according to the hospital's schedule and consultation times.

I get comfortable in my chair and watch as Charlotte's chest rhythmically pops up and down.

"Hiccup. Hiccup." She sounds like a little dog squeaker toy.

This is so … human. So visceral—this hiccupping.

When I was pregnant she hiccupped several times a day and almost always around 9:00 p.m. My rounded belly would bump up and down, reminding me she was very much alive in there, feisty, and full of life. Seeing her hiccup now is like an injection of hope, reminding me she is not just a litany of lab numbers. She is not just a portfolio of parading specialists. She is not just a looming OR trip. She is not just facial tape and nasal hooks, tubes and wires, leads and lines, medications and TPN.

She is human. She is beautiful. She is strong. She is Charlotte.

Journal Entry - Monday, December 11, 2017

Father, Abba,

Praise your name. For countless wonderful people who have helped us get to today. For our health and for Charlotte's health. For another day being a family of three. Lord, praise your name for your presence. For your grace. For your love.

Forgive me for my lack of faith. For my fear and anger and sadness and hurt. Praise your name for helping me cope with all of these things. Lord, please help me to feel 100% tomorrow so I can be fully present with you, Dan, and Charlotte. Help me to be healthy so I may serve you and love my family. Help me, oh Lord. I've never needed you like I need you now. I cannot face this alone. Only with you.

Chapter 26 Family Meeting

Wednesday, December 13, 2017

"Thank you everyone for coming today, and Emily and Dan for making this priority, too," Dr. Rick opens the meeting as everyone takes their seats and falls quiet. His comment strikes me as odd. Of course, this is priority. This is our daughter we are meeting about.

My eyes are starting to open to the reality that we are beyond blessed that Dan and I are able to be here. I'm realizing many other parents find themselves pulled back to work due to financial, insurance, or job security strains, some have other children they need to be with at home, while still others feel intimidated to sit at a conference table filled with specialists discussing medical terms they've never heard.

I find it a little exhilarating in a weird kind of way. I'm used to high pressure meetings with suit-wearing executives at multi-million-dollar companies, discussing business plans and sales strategies, so sitting around a table filled with white-coats feels familiar, though the topic is incredibly personal and the medical jargon is often over my head.

I sit up straight on the edge of my seat, pen in hand and a brown leather-bound journal open to the first, crisp page, poised to take notes. Our social worker met with me this morning to prepare me for this family meeting, arming me with this new notebook and pen so I could feel equipped to take notes, ask questions and keep record of key conversations.

"I believe everyone has met by now, but in case you haven't had a chance to talk with Emily and Dan yet, let's go around the room quickly and introduce ourselves and our role in Charlotte's care. Then we will start back around the room to discuss specifics regarding each subspecialty, diagnoses, and next steps," continues Dr. Rick. "As we all know, Charlotte is a unique and complex patient, so the goal of this family meeting is to collaborate on her needs and walk away with a care plan, recognizing it will adjust and change as needed."

He proceeds with introducing himself and his role as Charlotte's attending Neonatologist, then going clockwise around the room, each specialist stands up one by one and does the same, until all twenty-or-so have spoken. I knew there were a lot of people assigned to Charlotte's case but it's shocking to see them piled in one room, all for one five-pound patient. I'm whelmed with gratitude that the hospital has given my daughter such time and attention.

Maybe I should write all the names down. Before I even try I realize I can't spell most of the foreign names I'm hearing. This board room is truly a melting pot of nationalities, accents, perspectives, and insights. I feel honored I get to be part of it, and also a little guilty that I'm enjoying such a meeting when I know it's about my daughter's health.

I can't keep up with the speed at which they make introductions so I just put my pen down and listen. After everyone is introduced, Dr. Rick turns to Dr. Fuhrman first. "Urology, let's start there…"

The next 90 minutes fly as Dan and I listen intently to each subspecialist give their report. My head grows heavy, and I notice an increasing throb between my eyes like a headache is looming. For as much as is known about Charlotte's condition and next steps in her care, there is even more unknown.

I'm blown away by the collaboration between specialists while simultaneously taken aback by their disagreements with each other. It shocks me there is not a clear path toward her recovery. It just seems like with this many years of schooling in one room there should be more answers to all the questions. More clarity. I'm beginning to see medicine is a lot of educated hypothesizing. Gray area far outweighs the black and white.

The Urologist and General Surgeon hash out which should come first, the ureter-bladder implant surgery or the bile duct, cyst and liver surgery. Two cardiologists disagree, one saying Charlotte will surely need surgical intervention for her narrowed aorta within a year, while the other says she may not need cardiac surgery until her teens. Or maybe ever.

Genetics rehashes all the tests they've done and concludes they still don't know why Charlotte's symptoms present the way they do. "There's no other recorded case around the world that we've found, with the same diagnoses combination matching Charlotte's," they say.

Amidst all the conversation, there is one common phrase each doctor repeats: *if this… then that.*

"*If* the biliary obstruction begins blocking bile flow, *then* we have to remove it before addressing any other health concerns," says the Gastroenterologist.

"*If* we wait too long to attach the ureters to the bladder and get the bladder cycling with output, *then* the bladder muscle will dystrophy and lose its pliability," says the Urologist.

"*If* renal function returns and filtering units gain function by one-year-old, *then* we may not need to do dialysis," says the Nephrologist.

"*If* ventricular function decreases with the myocardium, *then* we may use medications for long-term management," says the Cardiologist. "And, *if* the aorta doesn't grow large enough with Charlotte's overall growth, then we will either place a balloon in the aorta or surgically intervene by the time she's one."

Plastics chimes in, "We need to complete a lip adhesion surgery around three-months of age, then a complete adhesion at six-months and a palate repair at twelve-months. We can work around the other systems and priorities, but we don't want to venture too far from those times in her growth and development."

Discussion volleys around the table as various cross-system implications arise. "We will need Cardiac Anesthesia involved in all surgeries to monitor her heart closely while under anesthesia," comments Cardiology.

"We will have to avoid NSAIDS for Charlotte because her kidneys cannot process that much potassium, given their compromised condition," adds Nephrology.

"With the liver compromised we will have to be careful what medications we use that are processed in the liver, until we know more about its overall function," chimes in Gastroenterology.

It's one massive puzzle, prioritizing treatment plans while ensuring intervention for one body system doesn't negatively impact another. The tension and conflict between specialties is uncomfortable but it also gives me great confidence in our care team. They don't seem phased by disagreement. They aren't afraid to hash it out, to hear each other's perspectives, to take in additional information and go back to the drawing board to rehash a new treatment plan. In my team leading experience, that's what makes a great team, one that can trust each other enough to disagree, work it out and come through with a better plan because of the honest and forthright conversations.

I begin sensing everyone getting antsy to close the meeting and get on to the next thing in their days' schedules. But I desperately want closure on the immediate next steps.

"So, am I understanding correctly that as of now, our next big surgery will be in a few weeks after the holidays, working on her kidneys and related anatomy, unless for some reason the cyst in her abdomen presents problems, in which case we will address that first?" I jump into the conversation. "Am I hearing everyone right?"

All heads nod in agreement.

"So, we obviously have a lot of surgeries ahead of us," I press. "One of my top concerns is trying to limit the number of surgeries to as few as possible. So, can we merge any of these and accomplish more in one OR visit? Kill two birds with one stone so-to-speak?"

Dr. Rick jumps in, "Studies on infants and anesthesia are limited, however, what we do know is length of time under anesthesia is of greater concern than frequency. So, while we will merge what we can in the OR, doing more surgeries that are shorter in length is better than doing fewer but longer surgeries."

"And how many surgeries are we looking at, do you think, by the time it's all done," Dan speaks up.

Everyone looks at each other and silence ascends over the room as we all do head math, calculating.

"It appears at least six in the first year, between Uro, Gastro and Plastics," Dr. Rick finally says. "Then perhaps six or more by the time she's eighteen."

I sit back and process this large number. Twelve or more surgeries. The room seems to close in on me. How are we ever going to make it through twelve or more surgeries? I reach for Dan's hand and take a deep breath. Grandma's words resurface in my subconscious, "One day at a time, Emily." Now I think I'll take that one step further. It's not just one day at a time, it's one hour, one minute, one second at a time. That's all I can physically, emotionally, and mentally process.

"We will be with you every step of the way and Charlotte is a tough kid. She's shown us that already. She has a highly skilled team surrounding her. She will be okay. Let's take it one step at a time," Dr. Rick seems to know what's going through my head and echoes my exact sentiments. "We're going to do all we can for her."

Journal Entry - Wednesday, December 13, 2017, 10:00 p.m.

Lord, this is difficult. The most challenging thing you've ever asked of me. And I am too weak to accept the challenge on my own. But Lord, please don't take the suffering away from me. Refine me in the fire. Teach me in the midst of the struggle. Praise your name for trusting me with Charlotte. Thank you for granting me the opportunity to learn true trust in you. Lead me, oh Lord. For I am weak and in my weakness you make me strong. Thank you so much.

 Desire to Run This Race Well

At first, I thought taking away this challenge meant Charlotte healing completely. Once I realized that was not going to happen, I started fearing God might just take the situation away completely by letting her die. The idea that maybe he would take this opportunity from me to suffer for Charlotte and for the Lord crippled me. It is so hard to put into words or really even make sense of, but I had this strong desire to run this race I was given, and a fear that I may be pulled from the race because I was not up to the task. Maybe it was again my recognition of my complete lack of ability to do this on my own, but also my deep desire to do it well.

Journal Entry - Saturday, December 16, 2017

How do I place my hope in God?

Hope in you, Lord, is the only thing that gets me through each day. Hope in you is the only thing that keeps me focused and purposeful.

Lord, help me to never act religious but reject the power that could make me godly. (2 Timothy 3:5)

"And how from childhood you have known the sacred writings that are able to instruct you for salvation through faith in Christ Jesus." (2 Timothy 3:15)

"As for you, always be sober, enduring suffering, do the work of an evangelist, carry out your ministry fully." (2 Timothy 4:5)

Chapter 27   Holiday Expectations

Journal Entry - Monday, December 18, 2017

Hello God,

I am so grateful, Lord. For two sets of amazing grandparents who love us and love Charlotte. For my aunt who has postponed her travels just to watch our dogs while we are in the NICU. For another aunt who has traveled up just to help with Charlotte's medical needs and who has been on the phone helping us understand medical terms and next steps even when she can't physically be here. For even another aunt who has fed Oscar for us while we've been gone. For our work that's both been so supportive. For my brother, Dave, picking up family Christmas duties so I can focus on Charlotte. For Ronald McDonald—the room, the meals, the shuttle, and the kind volunteers. For family, friends and strangers who give us money to help pay for Charlotte's medical bills.

God, you always provide, and you certainly have provided in abundance. We are so blessed, and I am so grateful. I've not even listed half of our blessings. They overflow. Our cup overflows. Praise your name Lord. Hallelujah. Praise your name.

Amen

Sunday, December 24, 2017, Christmas Eve

A cold shiver courses through my body as I pull my red and black Christmas dress off of my shoulders so I can pump. As I hook up all the parts I look up to see snow falling outside the third-floor bedroom window. Laughter and the hum of our large family's lively conversations radiate up through the floorboards from the kitchen and living room two levels below. Along with the joyful sounds come tantalizing aromas of sweet and sour meatballs, Grandma Helen's highly anticipated cheesecake, Uncle Mikey's homemade sausage, Aunt Gail's fresh hot pretzels and a whole host of other festive foods. Everything seems so beautiful and wonderful on this crisp Christmas Eve, yet the cold of the room matches the frozen state of my heart.

I've been trying to hold it together today, trying to focus on the reason for the season and not on the fact that my daughter is stuck in the NICU on the other side of this city, twenty minutes from my sister and brother-in-law's home where we are staying the night to celebrate Christmas. I knew this day was coming. I knew Charlotte wouldn't be with us for holiday gatherings. I've had weeks to prepare for this mentally. I've been trying to focus on all the good things, and there are many. Why is it still so hard?

I look down to adjust the pump bottles and flash back to a couple days ago, watching my child learn how to nurse.

"Bilateral cleft babies can't make a seal in order to form suction and successfully breastfeed," our plastic surgeon told me. "You can try, but I don't want you to be too disappointed when she can't."

I took that as an invitation to see what Charlotte was capable of doing. To see what God could do. I knew back when I was still pregnant with Charlotte that she likely would be unable to nurse, but I was dead set on giving her a chance and letting her prove to us what she could and could not do. Was I being stubborn and stupid for not just accepting Charlotte's limitations and the fact that I wouldn't be able to breastfeed? Maybe. But on the other hand, I felt I owed it to her and myself to at least give her a chance. After all, breastfeeding is so hyped up these days as being the best thing for mama and baby, so why shouldn't I try?

There are a lot of things I can't impact in Charlotte's health and care, but how she is fed is inherently and instinctually a mother's job, and I so desire to live up to that job as best I can. For her and, if I'm being super honest, for myself. So, earlier this week when I was cleared to do so by Dr. Rick, I asked Marla the Speech Therapist and Sally the Lactation Consultant to help me attempt breastfeeding.

After the nurse settled Charlotte into my lap, adjusted her IV, three heart monitor leads, pulse ox and two nephrostomy tubes so nothing was pulled or twisted, Marla and Sally got to work coaching me. "The tape on her upper lip will actually help her potentially form a seal," encouraged Marla.

"Now, you're going to want to make sure she opens really wide, and you get a deep latch," coached Sally.

Bless them. They were well aware of the fact they were helping me try something that likely was impossible. The first couple of attempts to latch were futile, as Charlotte tried to figure out what in the world I was doing to her. She screeched in frustration, not familiar with being held in the football position and having a breast pushed to her face. "Let's put a drop of hand expressed milk on her lips and see if that gets her going," suggested Sally.

As soon as Charlotte smelled the milk and felt it on her lips she opened her mouth wide, and Shirley helped position Charlotte quickly. Right away Charlotte started sucking, or at least trying. "She's doing it!" I exclaimed, beside myself with excitement. Marla and Sally stayed with me for thirty minutes, coaching me through how to encourage Charlotte to eat. We had no way of knowing how much she actually extracted, or if she just drank what my body naturally let down, but she gave it her all and was left in a blissful sleepy milk coma by the time we were done. I was over the moon.

"That's amazing!" exclaimed the plastic surgeon when we told her. "That's a first for me, having a bilateral cleft kid successfully breastfeed." She shook her head in awe and disbelief. Pride swelled. I kept thinking, that's the power of assuming someone can do something until proven otherwise. That's the power of assuming anything is possible. Of not taking no for an answer.

After that, I wanted to breastfeed her all the time. It became my mission to be there for as many feeds as possible, so she could nurse rather than eat from a bottle. Of course, she still had an NG tube and was fed via the syringe and tube too to make sure she was getting enough calories, but the high of being able to feed her myself became addictive.

So, naturally, sitting here pumping and knowing she's eating from a bottle with the nurse stuck with the Christmas Eve shift stirs a swirl of emotions in me that I can no longer contain. I've held it together all day, not wanting Charlotte to know my turmoil while I was with her this morning and afternoon, and also not wanting our family to think of me ungrateful for them hosting Christmas here in Cleveland so we can be near our daughter. But I can't hold my emotions any longer. Sobs begin racking my body and wails escape my lips.

Thank God I'm on the third floor. No one can hear me over the racket of the party downstairs so when I realize I can't contain them anyway, I let them go. It seems the volume of tears and snot excreting from my face just about match the amount of milk I'm collecting in the bottles. Disgusting. I pull the box of tissues from the bed stand, place them beside me on the bed and attempt to soak up this mess as the waves of grief overtake me. After each nose wipe I squirt hand sanitizer on my dry, cracked hands, obsessively trying to keep germs away from my pumped milk. It is flu season and Charlotte doesn't need that on top of everything else.

I have no idea how long I cry, how long I've been pumping or how many times I've sanitized, but eventually, the sobs subside to sniffles. I sit there on my sister and brother-in-law's guest bed trying to deep-breathe and regain some composure when I hear a soft knock on the bedroom door.

"Emily, are you in there?" Dan asks quietly.

I breathe a sigh of relief. I subconsciously was hoping someone would come save me from drowning in my own grief.

He opens the door and sees the pile of soaked tissues stacked beside me, seeing, no doubt, the hot mess I've become. He quickly crosses the room and sits beside me, pulling me in for a side hug because my front is still attached to plastic and tubing apparatus. I chuckle between sniffles at how ridiculous I must look. I start slowly pulling the pump off me. Dan silently helps, taking the bottles of milk and dumping them into a storage bag. Both of us working on autopilot from having done this hundreds of times by now. I pull my dress back on and turn my back toward Dan so he can zip me back up.

When I turn back toward him tears are welling in his eyes, too. "This is so hard, not having her here with us," he says.

"I feel like a horrible mother, leaving her in the hospital while we come eat and drink and act like everything is fine. Why do we get to enjoy Christmas while she stays in the hospital? We should be with her," I blubber.

"You're not a horrible mother, Emily. We were with Charlotte all day today and we will be with her again tomorrow morning before we go to your parent's. She knows she is loved and to her this is just another day. She doesn't know it's Christmas Eve," he soothes.

"But *I* know it's Christmas Eve and I don't want to do Christmas Eve without her!" I say, sounding like a total brat. I expect him to get frustrated and leave. Instead, he pulls me in closer.

"I don't want to do Christmas Eve without her, either," he whispers. I break at his vulnerability and love, and a whole new rush of tears start flowing down my red, chapped cheeks. We sit and hold each other until both our tears run dry.

230

"Whenever you're ready, we can rejoin the party together," Dan offers. His gentleness is so touching that it keeps making me cry all over again, just when I finally think I'm done.

"I'm leaking, again!" I say with a laugh and sob at the same time as I pull yet another tissue out of the box and dab my soaked cheeks and chin.

"You don't have to stop crying to go back downstairs. I think everyone will understand," he reassures. We sit there for a few more minutes, each in our own thoughts, before I break the silence.

"I've been reading the Christmas story to Charlotte every day for a few weeks now, and this whole experience has caused me to rethink it on a new level," I say. Dan nods, listening. I go on, "I've always known the story, but I never really thought about it from Mary's perspective until this year. I keep thinking Mary probably didn't plan on having Jesus in Bethlehem away from her home, either. She probably didn't plan on having him in a stable. I bet she didn't expect to have to run away and hide in Egypt while Jesus was young. Christmas was messy, emotional, and full of the unexpected for her and Joseph. So, what makes me think it should be anything less for me? I have a whole new appreciation and respect for Mary and Joseph." I think for a minute, then add, "I am in awe of them, actually."

I was raised Catholic, and I always had an appreciation for Mary, but I've never formed a real relationship with her. This whole experience of motherhood, as traumatic as my introduction to it has been thus far, has caused me to think of her often. I have noticed a subtle but very real awareness of her presence with me since

Charlotte's birth. I can't explain it. I don't pretend to understand it. But, somehow, it's like she's drawing near me in my suffering and loving me like only a mother can. I sense the beginning of a relationship that is likely going to get stronger and more present with time, especially as I keep navigating this life as a mom of a child with major medical complexities. A child who does and will suffer greatly. I think Mary can relate to that more than any other mother, considering she watched her child be murdered right before her eyes, in the most painful, hideous, and heartbreaking way. She knew when Gabriel announced she would be the mother of our Lord, that her son would ultimately sacrifice his life for us. She knew she would get a front row seat to watch her son endure unthinkable suffering. And she still said yes. I'm blown away. Of course, she also knew through his suffering, he would rise again and save us from death. But just because she had hope doesn't mean the suffering magically went away. Oh, how I can relate. I have hope Charlotte will heal. God even told me so. But that doesn't eliminate the suffering she has to endure in order to get there, and it doesn't remove the suffering for me who has to stand by and watch with very little I can do to help.

Oh Mary, teach me your ways. How did you do it? I need your strength. I need your grace. I need your hope. Help me love and care for my daughter the way you love and care for your son.

Her presence is an unexpected gift that I'm so thankful for. Her's and the presence of so many both physical and spiritual, carrying me through this.

"I have not left you ... I have sent literally hundreds of people to be my

hands and feet for you, Daniel and Charlotte," God said. I believe him. I'm starting to realize maybe the hundreds of people he's sent are not only people here on earth, but also people in heaven. He's sent an army to carry us through this. Will I let them?

Something funny must have happened downstairs because an uproar of laughter knocks me out of my reflective state-of-mind and reminds me our family downstairs is part of that very army. I need to let them be here for me. To Dan's point, I don't need to keep it together to rejoin the party. So what if I'm crying? It would be alarming if I wasn't! With a newfound peace, I stand, smooth out my dress, grab a fresh Kleenex, reach for Dan's hand and together we descend the steps.

Our four nieces and nephews, between the ages of three and five, run past the base of the stairs into the dining room as Dan and I step into the foyer. Then comes Grampy stomping behind them exclaiming, "I'm gonna get you!" in a deep gruff voice. Their squeals and giggles are magical.

We follow them into the kitchen where Grammy sees our faces and wraps us in one big group hug. She steps back, looks at both of us and says, "What can I get you two to drink?" We all laugh, and I sniffle and wipe another loose tear away, saying, "Chardonnay if you have it, please."

"I'll take a Christmas ale," Dan says.

Grammy hurries to collect our drinks and Aunt Sheila walks in from the living room carrying a huge basket overflowing with little gifts neatly wrapped, with a gorgeous handmade bow on top.

"There you guys are!" she says, setting the basket at our feet. "I was wondering where you went. This is for you."

"All of this?" I ask, incredulously. She waves her hand dismissively.

"Oh, it's just a few small things to help you guys feel at home at the Ronald McDonald House."

I stare at the basket that comes up to my knees, brimming with beautiful packages. "Should we open it now or later?" I ask.

"Well, it looks like you two could use some cheering up so open it now," she smiles.

Dan kneels down and lifts up the gift basket tag to read. It's a hand stitched pink felt ornament with Charlotte's monogrammed initials. "Did you make this?" he asks.

"Yes, she needs her first Christmas ornament," Aunt Sheila says matter of fact.

I pick up the top package and start to unwrap. It's a box full of flavored hot chocolates. "Those are for after your cold walk in the snow back to the Ronald McDonald House when you've been at the NICU all day," she says. Dan unwraps the next gift. It's two green, blue and white painted and ribbed pottery mugs. "A little bit of home for you guys, so you don't have to drink out of styrofoam," she comments.

Now my tears have turned from sad ones to grateful ones. "You've thought of everything!" I whisper as we unwrap to-go packs of Kleenexes, chap sticks, travel soaps, gum, chocolates.

"Pick a number from the hat," my sister-in-law Margaret says as she walks up to Aunt Sheila, Dan and me. "We are going to start the annual Whiting white elephant gift exchange in a few minutes," she explains.

Dan looks at me with that expression that says, oh no, we forgot to get gifts! Margaret leaned in and quickly whispered, "I bought you two white elephant gifts so you can participate." She shakes the upside-down hat toward us, encouraging us to put our hands in and draw out a number.

Our family has thought of everything. Their expressions of love make me want to sit in a corner and keep crying tears of joy, but before I can even process this emerging emotion, Dan and I are swept into the living room, handed drinks, plopped in the middle of the couch and the game begins.

Chapter 28   Accepting Help

Journal Entry - Friday, December 29, 2017

Serve, Fear, Obey, Listen, Cling.

Lord, help me to listen more than I speak. To hear you more than I hear myself. Lord, I cling to you. Help me to never let go. Loosen my grip on my own strength. Loosen my grip of control. Loosen my grip of what the world says is normal. Teach me faithful obedience. Silence me so you may speak. Center me on you, Lord. Teach me true obedience. Faithful obedience out of love. Teach me to fear you, to respect you, to love you, to hope only in you, to serve only you. Lead me, Oh Lord.

I will follow. Help me to follow.

Abba, Father, Lord.

Monday, January 1, 2018, New Years' Day

She's so beautiful. I gently rub lotion on Charlotte's cheeks and belly, trying to soothe the red, angry skin where we removed the tape from her face and the monitor leads from her abdomen. She's chewing aggressively on her pacifier. She's tired and no doubt hungry, too.

It's been a big day so far, already having a blood draw and an ultrasound of her liver and upper quadrant. The nurses skipped the last two feeds to give the sonographer a clear image of Charlotte's liver and bile ducts. Poor baby hasn't eaten in six hours, and she spent the last hour screaming while the sonographer worked to get good images.

"Can we use warm gel this time?" I asked as I watched the sonographer open a packet of the blue gooey stuff and cover the ultrasound probe with it.

"I wish I could," she said. "We can't use warm gel in the NICU for sterile purposes."

"Seriously?" I said, annoyed. This kid has been through so much and the least we can do is warm up the gel before we make her lay still and hungry for an hour, getting pushed and prodded. How can warming the gel possibly be unsanitary? Yet, I obviously didn't want to do anything that could compromise Charlotte's health or give her any additional risk for infection. I was tempted to snatch up the bags of gel, which looked like fast food mustard and ketchup packets, and hold them in my hands to warm them at least a little. What harm could that do? Instead, I focused on soothing Charlotte as best as I could with the pacifier and a few drops of breastmilk. It was futile.

As soon as the sonographer finished, I asked the nurse if she could help me bathe Charlotte and get her warm and cozy for her hard-earned and long-awaited meal. I was proud of myself, getting fairly skilled at helping care for Charlotte, wiping her down gently with

Johnson & Johnson baby soap and navigating the nephrostomy tubes. Then the nurse brought out baby oil and helped me carefully remove the DuoDERM, also called plastic skin, from her cheeks. The steri-strip tape that holds her lips together rests on the DuoDERM, and while the steri-strips are changed almost daily, the DuoDERM can stay on for a week at a time, sparing her skin from always having tape pulled off and reapplied. But, once a week we do have to replace the DuoDerm, too.

I can't imagine how it must feel, having adhesive removed from her cheeks and lips. Her entire body gets red, and she screams bloody murder every time. But the timing of redoing the tape is perfect because today the hospital photographer is coming to capture a couple newborn photos for us.

We pat Charlotte dry, and I put a big homemade felt flower bow on her head, a gift from my sister-in-law's mother, in anticipation of the photographer. There is something about putting a bow on her head that satisfies me, as if it's a statement telling all the hospital staff she is not just a medical phenomenon. She is not the hospital's. She is a beautiful baby girl, and she is my daughter.

I look at Charlotte with admiration as I do some baby massage like the occupational therapist showed me, slowly and gently rubbing lotion down each of Charlotte's arms and across her tiny palms. "Positive touch is very important for her healing," the therapist had said. "She gets lots of negative touches all day, and we want to give her positive ones, too."

How many babies can say they get massages? Not many. Then

again, I suppose most babies also don't get daily pokes from needles, probes, thermometers, stethoscopes, tubes and catheters. So, there is that.

I slowly and gently velcro one of our new 'NICU shirts' around Charlotte's arms and abdomen. One of my mom's friends, whom I've never personally met, heard Charlotte is unable to wear typical baby clothing because of all the wires and leads, so she took it upon herself to find a pattern and sew four outfits together that would fit Charlotte. She made soft fleece tops that work beautifully over all the medical paraphernalia, adorning her with sweet mint green, white and pink sheep, and pink and brown owl prints.

I'm so amazed by this woman's generosity and thoughtfulness. It makes me wonder, before all this craziness happened with our daughter, did I stop what I was doing in my daily life to do something so kind and intentional and time consuming for someone in need, as this woman has? I'd like to think I did, but then, was I so absorbed in my daily to-do list that perhaps I didn't look up long enough to notice these kinds of needs around me? And here this distant family friend heard through the grapevine that I couldn't dress my child, and she went out of her way to provide a solution. Astounding.

My hands continue gently but firmly caressing Charlotte's legs from her skinny thighs down to the balls of her feet. Her sweet, soft calves glide through my hands. I have to be careful to avoid her heels. They are bruised with pricks from the hemoglobin needle each morning. They look like purple and blue pincushions from all the tiny pokes.

She is wide awake, alert and watching my every move, but now peaceful. Looking at her with great admiration, I realize this is the first time I've seen her skin with no monitors or tape stuck to it since the few moments after she was born.

She's stunning.

But, with no wires in the way, I also more clearly observe her distended belly and herniated umbilicus. Her belly is rounded like a milk-drunk kitten's, pushing her belly button to be an outie. Too much milk is obviously not why her belly is big, though. It could be due to the swollen kidneys or the cyst in her abdomen, or something else. We don't know yet.

My phone vibrates, interrupting my thoughts. I wipe my left hand off on a towel so I can pull the phone out of my back pocket and read the text. It's my friend from high school whom I haven't seen in months. "I'm pulling into the parking garage. Be there in a few mins," her message reads.

Melissa reached out a couple days ago asking if she could drive up to visit. She wanted to come an hour north on her day off, just to see me. But it doesn't surprise me. She's always been the selfless kind, the kind of person who drops everything to be there for the people she loves. I love her for it.

Did I ever drop my schedule to be there for her? I think back over the years but struggle to recall. My sense of being a selfless person who helps others is starting to crumble. I'm beginning to see the reality, that maybe I've been pretty busy building my career, traveling all over Timbuctoo, rather than showing up for the people I love when they needed me most. Not that those things were bad, but maybe I'm not as selfless as I like to think I am.

"I want to see you but unfortunately you can't come in the NICU to meet Charlotte due to limited NICU visitor rules," I told her when she called to ask if she could come a few days ago. I was disappointed that I couldn't at least let her meet Charlotte.

"That's alright!" she said. "I'm coming to see *you*. I can just sit with you in a waiting room for a few minutes to say hi."

Thinking back on that conversation, I smile as I respond to her text now, "I'm so glad you're here! It might be a few minutes before I can come out to meet you because we are feeding Charlotte and taking her pics but let me know when you're on the third floor and I'll be out ASAP."

My phone dings almost immediately with her response, "No rush! Take your time. I have the whole afternoon off."

I sit down to breastfeed Charlotte while the nurse preps the syringe and NG tube. "After we fill her belly she's going to be so content and sleepy for the photos," the nurse comments. Just as we get started feeding Charlotte, a short mid-thirties man who looks harried and uncertain walks in the room holding a large camera.

"We just started feeding Charlotte so it's going to be a few minutes. Can you wait?" the nurse asks the photographer who looks at his watch and nods, seeming impatient. I feel a pang of guilt and a rush of familiar, very confusing thoughts and emotions. I feel guilty having the hospital photographer take our newborns' photos because his job is really to capture pictures of loved ones who will not likely make it back home. It feels like asking for his services is somehow admitting our daughter is not going to survive. But the reality is, by the time we are discharged, Charlotte will no longer be a newborn and I really want professional pictures of her as a newborn. I want the cute images of her tiny fingers and toes, with an oversized bow on her head and no tape on her face. We tried to bring in our friend who is a photographer, but that was not allowed, so this is our next best option.

Then I feel guilty that I'm taking this man's time when there may be another family in the hospital whose loved one is breathing their last and I'm selfishly occupying him with my own silly desire for professional photos. Then again, why shouldn't I be able to get images of my child when she's an infant? With so many things stripped of me in this early motherhood experience, I feel indignant that the least I could get is a couple of photos to remember how small she was.

In the back of my mind is the unwanted but lingering question, should I even be capturing professional photos right now, before Charlotte's lip surgery? The thought makes me feel ashamed, like somehow I'm not proud of my daughter's looks because she has a cleft. But I know that's not why I hesitate. I hesitate because I wonder if she will want photos of herself with her cleft. Will she one day wish I hadn't captured these images? Does it seem like I'm almost making fun of her cleft by photographing it? Like I'm mocking it somehow?

How ridiculous. The cleft is part of who she is, and she is beautiful.

In desperate need to know whether I was the only crazy mom in this conundrum, I obsessively researched cleft Facebook support groups. Were other mothers wondering this same question? It turned out many were, and without fail all the mothers of grown kids with cleft replied with confidence that yes, we absolutely should capture professional photos of our babies before the lip repair surgery, because after the surgery, we will miss their original smile, cleft and all. Their responses encouraged me to move forward and book the hospital photographer.

These confusing and conflicting thoughts jumble in my mind and make me anxious as I try to feed Charlotte quickly, so we don't hold this photographer up any longer than necessary. As soon as she finishes eating I gently place her on my mom's homemade quilt that the nurse beautifully spread in her new crib. Charlotte graduated to a crib over Christmas, no longer needing the temperature regulation of an isolette. She looks tiny in this huge bed. The nurse gets the photographer from the hallway where he is waiting.

He doesn't make eye contact as he walks to our bed space and fidgets with his camera. I stand awkwardly, waiting for him to tell me what I need to do, while Charlotte sleeps soundly. Feeling the strain of the silence, I blurt, "Unfortunately we can't remove the orange NG tube from her nose for the photos, or her nephrostomy tubes from her back, even though we were able to remove most of the other things. Maybe you could photoshop them out?"

He looks at Charlotte and then to me and says, "I can't photoshop the orange tube." I'm taken aback by his briskness. Does he really not want to be here and do this right now? Does he think this is ridiculous, taking my daughter's photos when there are probably others in the hospital who need him more? "But we can cover her diaper and the tubes with the blanket so you won't see those," he adds. He backs up and gestures for me to lay the quilt over Charlotte as he described.

He takes a few initial shots, assesses them on his camera, then turns to me and asks what kind of images I have in mind. I show him a homemade hat a distant family friend made us, along with a beautiful matching bow and blanket set we were given, as well as the flower bow and mom's quilt she's currently adorned in. "I was hoping we could capture of few images of her in each of these, so three different outfits, if you will." He takes a deep breath and gets to work. I watch, feeling like a huge inconvenience.

"You can put the hat on now," he says after taking two or three shots of Charlotte in her bow and quilt. I am taken aback. I thought he'd take more images like in a real newborn photo shoot. Not that I've ever been to one, but based on what I've seen from friends who have babies, they take a lot more than three images in one outfit, moving the baby around in all kinds of cute positions. But that is clearly not the service he provides. This is not what I expected at all. I don't say a thing, but gently swap out Charlotte's bow for the hat and step back again. As I watch him angle the camera a few different directions and walk gingerly around the crib to get the best shot, it dawns on me.

Maybe he's not judging me for taking up his time. Maybe he's not being rude or curt on purpose. He probably simply doesn't know what to say or how to act. I mean, it's not every day you see a tiny baby in the NICU with so many medical needs and interact with her obsessive and exhausted mother. Maybe he is not cold hearted, but in fact just doesn't know what to say or what to do, so he's doing what he can for us. It makes me think of the Little Drummer Boy Christmas song. "I have no gift to bring … shall I play for you?" Perhaps he's giving us the best gift he can, and that's using his photographing skills like the little boy used his drumming skills.

Now I feel stupid. Of course, he's not repositioning Charlotte like a typical photographer would. He's probably not allowed to touch patients, especially infant ones, and he's probably terrified of screwing something up with the nephrostomy tubes, too. Of course. Why didn't I think of that? I was terrified to touch her when I first saw them, too. Wow, I really jumped to some ridiculous conclusions. My misguided perception of him is more of a reflection of my own anxieties and insecurities than a true reflection of him. I fight feelings of disappointment, in myself for being so judgmental and in this photo shoot for once again being nothing like the typical experience. But then, why did I expect it to be anything close to typical? Her kidneys are draining into attached tubes, for crying out loud!

He snaps his last photo and says, "I'll email you the images by the end of the week. Take care," and he leaves. I try to shake my disappointment as I settle Charlotte in for a good and hopefully undisturbed nap, so I can go spend a few minutes with Melissa. "I'll be back before her next feed," I tell the nurse as I give Charlotte a kiss on her forehead and walk out.

"Hey!" Melissa exclaims, standing up and giving me a huge hug. She's holding two Starbucks cups. "I thought I'd bring you a coffee," she says and hands me one. Of course, she did. She even knows I like it black. I lead her to the Ronald McDonald Family Room, and we sit on the couch to catch up. We start chatting like the old friends we are. I catch her up on the craziness of the last few weeks while she absorbs what I'm telling her with wide eyes. Then I ask her to tell me about what's happening in her life. She fills me in on her work and family. We start talking about horses, which she and I have shared a passion for since grade school. We used to race our horses through neighbor's corn fields, ride them into ponds for mid-summer swims on horseback, and we even camped out in a tent in her barn once. We were crazy about horses. I drifted from horses since leaving for college, but she still owns several and she tells about the latest training mishaps with them. She tells me about her involvement in our high school agriculture program, FFA, which she now lends a helping hand as a coach for their extracurricular activities.

"Actually, I wanted to ask you something," she says. "They are doing a fundraiser this Spring for a community family in need. They are wondering if they can raise the money for you guys?"

I sit back, caught off guard. A fundraiser? For us? "Oh, I'm sure there are other families who could benefit from it more than us," I quickly say, grateful they thought of us but not really sure how to react. Are we a family in need?

"I can only imagine how many added costs you guys have from being in the hospital and the FFA team really wants to give the money to you, but only if you're okay with it," Melissa says.

"What does the fundraiser entail?" I ask, almost feeling greedy even considering saying yes. We really don't *need* the money. We are doing okay. I think we are okay. Are we okay? I fear whether we will remain financially stable as the medical bills start rolling in, but thus far, we've been able to stay afloat. Then again, I haven't opened the growing stack of mail from the Cleveland Clinic billing department yet.

"Well, it's an Easter family event so there will be the Easter Bunny, an egg hunt for the kids, raffle items and food," Melissa explains.

I envision a small gathering that maybe raises a couple hundred dollars. I can get on board with that, since I don't want to disappoint them or Melissa by saying no.

"Yeah, I think that would be okay," I say hesitantly. "But if there is another family that you know of who could benefit more, please don't feel like you need to raise money for us," I add.

"Nope, they have their hearts set on doing it for you," Melissa says. How strange, to be the benefitting family from a community event. I've often donated to such causes and even helped put them on a time or two, but I certainly never imagined myself being the benefactor one day. It'll be a small event, I justify, and it's important to the local FFA kids so the least I can do is say yes.

"Great! They'll be so excited," says Melissa with enthusiasm.

She seems relieved I said yes to the fundraiser, like it gave her something to do to contribute to my otherwise helpless situation. This is becoming a theme. People offer to help and if I accept, regardless of the offer—whether it's to send a gift card, organize a fundraiser or bring me a coffee—they seem energized and grateful for the opportunity to do something.

Likewise, when I turn down offers, people react in a way that seems almost deflated. Like I stole their opportunity to help.

I mentioned this to Mom the other day, to which she advised, "Countless people want to help, and they don't know how. So, you accepting their help is actually selfless of you, as contradicting as that might seem." What a shocking perspective, that maybe accepting help isn't selfish in any way, but rather it is selfless to humble myself and say yes, I do need help and whatever people have to offer is more than enough.

Why is receiving help so hard? Why is it so hard for me to simply say yes? I suppose I'm not used to being on the receiving end. This is whole new territory. It's terrifying. It feels like with each yes, I'm also inadvertently announcing, "I can't do this on my own," which I obviously can't, but making that so painfully clear to the public is, well, painful. Especially in the form of a community fundraiser. Everyone will know just how helpless I am! But each time I lay my pride aside and accept what's offered, I see the benefit reaches far beyond simply our family gaining whatever is given. The giver also gains a sense of purpose and satisfaction. That alone is worth accepting the help, isn't it?

From now on, I vow to always accept help regardless of how big or how small or whether I perceive we need it. God said he would provide, and if I continually turn down those who offer to help, those he sends as his army of supporters he said he surrounded us with, then I'm turning down his help and telling him inadvertently, "I've got this, thanks anyway." And for heaven's sake I don't have this at all! I am 100% incapable of managing this situation without an army of help. So, I need to die to myself here and now. Die to my pride and humble myself. That's what I'm going to try and do.

Lord, help me to do it.

Still, I hope this fundraiser stays small and doesn't make too much of a fuss over us.

 ## Telling Pride to Take a Hike

The fundraiser turned out to be a very large event with people pouring in from all corners of the county and state. Hundreds of people attended. So much so that the Easter Bunny ran out of candy. Even my first high school crush showed up, having no family or children of his own, just to support us. At the sight of him, I couldn't help but cry on the spot. He had no interest in seeing the Easter bunny or collecting eggs, but he was there nonetheless, to support us. Who does that? Apparently, he and countless others.

By the end of the event, I saw numerous old friends, acquaintances, and friends of friends whom I didn't know, but our story reached them, and they donated to Charlotte's cause. I learned from that experience that when God says he'll provide, your job is only to say yes and don't let your pride get in his way. He'll do the rest.

And my goodness he'll provide more than you ever dreamed. The FFA kids didn't just raise a couple hundred dollars for us, they raised $16,000. And it wasn't just an intimate little get together. Our family was featured on the front page of the community section of the local newspaper. After the event, checks kept rolling in with notes saying things like, "We hoped to come to the event but weren't able to, so please accept our donation now."

The moral of the story is, when someone offers you help, your job is only to say yes and then tell your pride to take a hike. What happens next will astound you.

Chapter 29   Emergency Baptism

Dan's Text Message, Thursday, January 4, 2018

"Good morning, Love. I hope you are having a great morning. You are doing a great job being a mother. I know it's tough with all the doctors and nurses, pumping all night, thinking about all her upcoming procedures. I know it's hard to trust God in these moments. Look at where he has got us? We have an incredibly strong marriage in spite of things not being perfect, we have a beautiful baby despite her challenges, we have an amazing family that lets go of personal schedules to get us through this tough time. We have a comfortable place to stay and warm meals. Our blessings go on and on. We need to continue to trust him and trust that he is acting through us, our doctors, nurses, and family. I trust your love for me and your love for God, Babe, and wouldn't want to go through this with anyone else. I love you, Babe."

My Reply:

"Thank you for this text, Love. It means the world to me this morning. You are right, our blessings overflow. God has brought us this far and he'll continue to carry us. I trust him. I trust you. And I love him and I love you. Thank you for being

there for Charlotte and me yesterday. We are so blessed to have you. I may feel broken from the battle of the day, but I know the war isn't lost. I'm so grateful we are in this together. With God, we will prevail. I love you."

Monday, January 8, 2018

"Charlotte Jo Whiting, I baptize you in the name of the Father," Dan squirts holy water from a pink plastic bottle onto the back of Charlotte's head. It thuds into an empty white paper bucket held in his left hand. "And of the Son," Dan pours more water on Charlotte's downy head. It rolls off her sweet dark infant hair. "And of the Holy Ghost," Dan concludes with a third squirt from the bottle of Holy Water our cousin gave us before Charlotte's birth. I am holding Charlotte horizontally in the football position, watching as Dan nervously and carefully takes a well-worn hospital wash cloth to pat our almost six-week-old dry.

He kisses her head and I pull her close to kiss her, too. Dan and I lean our foreheads on each other and whisper prayers over our daughter. "Oh Lord, thank you for this beautiful baby you've blessed us with. We pray she is filled with the gifts of the Holy Spirit and she grows to have a deep personal relationship with you. Lord, please fill the OR today. Be by her side, guide the hands of the surgeons and the nurses. Let them be your hands of healing for Charlotte. You said you'd heal us, all three of us." I pause, then quietly choke, "Lord, I believe, help my unbelief." Silent tears fall on Charlotte's blue and white striped hospital swaddle blanket.

How can tears be so bitter and sweet all at once? I am filled with great peace, hope, and a deep joy of knowing where, and in whom, our hope comes from. Knowing Charlotte is a beloved child of God. Knowing regardless how today's surgery turns out, she is in his loving hands and she will ultimately be okay, whether here with us or in heaven with him. Yet I simultaneously experience dread and deep sadness knowing the suffering that is to come. I've stopped being surprised when these emotions cohabitate.

Regardless of the outcome, Charlotte will experience great pain and that destroys my mama heart. How I wish I could take this pain from her. I wish it were me who could be cut open for exploratory surgery. I wish I could take her place. I would a million times over. That sounds valiant and selfless but it's not. It's selfish, truly, because the pain of watching her go through all this seems like it's 1,000 times worse to watch her endure than if I could just take on the pain myself. If I could only take it away from my daughter.

Lord, why can't I be the one who suffers in her place?

Dan concludes our prayer, "*Let your will be done and give us the strength and courage to face it. You love Charlotte even more than we do, so Jesus, we trust in you. Amen.*"

She's peacefully sleeping through it all as if she doesn't have a worry in the world. Thank God. I'm surprised she didn't even wake from the water. But Dan intentionally warmed it as best he could before he poured it on her, so that surely helped. The lights are still dim in the room. It's only 6:00 a.m. Besides the rhythmic hum of monitors and machines, the room is almost peaceful. I hope we can keep her asleep until they put her under anesthesia, which should be within the next hour or so.

She has to be NPO for the surgery so we work quietly and slowly in hopes we don't wake her, so maybe she won't even know she's hungry before surgery begins. This being our third procedure in five weeks, and who knows how many NPO tests at this point, we're learning the tricks to help Charlotte's experience be at least slightly less traumatic.

It does feel a little sneaky, keeping her sleeping and then putting her under anesthesia before she even knows what's coming. One moment she falls asleep peacefully in her NICU bed and the next she wakes up in a post op recovery room with a line of stitches stretching from her right side all the way to her belly button. It seems like a betrayal of her trust. But then, what is gained by waking her before surgery only to make her aware of her empty stomach?

Dan and I rolled out of bed, huffed our snow boots on and hurried to the NICU super early this morning so we could spend time with her before she is wheeled into the OR. We are painfully aware of the fact that this surgery could end in a lot of different ways, including her possibly not surviving. While we are trying not to let our minds go there, it seems only responsible for us to act accordingly and conduct an emergency baptism.

On December 8th, a month ago today in-fact, the priest who conducted our marriage ceremony, Father Jack, visited us in the NICU. Charlotte was only a week-and-a-half old. He offered at that time to baptize her, which Dan and I declined. It felt like doing an emergency baptism was admitting she might not make it, and we weren't ready for that. Then again, as a parent is anyone ever ready for that?

Father Jack was surprised we turned down the offer saying, " If you change your minds or things get dire, you can always conduct an emergency baptism yourselves. You don't need a priest to do it." He then proceeded to teach Dan and I exactly what to do in such a case. I remember feeling conflicted at the time, wondering if we were sticking our heads in the sand and refusing to acknowledge reality, or if we were being faith-filled and trusting she would heal. Sometimes the difference is hard to decipher. As he told us the bible verse to say from the book of Matthew to conduct the baptism, I was touched by his diligence to prepare us for the worst, while I simultaneously dismissed it as something I'd never need to remember.

But things change, just like how surgery plans change. We began the new year last week thinking Charlotte was headed to the OR on January 3rd for a ureter implant surgery. The plan was to connect her ureters to her bladder and if the bladder began cycling successfully as a result of the surgery, they would remove the nephrostomy tubes from her back. We eagerly awaited the elimination of these pesky bags, which present risk of infection and also of falling out. But, on January 2nd surgeons conferred and changed their minds. The abdominal cyst needed to go, now.

Exploratory gastrointestinal surgery was scheduled with the pediatric general surgeon for January 8 and instead of going to the operating room on January 3rd for ureter implantation, Charlotte went to Interventional Radiology (IR) that day to have new nephrostomy tubes placed under x-ray and ultrasound guidance. The idea was this would buy Charlotte's kidneys more time to drain via the tubes while doctors addressed the abdominal cyst. Apparently nephrostomy tubes only last for about a month and hers had already pushed beyond that limit because we had held off on replacement, thinking we could just eliminate them altogether. Plans changed.

As we rocked Charlotte yesterday in anticipation of today's surgery, Dan started rethinking our decision about baptism. "We probably should baptize her like Father Jack showed us," Dan said. At first I was taken aback by his suggestion, but then I realized I had no valid reason to object besides my own fear of what baptism was admitting.

The NICU nurse assigned to prepare Charlotte for surgery this morning is standing back, watching at a distance with reverence as the three of us cling to each other in prayer. Bless her.

When we came in this morning she was moving Charlotte to an isolette that could transport her to the operating room. She was gathering up all the mobile monitor units and anything else needed bedside. We didn't even tell her we were about to baptize our child. I just scooped Charlotte up and stood close to the isolette so as to not pull on any of her lines and leads, and Dan went about gathering supplies.

When she realized what we were about to do she said, "Wait just one moment," and walked briskly back to the supply room. A few minutes later she returned with a clean white rag and a bucket. "These should help," she said with great kindness. "I can call the hospital clergy if you'd like a pastor to come," she offered.

We both shook our heads no. "We are prepared to do it ourselves, but thanks," Dan said.

He fumbled on his phone, pulling up the instructions for how to perform an emergency baptism, which he had found and thoroughly researched the night before. My heart explodes with love for him, for his diligent desire to baptize her correctly.

"Surely we can just pour water on her and pray and then she's baptized, right?" I asked him last night, wondering why he was so absorbed in researching it.

"No, Emily, there are specific words we need to say to make sure it's valid."

I must admit I feel very unknowledgeable about the ins and outs of baptism, but I do know I trust in the Lord and I also know the Church is wiser than I, so I am happy to follow our priest's guidance. I'm grateful Dan is taking this so seriously, because I think if it were up to me I would screw it up.

Seemingly the moment we say "Amen," a group of three Plastics Team residents walk in the room, past the nurse and right up to Dan, me and Charlotte, oblivious to what is going on. One of them speaks loudly saying, "We are here to redo Charlotte's tape."

Of course they are. Isn't that the way of NICU life? There is no time to just revel in the moment before we are back to navigating the demands of specialist schedules and care regimens. I see the nurse come forward, trying to head them off before they wake Charlotte. My inner mama bear comes out full force.

"I appreciate your diligence on her taping, but I don't think it matters much right now. She's heading to the OR this morning and we need to keep her asleep before then," I pull Charlotte in close to my chest and turn my shoulder to them, putting myself between them and her. My body language communicates "Back off!" without saying those words, exactly. Instead, I say, "Can we redo the tape after the surgery?"

Why are we even worrying about her tape right now when she may or may not make it through the day? Did they not get that memo? It's kind of an important one! What does tape matter? We don't care whether her lip stretches to make for a pretty adhesion in a few months.

The resident takes a pause and looks around the scene, observing the holy water and bucket still in Dan's hands and Charlotte's damp head. "Oh, we are so sorry. We didn't realize … we will retape later," he stumbles on his words and turns around, ushering the group out like a hen with her clutch of chicks.

As if on cue, the Pediatric General Surgery Team walks in as the Plastics Team walks out. They are dressed in their blue surgery garb and have a quiet but determined air about them. Dr. Cressefulli, the head surgeon for today's procedure greets us and begins walking us through all he will accomplish.

"As we discussed at length yesterday, today's procedure will last a minimum of 3 hours. Likely longer. I plan to explore the abdominal cyst and remove it. Until we get in there, we won't know exactly what it is or how to proceed with rebuilding the biliary tree, since the cyst currently envelops it. We will also do a Ladd's procedure, correcting the malrotation of the gastrointestinal tract. With that, we will perform an appendectomy because Charlotte's appendix is in the left quadrant of her abdomen rather than the right. This will eliminate the variability of possible future appendicitis going undiagnosed since her appendix is not correctly positioned. We will repair her herniated umbilicus as well. And I understand we will be placing a Broviac catheter before we are finished." Dr. Cressefulli concludes, looking Dan and me right in the eyes. "We will take good care of her, and if the surgery takes longer than expected, it's because we are working diligently to give her the best possible outcome. Dr. Carter will scrub in with me."

We complete all the formalities and signatures of consent, robotically going through the motions. Then the nurse tells us to take a moment with Charlotte before we are to put her back in the isolette to be wheeled off to the surgery unit.

How do you say goodbye to your daughter, when you know where she's going and what she's about to face? My head scrambles, wondering if we are doing the right thing. Should we go through with this? What if we say no and stop this whole thing from happening?

She would die. I know that. She can't go on with this cyst in her abdomen and with her GI tract backwards. She has to have this surgery. This is the logical next step in her healing. But logic is hard to reason with when your heart feels like it's lying in your arms, breathing peacefully and trusting you as her mother to take good care of her. I look down at her sweet sleepy face, innocent and naive to what is about to happen. How do I place my heart back in that isolette and let her be wheeled away by a group of strangers and trust that they will do what it takes to help her live?

If I place my trust in them, I absolutely cannot go through with this. They are merely human, and though they all mean well and have years of schooling to make informed decisions, I cannot fathom trusting them with my daughter. With my heart. Yet I know it's not just this group of surgeons and nurses that I'm sending my daughter with. I know God is going, too. I know he's going to hold Charlotte. He's going to guide these surgeon's hands and inspire their intellect to make the right decisions. The only way I can possibly let go of Charlotte right now and put her in that isolette as the nurse is beckoning me to is by trusting this truth. "*Jesus, I trust in you,*" I whisper as I rock Charlotte back and forth for one more moment before reluctantly lowering her into the nest of blankets.

Dan kisses her forehead, cups his hands around her head and feet for a few moments, then closes the isolette doors. His face wrecked. Realizing she's been set down, she begins to protest, wiggling and squawking. Her small cries turn to vehement screams, though they are muffled by the plastic cocoon that seems eerily like a hearse. I resist the urge to pick her right back up. Instead, Dan and I cling to each other, and we slowly follow the beeping mobile infant bed, along with the herd of staff, out of the NICU, down the elevators and onto the surgical floor.

Chapter 30 Guilt

Monday, January 8, 2018

"What did I do to cause this?" I mumble with my forehead in my hands and my elbows on my knees, trying to think of anything. What? What did I do?

The image of Charlotte screaming at the top of her lungs and flailing her naked arms and legs while the anesthesiologist covered her mouth and nose with a mask is ingrained in my brain, replaying over and over like a scratched compact disc. Like the punch line to a cruel joke, making it obvious there is nothing I can do to help her. Nothing I can do to take away her struggle. Then her cries muffled, and her limbs went limp as the OR nurse closed the big steel doors and left Dan and me standing in the empty hallway, simultaneously wanting to scream and throw the doors back open while also feeling numb and frozen in our shoes.

Another nurse beckoned us to walk to the waiting room, chatting as if everything was perfectly normal, trying to distract us from this nightmare. Did she have a clue what was happening? My anger flashed as I listened to her go on about the snow and whatever storm was supposedly headed our way tonight. As if I care in the slightest about what's happening outside. She was trying to help, but the complete lack of recognition that this is straight out of a horror film made me want to shake her into silence.

Instead, I thanked her after she led us to the waiting room and now I find myself here on this gray leather hospital couch wanting to crawl into the fetal position. Did I take medication during pregnancy that I shouldn't have? I shouldn't have taken that Tylenol when I had a headache that one time. Did my pansy-self who couldn't handle a measly headache without Acetaminophen cause my daughter to endure unthinkable pain now?

Did I breathe in some kind of chemical that I shouldn't have? Does our house have some kind of toxic substance I don't know about? It was built in the mid 1800's, so that's not too far of a stretch, is it? Why did we choose to buy such a fixer upper as our starter home? Why did I insist on painting while I was pregnant? Maybe that was the demise of our child.

What about those handful of beers I drank the week before we knew we were pregnant? Did they cause Charlotte's anomalies? I used to drink way too much caffeine before I was pregnant. Could that have altered my egg's genetic code somehow?

Or, what about that summer vacation we took when I was sixteen-weeks pregnant? It was in Utah and there was a distant wildfire. I breathed in smoke all week. Did that do it? I remember getting insanely hot and tired during a hike on that vacation. I was stupid for thinking I could hike four miles in 100-degree Fahrenheit weather. Did heat stress cause all this?

Doctors say whatever happened to Charlotte's genetic coding that led to her anomalies happened very early on when all the tiny cells were dividing and preparing to build organs and limbs. Likely when she was four to eight weeks gestation, still smaller than a pea. But why did Charlotte's genetics code build her the way they did? The way that led to her needing this emergent surgery. The way that may lead to her death.

I rock back and forth, wracking my brain, lost in my own self-deprecating thoughts. I should collect myself. Both sets of our parents are here waiting with Dan and me, passing the hours by while Charlotte is splayed on the OR table. But I cannot shrug this question and the resulting crushing guilt. My daughter is undergoing a massive surgery and she's about to face an unspeakable recovery journey, at least we hope, assuming she makes it, and I cannot live with myself thinking that perhaps I did something to bring such pain upon her.

"What did I do?" I mutter again. My hands shake. I am overwrought with self-blame.

My mom is sewing the binding on a quilt in her lap. Her hands stop their busy work immediately, and she looks at me through questioning eyes. Grammy Nancy was telling a funny story about the farm market she and Grampy own, trying to keep us upbeat and distracted with the mishaps of pumpkin butter and Christmas tree sales. She falls silent at my outburst. She looks at me curiously. I sit up straight and try to brush the debilitating weight of guilt off of my shoulders but can't seem to engage in any conversation besides the one that's racing through my head.

What did I do?

Before either woman can ask what I meant by my comment, the pager buzzes and vibrates. I snatch up the pager that's sitting in the middle of us all on the littered coffee table and quickly scan the OR nurse's message, "Charlotte is doing great. She is under anesthesia and surgeons are about to begin." I pass the pager to Dan who reads it aloud for everyone. He sets it back on the table in the midst of a spread of coffee, half-eaten breakfast sandwiches and newspaper pages.

My mom sets her quilt aside and leans over the table toward me, "Say that again, Emily? What did you say?" She has great concern written all over her face and I know she heard me right, but she wants to clarify.

"Genetics says they can't find an explanation for Charlotte's diagnoses. The doctors all reassure me there is nothing I've done to cause this. But I can't help but think I did. There's got to be something that explains why Charlotte is facing all these challenges, and what if I'm to blame?" I spit the ugly words out. Until this moment, I haven't let myself really process this question. Sure, I've felt the guilt and wondered why, but I haven't allowed myself to stop and really think about it. Now the self-accusing thoughts are relentless like aggressive ocean waves swallowing up the shore.

Mom's eyes well and color floods her cheeks. That look is familiar. It's the one I feel almost daily—the mama bear look. I get it honestly. "Emily, you know you didn't do anything to cause this.

Absolutely not. You did everything you could to be cautious during the pregnancy and there is nothing you could have done or not done to make her develop the way she did," Mom says with conviction, determined to convince me of her words' truth. I hear the pain in her voice. She's hurting for me. It's ironic, how she hurts for me as she sees me hurting and meanwhile, I'm hurting for my daughter as I watch her endure all of this.

"It's not logical, but I feel so guilty," I admit.

Grammy Nancy jumps up from her chair that's on the opposite side of the table and sits beside me, rubbing her hand on my back. Dan is on the other side of me with his hand on my knee, but he seems unsure what to do. Poor guy. I don't blame him. His wife is having a total meltdown while his daughter is fighting for her life. What is he supposed to do? Mom leans forward and puts her hand on my opposite knee, too. I sit back and reach for a Kleenex, trying to regain composure. I feel foolish, making this about me. I laugh, which comes out sounding like a snort, feeling awkward now. I didn't intend to make such a scene or to garner this much attention.

I'm tempted to brush my mom and mother-in-law away and act like I'm fine, like I don't need their help. But I do. I do need their help. I am far from fine. How annoying that I am a basket case when really we should all just focus on Charlotte. But the reality of waiting during my child's surgery is that there is nothing to do but wait, and in that waiting, the thoughts and reflections that haven't been given the time of day thus far crop up with a vengeance. They haunt my mind and as much as I don't want to acknowledge them, they refuse to

265

relent.

I suppose this is a continuation of my lesson to let people help me. Let my family hold me for a bit and see my brokenness and pain on ugly display. Let them hurt with me and stop trying to shield them from how deeply I ache. I cannot protect them from my pain any more than I can protect Charlotte from hers. I cannot carry myself right now, so I acquiesce and let these beautiful women carry me in this moment, even if it's just by them sitting with me and telling me on repeat that I am not to blame for this. There is nothing I have done to cause this. I did not do this to our daughter. I know this. I know this. I know this.

I don't believe it.

Help me to believe it. Oh Lord, I need this guilt to go away.

Chapter 31 Oh God

Tuesday, January 9, 2018

I fumble to hit snooze on my cell phone alarm. Green neon numbers on the bed stand digital clock glow 4:30 a.m. It's pump-thirty. I roll over. Five more minutes. Before I know it, the phone relentlessly buzzes at me again, telling me to get out of my warm bed and collect milk for my baby. I turn off the alarm and see two missed calls from the NICU—one at 2:30 and one at 3:00 a.m., plus several texts from Dan. I sleepily roll over and reach for Dan but instead of landing on his strong chest, my arm finds empty cold sheets.

I shoot up. Where is he? My chest pounds as I recall our daughter is only a few hours post-op. I press the phone to my ear and strain to listen to the voicemail.

"Hello Mrs. Whiting, um, this is the attending Neonatologist at Cleveland Clinic," his heavy Russian accent is hard to understand in my sleepy, frenzied delirium. I've never heard this accent before. He must be new to the rotation since we've been hospitalized. "Um, I'm calling to inform you Charlotte appears to be experiencing seizure-like activity. She is stable now, but you may want to come to the NICU as soon as you receive this message. Um, I'll try Dad's cell, too. Bye."

I throw off the bed covers and pull on my jeans while skimming Dan's texts. "I am at the NICU. Come when you get this." Why didn't he wake me before he left?

Then his next text, "Sorry I didn't wake you. I figured you could use the sleep and I'd come get you if I needed to."

I check the time of his messages. 3:00 a.m. I had just pumped at 2:00 a.m. and must have fallen into a deep, albeit short, sleep. Panic rises. My chest tightens.

I still have to pump. Gah! I don't have time! I'll have to do it when I get there. I snatch up all my bottle and hose supplies, stuff them in a bag and shove my feet in my winter boots. I throw my knotty hair up in a messy bun on the top of my head and rub my hands over my sleep-deprived eyes.

I feel old. I'm only twenty-seven. I feel like the last few months have added a few decades to my age. I should wash my face and brush my teeth. Instead, I pop a piece of mint gum in my mouth, open the bedroom door and walk briskly down the empty Ronald McDonald hallway, descend the dimly-lit stairs and go through the sleepy lobby into the dark, brisk air. The front desk night shift volunteer calls after me, asking if he can order me a shuttle. I will get there faster if I just hoof it through the ankle-deep snow and sludge the half-mile to the hospital. I wave over my shoulder and yell, "No thanks!" before picking up into a jog.

I have been warned numerous times not to walk these streets

alone, especially in the dark. Apparently this is a bad part of town where muggings happen frequently. Whatever. They can take my pump bottles and coat. That's all I have anyway. I don't think anyone is going to mess with me. Let them try.

By the time I get to the third floor of the hospital and gain access through the security desk, sweat drips down my bra and forehead. I huff and puff, trying to catch my breath as I buzz the doorbell outside the NICU. My snow boot taps the floor as I wait impatiently for someone to let me in. I peer through the small window in the door. Doctors and nurses fill and overflow Charlotte's room.

A night-shift front desk manager answers the door. "Mrs. Whiting, I want to prepare you for what you're about to see. Charlotte has EEG leads on her head to monitor brain activity. It can be shocking when you first see it," she trails me. I nod in acknowledgement but keep walking down the hall to my daughter's bed.

I push my way through the small crowd and find Dan standing beside Charlotte's isolette. He grabs hold of me in a hug, blocking me for a minute. I look past him over his shoulder. I need to see my daughter. From just five feet away, all I see is wires, lines, tubes and splayed limbs.

"What's happening?" I ask, pushing Dan aside and going straight to Charlotte's bed. I try to take in what I'm seeing. Her head is covered in fifteen or more little electrodes, each secured with white gauze-looking tape and thick glue, connected to individual white, red and blue wires. Her scalp looks like someone got carried away with a blue permanent marker, flagging where the electrodes go. In addition to the nasal elevator, DuoDerm, tape and NG tube that were on her nose and mouth preoperatively, Charlotte has two more tubes in her mouth—one a breathing tube and the other a stomach pump. Both arms have IVs as well as one foot. The three heart monitor leads I'm used to seeing on her chest are joined by two more, along with the Broviac now implanted on her chest with a white tube protruding. She has one large surgical site tube coming out of her lower abdomen draining into a basin attached to the side of her isolette. It runs red and brown with blood and discharge. She has a four-inch-long white bandage spanning across her abdomen from her far-right side all the way to her belly button, covering a long row of stitches. Two nephrostomy tubes still protrude from her back and are joined with another catheter coming from her diaper, draining her bladder. A tiny blood pressure cuff hugs Charlotte's left thigh and her pulse ox glows pink on her left foot. Both heels have bandages covering her purple feet from all the needle pricks. There is not a square inch on her that isn't assaulted. I barely see the six-week-old, six-pound baby beneath it all.

This was all here yesterday when Charlotte returned from the three-hour surgery turned into eight. All except the EEG leads. Those are new and they consume the last part of Charlotte's body that didn't already have medical paraphernalia protruding—her scalp. Under all the apparatus, her tiny chest rhythmically pops up and down with the ventilator. Her skin looks ashen, like the skin of a preserved corpse in a wake.

Her eyes are open, but they look glassy, like she can't really see in her heavily medicated state. Her mouth wearily opens and closes around the tubes as if she's trying to say something, but no sound reaches my ears. Her arms and legs lay limp on the pink isolette bedding.

"The ventilator lays on her vocal cords," the night-shift nurse quietly explains. "That's why you can see her crying, but you can't hear her."

I watch the machine breathe for my daughter and my own breath escapes me. All oxygen sucked from my lungs, like I am hit head on by a Mack truck. The nurse quickly rolls her chair over and ushers me to sit.

"We are working to find the right balance of pain medication, to not overmedicate but to help her rest comfortably. Her natural drive to breath is suppressed with the medications so the ventilator is doing the work for her. We also have to be careful what we use to not compromise her healing liver. She's getting dexmedetomidine and morphine on continuous IV drip and we just gave her additional morphine PRN so hopefully it will help her get comfortable and fall asleep soon," the nurse adds.

Fall asleep but not kill her, I fill in the blanks of what the nurse is saying, and not saying. They are dancing between sedation and termination.

Dan puts his hands on my shoulders. "I didn't want to wake you because I knew there was nothing you could do anyway, and you needed some sleep. I got the call and came right away," he says gently, afraid I'm going to be mad. I probably would be if I had the brain-space to think about that now. He pauses and lets me have a moment to take in the reality of the scene. "They said she had two episodes early this morning that looked like seizures. They've been monitoring ever since with the EEG but haven't picked up on any seizure activity so far."

His voice cracks, then he starts to quietly weep. "The last part of her that we could touch, we can't anymore," he chokes. Last night when she finally came out of the OR at dinner time, we sat with her for a few hours with our hands cupping her head and feet, just like all the times before when we couldn't hold her. Now we can't even do that.

I open one of the isolette doors and whisper quietly, "Charlotte Baby, Mama and Daddy are here. We are here."

Her eyes wince.

"She's in a lot of discomfort right now, Emily," the nurse says gently. "Sound and touch are probably painful for her."

So, we can't talk to her either, or even touch her arm or leg to comfort her. There is literally nothing we can do. Nothing.

Dan sits in the chair beside me, and we stare at our daughter as doctors and nurses quietly buzz around us, telling us hypotheses of what may have happened through the night.

"It could have been seizures due to the heavy pain medications."

"It could have been her body in shock from coming out of such a long anesthesia."

"She received a blood transfusion during the surgery due to blood loss, perhaps it's her body reacting."

"Her breathing tube had secretions stuck in it, which we immediately resolved both times. Maybe her episodes were her trying to clear her airway."

The more they try to explain and comfort and help, the more I feel the room closing in around me. I have to get out of here. I can't do anything for Charlotte by being here. I have to go.

I abruptly stand almost knocking over the chair. I walk out without saying a word. I push through the NICU door into the hallway and walk into the nearest waiting room. No one is there except the noisy ice machine, so I sit down in the back corner chair and finally in this space of aloneness, I wail. I wail like I've never wailed before. I rock back and forth with my hands on my knees, feeling like I'm going to wretch. My cries come in loud waves, *"Oh God! Oh God! Oh God!"* Some escape my lips as moans and others as screams. I'm not sure if I'm praying or cursing. Either way the sobs keep coming.

My awareness of my surroundings and my care about others' reactions completely disappears as I am enveloped in an all-consuming despair. I vaguely notice a body come in to get ice chips and quickly leave before filling his cup. Then I am distantly aware of Dan wrapping his arms around me. My cries relentlessly continue, *"Oh God! Oh God! Oh God!"*

I don't have the energy or the wherewithal to pray for anything specific, or to even form a full thought. I'm done asking for anything from God or of him. All I can do is throw myself at his feet in desperate brokenness and recite his name over and over and over again. I'm completely humbled. On my knees. Emptied. Poured out. I have nothing left. Nothing but him. Who else do I turn to? What else can I do? Nothing. *"Oh God! Oh God! Oh God!"* my groans drone on.

 ## Simple Prayer

Sometimes our best prayers are the ones that come straight from the heart and with very little formality or explanation. After having time and distance to reflect on this, I have concluded this was absolutely a prayer, and not only just a prayer, it was possibly my most powerful prayer I have ever prayed.

God knows exactly what we need and when we need it, so a heart cry for him is sometimes the best prayer of all.

I don't know if two minutes or twenty go by, but Joyce the social worker comes into view and kneels in front of me. "Emily, what can I do for you? Do you need Kleenexes? Do you want to talk?" she asks loudly, trying to be heard over my cries.

I blurt, "Just let me cry!" My body racks with grief as she gets up and walks out the door. Quickly she returns with a blue pen, scrap sheet of paper and scotch tape. She sticks the paper on the door and writes in bold, "DO NOT DISTURB," before pulling the otherwise public waiting room door closed.

Space to Grieve

I kept the sign. To me it was the most loving thing anyone could have done for me in that moment—to let me cry. When we see others grieving, the best thing we can do is to give them the space to grieve— not to try and fix it or speak hope in that moment. Those things can be done after the grief subsides and the person is ready. In the moment of deep grief, all that's needed is the space to truly grieve and that's exactly what Joyce gave to me.

Journal Entry - Wednesday, January 10, 2018

Dear Lord,

I'm sitting here in the NICU staring at my sedated baby. She's two days out of surgery and, due to the immense pain, she's on a ventilator and heavy meds. My heart hurts. My baby hurts. And there is nothing I can do about it. I can't hold her. I can't feed her. I can't take away her pain. I can simply sit here and stare at her.

Chapter 32 Working Out Glue

Text Message from cousin Crystal, Thursday, January 11, 2018 (Lou is my family nickname):

Hi Lou. Just wanted to let you know you guys are on my heart big time. I'm sure you're so exhausted and just at your end. I'm praying hard for God to meet you there and give you some rest. No need to respond. You don't need another thing to do. He's going to bring you through this one day at a time. Love you all.

Thursday, January 11, 2018

"Here is some baby oil I found," Patty, Charlotte's NICU nurse today, says as she hands me a bottle, along with a diaper cloth and a black baby comb. "The diaper cloth is so much softer than the wash clothes we have," she explains. She brought two sets of materials from the supply closet, so she and I can work together. Patty starts gently massaging the oil onto Charlotte's forehead, demonstrating how to carefully work the glue out of her baby-fine hair.

There is a blob of glue cemented to Charlotte's head marking each spot an EEG lead resided up until yesterday when they finally concluded there was no seizure activity and removed the wires and tape. While the bundle of extraterrestrial-looking apparatus is now gone, the blue marker and glue is stubbornly cemented onto her head. No amount of water and soap beckons the adhesive off. Patty massages baby oil on top of and around the first blob of glue with experienced confidence, meticulously working it into Charlotte's scalp and loosening the glue's relentless grip with a mother's loving touch. She doesn't seem phased by the daunting task before us, so I take a deep breath and try to follow her lead, mirroring Patty's movements on another patch of glue on Charlotte's temple.

Charlotte's eyes are open with that glassy medicated look I just can't get used to, even though this is day four of heavy opioid use. Her cries reach my ears and are an audible expression of the state of both our hearts. Hoarse. Weary. But still fighting.

The sound is like the saddest song I've ever heard. It is still music to my ears, to hear her again. Doctors decided to wean Charlotte's pain medication enough today that her drive to breath returned and she no longer needs intubation. Her swollen and irritated vocal cords, which were unable to materialize sound while intubated, now produce a raw voice, making her sound like a chain smoker.

"I have something else that might help comfort you, Little Peanut," Patty talks to Charlotte as she thoughtfully opens a drawer and pulls out a small pink plastic tube. "Sweeteze."

She twists off the cap and gently squeezes a drop of the sugar water, proven to help infants deal with pain and discomfort, into Charlotte's mouth. Charlotte's quiet cries turn into a sucking sound as she uses her stomach draining tube as a pacifier and licks the sugar water down. Her little hands are swaddled near her face, and they have white socks covering them, preventing her from wrapping her long skinny fingers around her draining tube and pulling it out, which she's attempted several times even in her sedated fog.

"That's better, huh?" Patty soothes, satisfied that Charlotte seems content for the moment. She resumes the glue removal process. "We will just work out one piece at a time as Charlotte allows. It may take us a day or two, but we will get it," she assures me without taking her eyes off Charlotte. "Isn't that right Sweet Pea? You're going to feel so much better with all of this off."

Thank you, God, for Patty.

Her intentional loving care of my daughter touches a place so so very deep, like aloe on burning skin, like healing lotion on dry cracked hands, like stitching up a gaping wound. She cares for my child as if Charlotte is her own. Watching her meticulous, capable hands do their job, I sense Patty's care slowly healing my raw and hemorrhaging heart, too.

"*I have sent literally hundreds of people to be my hands and feet for you, Dan and Charlotte,*" God said. Patty is one of those hundreds. She is his hands and feet in this moment.

"One day at a time," Grandma's words resurface. "You'll do it one day at a time."

But a lot happens in one day at the NICU, especially post op. Today just in the short hours of this morning, Charlotte was extubated, she had an IV removed, she had bloodwork done and the Gastrointestinal Specialist visited us to review what they discovered in the OR.

"She's a unique one, your Charlotte," he said in his kind, Indian accent. "The construct of her liver and biliary tree doesn't fully match that of a Choledochal Cyst, but we treated it as such, and her numbers are responding well. She may need a liver transplant later down the line, or she may not. She will tell us."

Now I find myself trying to remove glue without ripping my daughter's hair out, all before lunch. Much like the glue that is barely holding me together—it's going to take a lot of massaging to slowly free myself. So yeah, one day is entirely too much to take on at a time.

Just like removing all this glue seems a daunting task. One minute. That's more doable. Just one moment at a time. One blob of glue at a time. From here on out, I'm going to work hard to just be present in this very moment. It's all I can handle anyway. One squirt of oil, one massage in a circular motion, breaking free one sweet baby hair from the grips of the adhesive.

I'm learning from Charlotte, who is not laying in her isolette worrying about what's going to happen in the next ten minutes, day or week. She is simply responding to her needs now and responding to us in the moment too. Like enjoying her sweeties as if it is the best treat ever. At this moment, it is.

Grandma, help me to stay in the moment, and do this one minute at a time. Lord, help me.

Journal Entry - Friday, January 12, 2018

"'Shall a fault-finder contend with the Almighty? Anyone who argues with God must respond.'" (Job 40:2)

Oh Lord, I know you promise healing. I know you promise love and hope. I know we don't deserve to have Charlotte let alone to care for her. But God, that doesn't take away the struggle of today. I am confident we will get through this, but I am struggling in this moment. To see your child in pain and be able to do nothing about it. And not just any child, but a newborn child. Oh God, help me. I am at my wits end. I am struggling. Help me. Oh Lord, help me.

Praise your name for a successful surgery. For her healing thus far. For the donor of blood she's received twice now. For my husband's faithfulness and love. For Ronald McDonald House and the abundance of food available to us. For a warm bed and for loving and knowledgeable staff. For family and friends. There is so much to be thankful for.

Amen.

Chapter 33 The Cavaliers Game

Monday, January 15, 2018

We gathered in a small circle outside the NICU door and clasped hands.

"*Oh Lord, we come to you today overwhelmed, tired and scared, but we trust in you. We pray you are with Sophie and all the doctors and nurses with her now. We pray you guide the hands of her surgeon and if it be your will, that she has a full recovery. We thank you for the life of little Sophie. She's small but mighty. We know you love her even more than we do,*" I paused as my voice squeaked into a high octave. After the lump in my throat passed and a couple tears escaped my closed eyes, quietly slipping down my cheeks and landing on the hospital floor, I took a deep breath and resumed praying aloud, "*So Lord, please take over in the OR, and comfort Sophie's parents and grandparents while they wait. We love you Lord, Amen.*"

I gave a reassuring squeeze to Koby and Rachael's hands before letting go. I lifted my head and opened my eyes, seeing Sophie's parents and grandparents huddled around. We all hugged and shared our tears in silence for a few minutes, while also laughing at the awkwardness of praying in the middle of the hallway where Sophie's isolette was moments before the OR and NICU nurses wheeled her away for her big operation.

I'd seen my daughter wheeled away far too many times and I knew too well the devastating feeling of watching your infant child be whisked away for a life-saving procedure that may or may not work. I didn't know these people from Alan. All I knew was they shared our NICU room in bedspace four, right beside Charlotte, and they were sending their child off to surgery, left to wait. I felt compelled to ask if they'd like me to pray with them.

They were lovely people. We exchanged a few pleasantries before that morning and related over the traumatic pregnancies and births of our daughters. But we hardly knew anything about each other.

That was a couple weeks ago now, and that simple moment of uniting in our fears and also in our faith began a blossoming friendship like one that can only be made in the NICU, bonding over shared trauma. It's nice to now bond over something entirely more fun— beers and basketball.

"Are you ready to go pump," asks Rachael who is now sitting to the right of me in the Rocket Mortgage Fieldhouse VIP section. The halftime buzzer sounds and the players' tennis shoes squeak as they trot past us to the locker rooms.

I wish I knew more about the game so I could really appreciate what I'm witnessing. I recognize the name JAMES on the back of one of the tallest player's jerseys. I'd have to live under a rock to not know who LeBron James is, but that's literally the only National Basketball

Association player I know anything about. He grew up close to my hometown in Akron, Ohio. Still, I feel so out of place but also exhilarated by this crazy once-in-a-lifetime experience.

"Sounds good! We'll be back, Dan," I say, standing up and shuffling past him into the aisleway. I hang back to let Rachael get in front of me, and then follow her through the crowds, up the stadium steps, up and down a few elevators and past several security guards who ask to see our family passes indicating we are allowed in the red roped off VIP sections of the stadium. Rachael waves hi and cracks jokes with many as we go. She obviously knows most of these people because her fiancé, Sophie's dad, is Koby Altman, whom I just learned last week is the General Manager for the Cleveland Cavaliers.

We had been hospital roommates for a couple weeks, laughed, cried, and prayed together and I had no idea he was the GM of our local beloved NBA team. We even gave baby gifts to each other, and they brought us homemade banana bread the morning of Charlotte's big exploratory surgery just seven short days ago. That's when Koby told us what he did for a living and he invited us to come to today's big game, the Golden State Warriors versus the Cleveland Cavaliers. "It's going to be a good game. Maybe it could be a distraction from all you two are dealing with. Something fun for you both," he had said.

I felt stupid for not knowing who he was. I bet everyone else around me knew he was THE Koby, meanwhile I was in the dark. Then again, I wondered if my not knowing was a good thing because we were able to strike a genuine friendship.

Rachael leads me to a backstage bar for the home team's family members and friends. She orders second beers for us both, hands me one and we continue to walk down the hall to a private bathroom and waiting area with our pump bags slung over our shoulders.

"This is my first time drinking since learning I was pregnant," I laugh. "I'm such a lightweight!" I've only had one Labatt Blue and I'm giggly.

"Me too," Rachael agrees. We find electric outlets and hook up our pumps. We nestle into the big brown leather chairs and start the hum of our pumps, talking and laughing together like we've been friends for years.

"Let's check on our babies," Rachael says as she pulls out her phone. We both open the NICUview app and coo at our girls, showing our daughter's off to each other. I am so relieved to see Charlotte is resting peacefully in her isolette, swaddled and asleep. After the week she's had, she needs good rest. I can't handle the guilt of being here having a good time if Charlotte is anything less than comfortably asleep.

It was hard for me to come here tonight, knowing I would enjoy myself. It's a weird thing, but the concept of having fun seems ludicrous and selfish, considering my daughter is still on pain medications and hooked up to tubes and wires in the hospital just a few miles down the road. The nurses caught wind of us having tickets and they insisted we leave.

"We have everything under control, and we will call you if anything happens," they reassured. "You enjoy yourself."

"Charlotte needs you to take care of yourself so you can come back refreshed tomorrow," they insisted.

But Charlotte's not just seven days post-op, though that would have been enough reason to hesitate leaving her. She also now has sepsis. Her blood work came back three days ago showing gastrointestinal bacteria in her bloodstream and the counts continue to climb each day. They started her on different antibiotics right away to combat the infection, but they now predict the bacteria has adhered to Charlotte's new Broviac line in her chest and continues to fester there.

"We just placed the line on Monday, but we will likely need to pull it to remove any risk of the infection growing in Charlotte's main artery where the Broviac is placed," said the infectious disease doctor earlier this morning. "We will also need to conduct a spinal tap to get a sample of spinal fluid. We need to confirm the infection has not gotten into the fluid around Charlotte's brain," he added. "The good news is, besides her elevated temperature, she is showing no clinical signs of infection thus far."

As if that wasn't enough, Charlotte was anemic this morning so she received another blood transfusion. Twenty minutes after the infusion completed, blood passed through her left kidney nephrostomy tube and sent the NICU team into a frenzy trying to figure out what went wrong. They ultimately concluded the blood must have been a result of irritation from the nephrostomy tube and not from the transfusion.

Amidst all of that, they decided to slow Charlotte's pain medication weaning schedule and increase dosage slightly, because she was showing signs of irritability.

Irritability. I wanted to spit the word *irritability* on the doctors who coined it. Of course, she's irritable, I wanted to scream. Wouldn't you be if you had all these tubes and wires and leads and you had sepsis and you haven't been fed in a week because your stomach is being pumped to stay empty until your gastrointestinal tract heals?!

When I heard the word irritability used to describe my daughter I felt it was inaccurately and unfairly used as a description of her personality, rather than a description of her current comfort level, or lack thereof. Of course, the doctors weren't referencing her personality and I knew logically none of this was their fault, but it is hard sometimes to resist taking my frustrations out on the medical staff who are all just trying to do their best. Words like *irritability* make me go mad. My daughter is not irritable, she is uncomfortable.

Sepsis. Pull the line. Spinal tap. Anemic. Transfusion. Weaning schedules. Irritability. How much can a baby take?

Should I really be gawking at my child on NICUview and having a drink at a Cavs game while my daughter faces all that? "We won't do anything more today," the nurse reassured me once they adjusted Charlotte's antibiotic and pain medications and settled her in for the night. "And you staying here isn't going to fix anything either. Go."

Rachael and I finish pumping and we take turns dumping the milk down the bathroom sink. "Now I understand the phrase 'don't cry over spilled milk,'" I say as we watch the liquid gold circle the drain, bubble and disappear.

"Ugh, I know. Not sure the beer was worth having to dump

that," Rachael echoes my thoughts exactly. Neither of us chance giving our babies milk that may have traces of alcohol in it but dumping the milk we both work so hard to extract every two hours round the clock definitely makes us want to cry.

"It's just this once," I say, trying to help us both shrug off the disappointment.

Back in our seats, the third quarter begins, and I settle in to watch this game of unbelievably talented basketball players. I may not know much about the sport, but I do know I'm watching the best of the best players duke it out in the NBA finals and their skill is a spectacle for sure. The Warriors and Cavs go back and forth on the court, matching shot for shot, keeping us at the edge of our seats wondering who will take the win.

Each time the scoreboard sounds I jump, flashing to the NICU when monitors alarm the nurses a baby's oxygen level is low or their heart rate is crashing. The squeaks of the basketball players' shoes remind me of the squeaks of NICU nurse tennis shoes as they work tirelessly to care for these tiny humans so dependent on their skillful and attentive hands.

The fast volley of the game, first the Warriors scoring, then the Cavs, the Cavs and back to the Warriors, has a dizzying resemblance to the frantic ups and downs of NICU life. Stephen Curry shoots a three pointer for the opposing team and the arena erupts at his performance. Then back to the Cavs hoops, LeBron slam dunks. Up and down, the Cavs continue to be in the lead by several points, then trail their rival. Lead, then trail. Amazing athletic feats followed by missed shots and disappointments.

Isn't that like life as we currently know it? One minute we are thrilled to lower pain medications and the next we are increasing them because Charlotte is irritable. One minute we are celebrating a victory, like liver enzyme numbers coming back within the normal range, and the next we are plummeting into the reality of sepsis. Who knew basketball could feel so much like life in an intensive care unit?

I observe the teamwork between players and coaches, witness the hours of practice time play out in this huge rivalry game. It's much like the NICU staff and us parents. Nurses and doctors practice for years, earning their degrees and learning how to save tiny lives that are on the brink of death. We as parents are plunged into this reality and have to learn on our feet how to collaborate with hospital staff for the best possible outcome for our child. Yet, all our lives have prepared us for this moment, this game-making play. Will we join the game? Will we fight for our child and team up with the doctors and nurses? Or will we crumble under the weight and sit on the sidelines in defeat?

I look in front of me and see a wife and children cheering on one of the players, no doubt their husband and father. What's their story? What are their hurts and challenges off court? I have a huge story and challenge outside of this arena, and it makes me wonder what others are facing while they distract themselves for a couple hours with the game. My level of empathy for everyone is through the roof, knowing I can't possibly be the only one with battles on my home court.

The end of the third quarter buzzer sounds. Will I ever be able to watch a game or participate in everyday life again, without constantly relating it to the situation I find our family in right now? I doubt I'll experience life the same ever again. Maybe that's okay. It's probably a good thing.

My perspective on life is changing forever. I sense it's changing for the better.

Chapter 34 Faith Doesn't Take Pain Away

Wednesday, January 17, 2018

I really should switch to decaf so I don't pass caffeine to Charlotte in my breast milk. Too bad the Ronald McDonald Family Room only serves full-strength, which is my favorite anyway. I pick up the large community coffee pot and pour a small amount in a white Styrofoam cup. Just eight more ounces won't hurt.

I've been kicked out of the NICU for the next thirty minutes while the nurses perform the sterile bedside procedure, removing the Broviac line we were so eager to place just a week ago. It was meant to limit the amount of pokes Charlotte would have to endure for the remainder of her hospital stay, allowing most blood draws and IV medications to be administered through the long-term port rather than the temporary IVs that need replaced every few days.

It seems the doctors will soon run out of good veins to use without the help of the Broviac, but we have no choice. It is either remove the Broviac line or sepsis will continue to fester in Charlotte's main artery and cause much bigger issues than a few IV bruises on each arm and leg. In not so many words, the doctors helped us understand this was a life and death thing. There really was no decision. The long-term port had to come out. Today.

I pull the cup up to my nose and draw in a long inhale while I eye the basket of soon-to-expire bakery treats donated from the Starbucks café downstairs. I'm still not used to being on the receiving end of donated goods, even for simple things like cake pops and coffee cakes, but I'm not about to turn my sweet tooth down out of silly pride. I pick up a slice of pumpkin bread and unwrap it. Over the steam from my cup I see Abigail sitting on one of the large brown leather couches on the other side of the family room. She has her head in her hands and her shoulders heave. Her seven-year-old son colors at a nearby children's art table, oblivious to his mother's distress.

Abigail's been a constant friend to me during our NICU stay, her four-year-old son in the pediatric oncology unit receiving spinal taps to deliver chemotherapy. I don't know much about her son's diagnosis, but I know this is the baby's second round of cancer, two different forms, in his very short life. On top of that, he was born with a congenital disorder. Abigail is a pro at hospital life, having basically lived here since his birth. The fluffy yellow Despicable Me Minion slippers on her feet are testament to the fact that this is her current home.

Abigail never cries, at least not that I've seen. She has been upbeat, social and joyful whenever I've been around her, which is nearly every day in this family room when we are both kicked out of our kids' units for one reason or another.

Seeing her like this, I exhale and recall what I want when I have my own emotional spills. I quietly set my coffee and cake down, pour another cup for her and add cream and sugar like I've seen her do countless times for herself, then set her cup beside her on the end table and sit next to her.

I don't say a word. I reach my arm out and place my hand gently but firmly on her knee.

I know she doesn't need me to say the *right thing* right now. There is nothing to say that is right. She doesn't need me to dry her tears. The tears are healthy and beyond warranted. She doesn't need me to bring her a tissue or ask her to talk with me about whatever is bothering her. She just needs my presence. Someone to hurt with her.

So, I sit, holding onto her knee in silence as she sniffles and cries. After a few minutes she sits back, just realizing I'm here. She wipes at her tears in futile attempts to stop them.

"You don't have to stop crying on my account," I say, my own silent tears of empathy slipping down my cheeks. I've never been able to see someone cry without crying myself.

I recall a fellow coworker once told me passing tissues to someone, while thought of as a generous gesture, actually signals your discomfort with someone's tears and subconsciously communicates to them that they need to stop crying. So, I don't hand her the tissue box. I wonder if Abigail thinks this rude of me to let her sit here blubbering. Perhaps.

Eventually her sobs do slow and she breaks the silence, blurting out angrily, "Everyone keeps telling me to keep the faith. To just keep praying. 'Take it to the Lord,' they say. Well, I have faith, dammit! I do believe. I know he's in control and I know he'll take care of us. But that doesn't make this any easier. This sucks!" She goes silent for a minute and then sheepishly says, "Sorry for my language."

I chuckle, "You don't have to apologize to me! You're just saying what we are all thinking, and *sucks* doesn't even begin to accurately describe it." She snorts out a small laugh.

Old Emily would have been shocked by her explosion of emotion. Old Emily would have held back in fear, not knowing what to do or say. I may have even tried to defend the faith in one way or another, thinking convincing her of God's faithfulness might help.

New Emily, current Emily, the me that's being dragged through this hell right alongside Abigail, couldn't agree with her sentiments more and I've come to learn feeling all the emotions of this journey, including and especially the ones of anger and frustration, are no threat to faith. In fact, really truly experiencing the depths of your pain and taking it to the Lord in all its ugliness is perhaps the most healing thing any one of us can do. He is the Lord of the universe. I think he can handle our anger and frustration.

"This does suck. It sucks so, so, so bad," I confirm, moving my hand from her knee to her shoulders, not so much in a comforting back rub as in a firm, 'I'm here in the suckiness with you' gesture.

Abigail's older son comes over excitedly showing off the dinosaur he drew, then returns to the art table to color a rainbow.

I add, "If this journey has taught me anything it's that faith doesn't make this easy by any means. I think to those from the outside looking in, it may seem that way, but the reality is, faith gives us something firm to hold onto while the world around us is spinning out of control and feels like it's crashing. Faith is the one thing we have to cling to when everything else seems lost. Faith gives us hope in this seemingly hopeless situation. But it doesn't make it easy and it certainly doesn't take away the pain."

Dan and I have often commented to each other how we don't know how people survive these kinds of situations without faith, because it is with faith that we know regardless of the outcome, God is in control and he is faithful. It is with faith that we remain hopeful. That we know God will use it all for good. We have agreed several times saying, "I don't know how people do this without God. It's hard enough with him, let alone without him." I break at the thought of just how lonely this journey would be without God by our side. When we have faith, we know our suffering is not for nothing and so we keep picking our feet up and walking, one step at a time, clinging for dear life to the Lord and asking him to guide each and every step lest we fall from sheer exhaustion.

Faith doesn't make it easy. Faith makes it possible.

She nods, takes a deep breath and reaches for her coffee. "Thank you," she says in visible relief, as if I just gave her permission to revel in the suckiness, knowing that doesn't mean she is any less faithful. I hear the deep sincerity in her gratitude.

Thank you, Lord, for teaching me how to be here for people like Abigail. I would have never known how without you showing me through all the people you've sent here for me when I needed them, too.

Chapter 35 The Fallout

Journal Entry - Friday, January 19, 2018

Good morning, Lord,

God, help me to affect what I can, let go of what I can't and recognize the difference.

Lord help me to raise our daughter the way you call me to even in these circumstances. Oh God, it feels like the nurses are raising Charlotte and I am a visitor. But, God, I am her mother and second to you, I know her best. So, Lord, help me to weather the next several weeks and to affect what I can and let go of the rest. Help me, Oh Lord. Help me.

Friday, January 19, 2018

"I know you are planning to come up later this afternoon, but now Charlotte has to go to IR," I say apologetically, knowing Dan really could use the morning off at home to rest and recover, physically and mentally, like we planned. I hope Dan hears my urgency through the phone though. "I really need you here now," I add, trying to keep my voice from matching the tremble of my hands. I hate that I've become so needy.

It's Friday morning and the first day since Charlotte's birth that I've been at the hospital by myself. When Dan returned to work a few weeks ago, our moms began taking turns staying with me in the NICU. Grammy Nancy and Grams Claire, each cover every other day. Their presence, indispensable. I cannot fathom surviving each day without them. But today both Grandmas have things to tend to and we planned for me to stay with Charlotte by myself. It was *supposed* to be a calm, healing day filled with kangaroo care snuggles.

Kangaroo care is all the rage here in the hospital. Doctors and nurses urge parents to hold their infants skin-on-skin as often as possible, saying the subsequent bonding and health benefits are significant for both baby and parent. Now that I finally can hold Charlotte again, after a week of staring at her through the plastic isolette during post-op recovery, I was overjoyed to have her to myself and hold her all day long.

Meanwhile, Dan was going to enjoy a day off at home, which he desperately needs. He's been coming and going from Cleveland for the last several weeks, working an hour south at his job in Barberton and driving back north to spend an hour with Charlotte in the evening before crashing in the Ronald McDonald room and doing it all over again the next day. Today is his scheduled every-other-Friday off, a unique and treasured perk at his job. We planned for him to stay home and use the time to recover a bit, putz around the house and take care of a few things before joining his girls in the hospital later this afternoon. It was going to be a chill day for us all.

Best laid plans. Welcome to hospital life, where the only thing you can count on is change.

This saying is used often at work, helping us grapple with the latest changes in our work environment, organizational chart or ever-evolving market dynamics. What felt like dramatic changes then pale in comparison to the changes I now navigate on a daily basis. Those changes were good practice rounds.

I've often thought my life before Charlotte, and especially my work, was all great practice for what I'm doing now, which is basically medical coordination and management for my medically-complex child. A job I never foresaw taking, one I would not have freely chosen, but one I find myself in nonetheless.

As an assistant director, my role was to support my team to be equipped and empowered to do the best job possible. I worked hard every day to learn leadership skills that would help me best support them in communication, working together as a team and of course succeeding in their marketing roles. Every single one of my team members was more skilled at marketing than I, and my job was simply to help them maximize their talents. I loved it.

Now I find myself in over my head again, working with doctors and nurses who all know way more about medical things than I ever will. My role is much the same: communication, working together with them as a team and hoping my contribution is lending toward their success with our daughter.

I can only hope my involvement is helping, not hurting. The NICU staff often remind me I am a critical part of Team Charlotte, so despite my lack of training and wavering confidence, I try each day to stand tall and actively participate in her care management. Perhaps I'm not doing a great job of it, considering Charlotte faces another urgent procedure today which could have been avoided. Was I not careful enough?

When my phone rang on my walk into the NICU this morning, Dr. Rick was on the other end of the line. My heart froze like the thin coat of frost that covered everything this brisk, cloudy Northeast Ohio winter morning. Last time a Neonatologist called me, Charlotte was walking the line between life and death, teetering by the minute. Was that a mere ten days ago? Feels like a lifetime ago.

"Charlotte's left nephrostomy tube fell out last night," Dr. Rick said.

My heart dropped. Fell out? That was our great concern ever since they placed the tubes when she was five days old. We've held her like a china doll that could break any second, petrified we would accidentally pull one of the carefully placed lines out of her kidneys. She was due for a tube replacement again but since doctors rescheduled her urology surgery for January 24, just five days from now, we hoped we could limp along with the current ones. Next week's surgery is supposed to eliminate the need for nephrostomy tubes all together, but we cannot make it even a day without them now. Without them, urine has nowhere to go. It builds up in the kidneys and causes irreversible damage to the already-compromised organs.

"We will need to replace them today," Dr. Rick told me.

"I'll be there in a few minutes," I said, breathless as I hoofed through the dirty slush on the sidewalk. "I'm almost to the main hospital entrance now." I picked up my pace, weaving through the usual morning rush of scurrying valet drivers, discharged patients awaiting their rides in wheelchairs and salt-covered cars arriving at the campus' wide front doors. The cold air was laced with exhaust from the long line of cars and my breath formed a dense fog.

It was 9:05 a.m. when I got inside and shrugged my large down coat off my shoulders. I was just a few minutes late for the start of rounds. Once inside the NICU, I found everyone huddled around Charlotte's bed, beginning their assessment with her. I glanced at Charlotte to make sure she was stable.

Though the IV was placed on her head yesterday, I still hadn't gotten used to seeing it there. The nurse practitioner said her veins on her arms and legs failed, just as we worried would happen, and they needed to give the veins a rest before trying again. The next best place was Charlotte's scalp. This is why we wanted a Broviac line, to avoid constantly needing to replace IVs and poke more holes in Charlotte's pale bruised skin and angel hair pasta-sized veins. But the long-term port was removed two days ago in an effort to stop the sepsis infection.

A rise of frustration threatened to consume me. There was no one to blame. No one to target my anger toward. These things just happen. They reassured me that while the IV on her head looked horrifying, it didn't hurt Charlotte any more than an IV anywhere else.

Still, it was disturbing to see the catheter, tubing and tape on her tennis ball-sized head. I had a hard time believing them. How could that possibly not hurt?

I ripped my attention away from my daughter and tried to stifle my emotion so I could focus on what Dr. Rick was saying. "I've booked the IR for noon. She will be NPO until then because she'll be placed under light anesthesia for the procedure. They'll need her to hold still to get the nephrostomy tubes placed in the kidneys. It shouldn't take long," he explained.

"How did the tube fall out?" I asked, trying not to sound accusatory in my tone but it was hard not to blame nurses for handling Charlotte too rough. There had been many times in the past when I cringed at how briskly they changed her diaper or how carelessly—it seemed to me—they moved her around on her bed. I regretted not saying something each time. I should have protected my daughter better.

"It was no one's fault," Dr. Rick said. "It's probably a result of a lot of small jostles that ultimately caused it to come out. I know it's disappointing, but it's really a minor setback and we can correct it quickly."

I took a deep breath and chastised myself for casting blame on the very people who work tirelessly to care for my child. Of course, no one did this on purpose. Everyone here is doing the best they can for Charlotte's care and yes, they change diapers briskly because they are good at it, not because they're careless.

"Did I cause this from holding her so much?" I blurted the real question at the root of my blame and fear. Did I inadvertently hurt my daughter? It could have easily been me, too.

"Look, Emily, you holding her is very important for her healing too, so even if holding her caused the tube to loosen, it was a calculated risk and one that presented minimal damage so long as we caught it quickly, which our nurses did right away. She will be okay," he reassured. "I wouldn't have let you hold her if it wasn't a risk worth taking."

I tried to internalize his words. This was not my fault. This was not anyone's fault. But it did mean another round of anesthesia, another morning of no feeds and another signed consent as I watched my daughter be wheeled away.

"Can I hold her while we wait?" I asked shyly, knowing I was pushing my luck. But I'd done this enough by now to know soon she'd get restless when she realized her belly was empty and if I couldn't hold her to soothe her, she would scream in angry defiance the entire time until she was put under. I couldn't handle standing idle and helplessly watching her cry for nourishment for the next three hours.

Dr. Rick didn't answer right away, but thoughtfully considered my question. "Typically, I'd say no because we don't want to cause any more damage to the remaining right tube and kidney until both are replaced, but even if the right tube falls out too this morning, it would be okay because they are both going to be replaced today anyway. So ..." he thought for another minute. "Yes, you may hold her," he concluded and threw me a smile, telling me he approved of my desire

301

to comfort my daughter as best I could.

I glanced toward the nurses station to see if Charlotte's assigned nurse for the day heard Dr. Rick's decision. I wanted to know she heard him so she would let me hold Charlotte, too. It's one thing to get the doctor's approval. But I've learned by now it's another to get the nurse on board unless it's specified in the orders. Nothing happens if it's not in the system as a direct order from the residing doctor.

I was disappointed to see she was tending to the other baby assigned to her care and was not listening to our conversation. I should have asked Dr. Rick to tell the nurse his decision, but thought better of it, not wanting to seem like a crazy mom with control issues. Surely I could just convey the plan to the nurse myself.

As soon as rounds finished with Charlotte and they shuffled to the next baby, I called Dan.

"I'll be there in a bit," Dan wearily responds. Standing here beside Charlotte's isolette, pressing the phone to my ear in earnest, I hear disappointment in his voice.

Of all of us, he had been the most protective over Charlotte's nephrostomy tubes, often checking over them to ensure they were not taut. Does he blame me for their falling out, since I am the one constantly insisting on holding her any time we have approval to do so? But her emotional well-being is important too and isn't that what babies need? Held? Dan didn't say a word of blame. Whether he cast it or not, the shadow of doubt hangs over my head like a gathering storm cloud.

Next, I call Mom. She will want to know. "Do you want me to

come up," she asks, concerned.

"No," I say. "Dan is coming, and you need a day off." Besides, I need my husband. I need our daughter's father with me.

Mom is silent for a few moments, considering her options. "Your dad is working from home today and he offered to spend the afternoon with you while he works. He said he can bring his laptop and just work right beside you and Charlotte. I'll ask him to come," Mom concludes.

"Okay," I say. Having Dad here certainly can't hurt.

Have I become so dependent on having help that I'm too weak to handle this on my own? Many other parents in the NICU navigate procedure days by themselves. Why do I feel the need to have someone here with me? And why do I feel a sense of urgency that it needs to be Dan? Yet, I know now is not the time to be the hero and try to take things on alone. Dan is my partner. He is Charlotte's father. I need him with me today.

Maybe I'm finally learning a little humility and recognizing my weakness as a strength. *"For when I am weak, then I am strong."* Yes, it's okay I don't feel equipped to handle today on my own. For when I am weak, I call on my army of help God has sent, starting with my husband Dan, and then I am strong.

I hang up the phone with Mom and turn my attention to my daughter. Surely Dan will be here in an hour or two, so I just need to focus on Charlotte. She's starting to wake and squirm. My anxiety rises. I look at the clock. 9:30 a.m. She's due for another feed at 10:00 a.m. Soon when her belly doesn't get the satisfaction of warm milk, she's going to start screaming. 10:00 a.m. to noon is going to be a long miserable couple hours trying to comfort my hungry baby, who also still happens to have a million other tubes and wires attached to her from the last surgery, sans the critical left nephrostomy tube. I desperately want every tube removed, but not like this. I sigh, releasing my disappointment and trying to adjust my expectations for the day.

The nurse returns to Charlotte's bedside and begins charting. "Can you help me get her out of the isolette to hold her?" I ask. I can't manage picking Charlotte up on my own. She has entirely too many attachments to juggle myself. "I want to keep her comfortable and asleep as long as possible so she doesn't realize she's hungry."

The nurse seems to assess my capability to hold my own child. We haven't had this nurse before. I've never seen her on the floor in our six weeks here. She appears to be mid-twenties, maybe a few years younger than me.

"Sorry I can't let you hold her," she concludes, matter of fact.

I am taken aback. "I asked Dr. Rick during rounds and he said I could," I say, trying to sound like I'm sharing useful information with her rather than forcing my will upon this nurse.

"I can't let you hold her because I don't want anything bad to happen on my watch," she says. "The other nephrostomy tube could fall out or you could hurt her because of the pressure in her kidney," she explains. "I'll get in trouble if that happens."

Heat flushes my face. A shot of rage races through my veins. Everything about her explanation was about her—about how *she* doesn't want something bad to happen on *her* watch, how *she* would get in trouble. What about what is best for her patient? For my daughter?

"If anything happens from me holding her it will be my fault, not yours," I say, trying hard, but likely failing, to remove any tone of confrontation from my voice. "We've had to withhold enough feeds by now that I know if I hold her I can keep her comfortable and quiet for as long as possible," I explain my reasoning, convinced that surely this nurse will agree with me if I help her understand the situation.

"I can't let you hold her," the nurse repeats with finality.

I see right through this nurse's abrasive facade and sense her fear. She is afraid and unsure so she's going the safe route. If the babe stays in the bed, risk of further complications decreases.

On some level, I empathize with her. The weight of doing her job well and proving herself as a fresh-out-of-school registered nurse has to be heavy. Not to mention, taking one look at Charlotte can instill fear in even the most experienced medical staff. She is, as all the doctors keep telling me, very *unique* and *interesting*, both great words to describe someone's personality, but not words you want used to describe your child's medical chart. If this were simply a nursing school exam I may have more empathy. But we are talking about a human being. My child.

I debate my options. I could defy the nurse and override her, but then will she provide the care Charlotte needs or will she lessen the quality of her care in rebuttal? Like when I fear sending an undercooked steak back to the kitchen lest the waitress spit on it. Ridiculous, I know. What well-meaning waitress spits on food, and even more-so, what well-intending nurse lessens care for a patient? Of course, this nurse intends well. She's a NICU nurse. No one becomes a NICU nurse unless they care deeply about young, critically ill patients. But it seems this nurse has her own interests in mind more so than my daughter's.

I need her to do the best job possible today and I need to find a way to work *with* her, not against her. Plus, what if she's right? What if I do hurt Charlotte or make things worse by holding her? Dr. Rick gave me the green light, but he hesitated. Maybe there was something to his reservation I should heed.

Everything in my body, my mama instinct, screams to hold my child. Sue, the nurse practitioner, reassures me repeatedly to listen to my gut, saying, "Mom's instinct is always right."

But do I really know what's best? It's hard to tell. Do motherly instincts still apply in extreme situations like this? And how hard do I push before I inadvertently make things harder for Charlotte when all along I intend to help? I decide to heed the nurse's decision, for now.

 Trusting Motherly Instincts

Yes, maternal instincts do apply even, and perhaps especially, in extreme situations like this. Yes, moms (and dads too) should always voice their concerns, ask questions and try to address whatever it is that's raising those little red flags in your parental brain, because more often than not, gut instincts are right.

Charlotte is now fully awake and squirming. "Good morning, Charlie Jo," I smile at her, momentarily forgetting about the nurse. I cup my hand around the other half of Charlotte's head that's not covered in IV tape.

"I see you made a big diaper. Let's get you cleaned up," I say softly as I reach for the drawer holding diapers and wipes. My hands work out of muscle memory, having changed her countless times before. I begin gently pulling the velcro tabs off the dirty Mickey Mouse Huggies that is carefully placed around the abdomen draining tube and the remaining right nephrostomy tube.

"I will change her diaper," the nurse says over my shoulder, positioning herself to usher me over so she can stand where I am.

I am confused. "Oh, that's okay," I say casually. "I can do it."

"No, I will do her Hands on Care until the tubes are replaced," she says.

What is happening? I hesitate to move out of her way. Really? Why can't I change my own child's diaper? All the doctors and nurses have encouraged Dan and me to "be as involved as possible in Charlotte's care." This comment always strikes me as odd. Of course, I'm involved in her care. I am her mother. I hate that I am *involved* and not *the* primary caregiver. It digs up those familiar feelings of being Charlotte's *visitor* rather than her mother. But if changing her diaper while I'm here is what I am able to do, you'd better believe that's what I'm going to do.

After a moment's hesitation, I acquiesce and step aside, watching her hands do my work. I try to muster my leadership coaching I received at work. What was I trained to do in a confrontation situation like this? Try to understand the other person's point of view. Right.

"Can you help me understand why I am unable to change her diaper like I usually do?" I ask.

"I don't want any more damage caused to Charlotte's tubing so I'm going to handle her care for today," the nurse says.

You've got to be kidding. Not only am I not allowed to hold Charlotte, I'm not even allowed to change her diaper. And though she doesn't say as much, her comment inadvertently fuels my suspicion that she thinks I caused the tube to fall out in the first place. That I can't be trusted to care for my daughter, even for a simple diaper change. Is that what she thinks, or do I?

"I need to pump, I'll be back," I finally say, needing to step away before I do or say something I regret. I need time to think. I hide in the pump room for 20 minutes, trying to collect my thoughts and rein in my frustrations. Surely Dan will be here soon, and he'll help me know what to do. He tends to have a more objective point of view.

Lord, help me to affect what I can and accept what I cannot.

I need to be strong for Charlotte and not abandon her out of my own fears and frustrations. I roughly scrub my pump bottle parts clean. If only washing away my anger was as easy as scrubbing milk residue from plastic parts.

When I return to Charlotte's isolette I find her screaming, just as I knew she would soon be. She's realized no one is feeding her. Her little body is flushed red with anger, expressing how I feel.

As her arms and legs flail, so too do the lines and leads. How is this any less jostling than me holding her? What can I do?

I can't control this nurse. I can't control how she wants to handle the situation. I can't hold Charlotte. I can't feed her. Maybe I can try to create a calming environment for her. I grab a blanket and lower it over the top of the isolette in an effort to make the space dark and calming. The nurse lifts a corner of the blanket to ensure she can still see Charlotte. She has to be able to keep her eyes on her patient, but her movement conveys she is in control here. I sense a power struggle between the two of us. This is going to be a very long morning.

Ignoring her, I search Pandora on my phone for the *Beauty and the Beast* soundtrack like the night shift nurse told me Charlotte likes. I play it quietly and place my phone near Charlotte's head. It may not help, but it's worth a try. I silently dare the nurse to tell me to turn it off. Minutes pass by at an excruciating snail's pace as I sit and helplessly watch my hungry, angry, and hurting child cry for me.

The desire to draw my infant child near is all-consuming. I want to hold her head near my lips, kiss her sweet soft downy hair, breathe in her baby scent, and hold her heart near mine until she calms into a sleepy peaceful rest. I want to tell her everything is going to be okay and know that it's actually true. I want to satisfy her hungry cry. I sense it's not just her belly crying for nourishment, but her heart, too.

Each time her bewildered eyes catch mine through the clear plastic isolette sides it's as if she's saying, "Why have you abandoned me? Why don't you respond to my cries?" At least when I couldn't hold her post-op she was heavily medicated and wasn't aware of my lack of interference for her. Now she's all too aware of my idle hands. How am I to sit by and not answer my child's call for her mother?

The clock finally ticks past noon but there is no sign of the IR nurse coming for Charlotte. "It seems they are running behind from another emergent case," Dr. Rick comes to tell me. "They'll be here as soon as they can." Should I seize the moment while he's here to ask Dr. Rick again if it's okay for me to hold Charlotte, knowing this time the nurse is here to hear the conversation and she will not defy the neonatologist? Surely it's a moot point now though, since Charlotte will be leaving for her procedure any minute. I decide to keep my mouth shut.

My stomach growls along with Charlotte's grumbles. I haven't eaten a thing today either. If one of our moms were here right now she would insist I go eat while she stays with Charlotte. But who will stay with her if I go now? I don't want Charlotte to feel even more abandoned while I go fill my belly, knowing full well hers is empty. Why do I get to eat while my child sits in hunger? Plus, what if the IR nurse comes while I'm gone?

Where is Dan?

As if an answer to my thoughts, my dad walks into the room. "Hey Lulu," he says and gives me a big hug.

I smile at the childhood nickname.

My dad is the kind of dad who always let me have the last slice of leftover pizza even though I knew he would like it. When he came home from his weekly work trips he'd get down on all fours and wrestle with me and my brothers. He spent hours with me in the barn when I was growing up, helping me care for my horse-loving obsession and all the manure that came with it. He taught me how to drive a tractor, shoot clay pigeons and change my car oil, just like he taught my three brothers.

His presence is a breath of fresh air in this otherwise oxygen-sucking room. "Mom sent you some lunch," he says over Charlotte's wails. "It's in the Ronald McDonald Family Room fridge."

Thank God. Dad settles into a chair next to Charlotte while I grab my water bottle and beeline for the door.

Please Lord, help the IR to come soon.

I can't wait for Charlotte to be put under anesthesia, so she is no longer aware of her discomfort and hunger, and my abandonment of her needs. What does her little mind think when she sees me stand idle to her cries? That I don't love her? That I'm a terrible mom?

I can't believe I'm wishing for my child to be put under, but I'm desperate for her to be relieved from her discomfort, and me from mine.

I sit down to eat and send Dan a quick text, "Still waiting for the IR. What's your ETA?"

His response comes quickly, "I'm doing dishes. Then heading up."

Excuse me, what? Dishes? So, he hasn't even left the house yet! My blood boils. I might lose it right here in the community Family Room. I'm wound so tight I might implode.

My appetite is gone but I shove lunch down anyway, knowing I may not have a chance to eat again for a long time and I have to eat to keep milk production up. On my way back to the NICU I stop at the front desk. "Do you know where Joyce the social worker is?" I ask the receptionist.

"Oh, I just saw her walk in. Let me go get her," she says reassuringly. Moments later, Joyce walks into view.

"Hey Emily, how are you? How can I help you," she asks. She was in rounds this morning with Dr. Rick, so I know she's aware of our nephrostomy tube situation.

"Can I speak with you in private?" I ask quietly. She's often offered to help us however she can, saying we can come to her for anything. Thus far, I've only approached her about practical things like insurance, medicaid and the like.

She and I walk to a quiet corner in the receptionist office, which is about as private an area as I'll ever find in the hospital. I muster the courage to say what's on my mind. "I'm not seeing eye to eye with our nurse today. I feel bad saying anything, but I'm not sure she has Charlotte's best interests at heart. I don't want to cause drama, but I don't know what to do." I spit the words out like if I say them quickly then I can't waiver and hold them back.

Joyce looks at me with concern. "I will tell the head nurse who all the nursing staff report to. She will take care of the situation."

I feel ashamed. I should be able to work well with any personality involved in my daughter's care. I pride myself in my ability to work with all personalities in my professional career. Why can't I work with this nurse?

Returning to Charlotte and Dad, a nurse practitioner stands

over Charlotte's isolette. Charlotte's scalp is swollen with a huge goose egg underneath the IV. "What happened?" I ask, panicked.

"The IV went bad and fluid is leaking around the vein," the nurse practitioner replies. "Since the IR is running behind, we are going to use the time now to place a new IV. She'll need one for anesthesia." My lunch threatens to come back up. Charlotte has to get yet another poke on her head. Can this day get any worse? Of course, it can. This is an intensive care unit for gravely ill newborn babies.

A team of three perform the sterile bedside procedure. I look at the clock. 2:30 p.m. Still no sign of the IR nurse, or Dan.

After the new IV is placed and Charlotte is left lying in her bed, her cries stop and she goes eerily silent. I reach in to hold her hand but she won't look at me. She turns her head to face the opposite direction. Her chest heaves.

She's given up. She's given up trying to tell me she's hungry. She's given up trying to fight off the nurse's painful pokes. She's given up trying to secure a meal. She's given up on me as her mother. I'm desperate to explain to Charlotte why I can't hold her, can't feed her, can't help her. She's despondent and it's far worse than her anger.

"Oh Charlotte, I'm so, so sorry," I cry in a barely audible whisper.

Finally, at 3:00 p.m., IR staff buzz in and in a flurry of activity shove consent forms toward me and prepare my now silent and emotionally disengaged baby to depart with them.

I finish signing the consent forms through blurred vision and lean over to tell her I love her. She doesn't turn her head to look at me.

Her eyes listlessly stare at the plastic sides of her isolette. Surely she's just tired, I tell myself. She hasn't slept all morning or afternoon.

"This won't take much time at all, and we will make sure she's comfortable," their words interrupt my despair as they wheel the isolette away, taking my defeated daughter, my defeated heart, with them.

With Charlotte no longer there, the room is awkwardly quiet. Dad and I pack up our few belongings and move to the more comfortable setting of the family room. He fires up his laptop and starts responding to emails while my anxiety scales the walls. I feel like a caged animal desperate for release. I try to distract myself with writing thank you notes I've been carting around with me for weeks, intending to show my appreciation to all those who have helped us in one way or another. But I cannot focus to even form a full written sentence.

I stand abruptly. "I'm going for a walk," I declare, feeling guilty leaving Dad who came to spend the afternoon with me but knowing if I stay for one more minute I might lose my ever-lovin' mind.

"Okay I'll be here when you get back. Take your time," he says.

I practically run down the two flights of cement steps, passing a steady stream of doctors and surgeons on my way. I burst through the doors out the main hospital building and am greeted with 30-degree Fahrenheit dry air. I fill my lungs, thirsty for any rejuvenation it might afford me. I don't know where I'm going, but my legs start pounding in any direction they please. For two long hours I wander the hospital campus, up and down sidewalks, through back alleys and along busy roads. If only I could run away and never come back.

I can't leave my daughter. It's like a gravitational pull. Every time I get to the edge of the hospital campus, I'm propelled back toward the main building.

I want to scream.

My phone dings with a text from Dan, "I'm here. Where are you?" he asks. I resist the urge to throw my phone into the nearest snow pile and instead shove it back in my coat pocket without responding. That's the question I've been wondering all day. Where are *you*?

Finally, when my fingers are frozen beyond feeling and my feet ache, I reluctantly return to the main building. It's dinner time and getting dark outside. "Is she back yet?" I ask Dan without saying hi or so much as making eye contact with him when I get to the Family Room. I'm sure he can feel my cold demeanor, matching my cold but flaming cheeks.

"Yes," he answers. "They are settling her back into the NICU and coming to get us when we can see her."

I sit between him and Dad on the couch with a healthy distance between us, waiting for Dan to apologize. Surely he owes me a huge apology. Instead, he opens our shared laptop and starts designing a pocketknife he plans to make in his metal and wood workshop at home.

"What were you doing at home?" I ask, trying to sound genuinely curious and not just spitting mad. Secretly, I hope he has some grand excuse for his delay, like he got in an accident or something tragic happened.

315

"I made pancakes and bacon, snuggled with the dogs, swept the house and watched some YouTube. Then I realized I had to do some laundry before I came back so I had to wait for the load to finish. I got packed up but realized I needed to clean up the kitchen before I could leave," he says. "It was nice to be home for a bit."

I bet it was.

"You do realize your daughter had surgery today, right?" I scoff. "And while you were taking your time at home eating pancakes I was falling apart here waiting for you to come." Hot tears threaten to consume me, releasing the tension from the day, but I will not give him the satisfaction of seeing my hurt. I will the tears to stay dammed. If I fall apart now, there is no telling when I will recover.

The head nurse pokes her head in the family room, saying, "Emily, am I interrupting?"

"No, no," I lie, grateful for a diversion.

"You wanted to speak with me? Is now a good time," she asks.

My face flames with embarrassment and my stomach rolls with dread. Should I have said anything to the social worker about today's nurse?

She crosses the room and signals to me to follow her to a quiet corner. We sit down next to each other, and she asks me to explain what happened. Where do I begin? I carefully form my words, trying not to sound like the crazy person I feel I am. I desperately don't want to cause any trouble for us or Charlotte in the NICU. But, I've gotten myself into this mess and now I have to follow through.

Maybe if I would have just kept my mouth shut we could have

gotten through today and never had this nurse assigned to us again. But then, she easily could be assigned to us many more times and I cannot bear that. No. Not even one more day. The thought fuels my resolve to tell this head nurse everything.

"I'm sorry you had that experience today," she responds with appropriate empathy as I recount the day's happenings. "We work hard to train nurses to involve parents in patient's care, but not all nurses are good fits for all families. We will assign her to other patients from now on," she says kindly. I expect her to get defensive of the nurse, but she doesn't seem ruffled in the least, like maybe this is a common situation she's dealt with in the past.

"This is a very stressful time for you, Emily. Being in the NICU is hard. We don't want to add any other hardship so if that means rearranging the nursing schedule, that's fine!" she says lightheartedly.

I don't have to try and work with this nurse ever again. That is great news. And it doesn't appear I've done any damage or caused undue drama.

"Truly it's no problem," she adds, seeing my turmoil. "And if there are specific nurses you think are great fits for Charlotte and your family, just say so and we can do our best to assign them to your case whenever possible."

Really? How did I go this long without knowing I could do that? "That would be amazing!" I say. "We've had Patty a few times and we love working with her. Could she be assigned to Charlotte?" I ask without hesitation.

"You mean Patty Clewell? Oh sure! I'll double check with her, but I assume she'll be thrilled. One of her long-term assigned babies has been discharged, so I think she's available. She loves her little Charlotte," the head nurse throws me a smile, claps her hands together in finality as if it's all resolved and says, "Is there anything else we should discuss before we go back and see Charlotte? She's ready for you."

 Learning to Advocate

Caregivers often worry about upsetting the medical staff, or we fear speaking up when we disagree with a medical professional's approach. But at the end of the day, we are our child's best advocate, and we have to speak up for them. If not us, then who? Our children are counting on us to be their voice.

I needed to learn to stop worrying about what people would think of me or how they would react, and just start freely sharing my input in Charlotte's care. This lesson would prove critical to her outcomes.

I can't believe my ears. Was it that easy to just ask to work with the nursing staff we love? A heavy weight lifts from my shoulders. Every morning has been a guessing game as to who will work with Charlotte that day. Now there may be some consistency in her care with a nurse we know and love. A nurse we've chosen. What a relief.

"There is one more thing," I say. "I really don't want our nurse today to know we talked." I imagine coming into the NICU each morning and scanning the rooms for this nurse, trying to avoid awkward exchanges with her for weeks to come.

She waves her hand in the air, brushing my concern aside. "I will handle it and you don't have to worry about a thing. You let me do my job Emily and you just focus on that sweet baby of yours," she says before standing up and encouraging Dan and me to follow her back to the NICU.

She has a good point. Maybe I've tried to do her job and taken on too much responsibility in collaborating with the nursing staff. Not that I shouldn't collaborate, but maybe I am better served to simply come to her with concerns in the future, rather than trying to resolve them myself. This goes against everything in me because it feels like I'm a little kid tattling on a classmate, but the reality is there is a chain of command at the hospital for a reason and it would behoove me to use it.

Dan and I trail her toward the door to the NICU. I glance back at Dad who waves us on. He knows the drill by now. He'll join us at Charlotte's bedside soon enough but for the next five or ten minutes, he will give us our space to reunite with our daughter.

Charlotte is lying in her isolette squawking quietly with two new nephrostomy tubes protruding from her back. The nurse is charting again, and I skirt past her. I just have to get through the next two hours and then it'll be shift change and she'll go home. I can do this. Two more hours.

Dan, he's another story. I can't skirt around him for much longer. I check my emotions and file them away for later. We will have to talk about it when we get back to our Ronald McDonald Room. For now, we need to focus on our daughter.

"They said she did great in the IR and now I'm prepping her bottle for a feed," says the nurse. I start to breathe for the first time since Dr. Rick' call this morning.

"Great!" I say, sitting down in the rocking chair next to the isolette and positioning a pillow on my lap like I've done countless times before, preparing to feed Charlotte.

When the nurse realizes what I'm doing she says, "I'm going to give her this first bottle. She just came out of anesthesia, and I don't want her to choke." The only reason I don't clobber the woman right then is because I know I don't have to work with her ever again after today.

Chapter 36 Reconciliation

Friday, January 19, 2018 Continued

The scalding water cascades over my head and pools at my feet. I watch it circle the drain, mingling with Dove and Tresemmé soap bubbles. I wish suds could wash away today's emotional grime.

My shoulders and thighs are fire red under the heat of the steady shower stream. It's oddly relieving to feel something so physical that matches the burning in my heart and the swirling in my head.

Dan's outside of the bathroom in our Ronald McDonald room. I wonder if he's aware of the conversation we need to have. I dread turning off the shower and facing him. Then we have to work through what happened today. And what did not that should have.

Oh God, help me.

How do I express to Dan just how hurt I feel without it becoming a huge fight? I don't know. My chest feels tight. My head heavy. I just want to crawl in bed and sleep for days, hoping when I wake this nightmare will pass. I linger in the shower until my skin screams for relief from the heat.

Showering has become my nightly ritual, a visceral cleansing of each day's worry and weight. It seems the length and temperature of my shower directly correlates with the intensity and struggle of each day. The harder the day, the longer and more scalding the shower.

Some of my most raw and real prayers happen here in this white handicap accessible space. It's the only place I'm alone, where I let my emotions go without worry of others seeing me. Where I'm literally naked and also where I feel naked and exposed to the Lord, letting him wash his love over me as I crumble at his feet in my mind's eye. It's become a space of worship, in an odd sense.

When we finally left Charlotte's bedside at 9:00 p.m. tonight, Dan and I barely spoke a word to each other on our shuttle bus to the Ronald McDonald House. A couple sat in front of us on the bumpy ride holding hands and exchanging intimate conversation. I watched with envy.

As soon as we got to our room I scurried into the bathroom before anything of importance could be exchanged between us. I needed time to gather my thoughts before I could face him head on. While the idea of just letting it all go without addressing it sounds great, that will only set us up for bigger and worse confrontation later. Better to just address it now, makeup and move on. Easier said than done.

It's been twenty minutes now. How long can I hide in here before I must face the inevitable? I sigh and turn off the water. I can't hide forever.

Lord, help me.

"Emily, I don't handle stress the same way as you do," Dan finally professes in exacerbation, after an hour of us sparring at each other and getting nowhere. My hair is mostly dry from my shower by now. "I can't sit there for hours on end in waiting rooms and being able to do nothing to help. I knew if I came today I'd just be sitting with nothing to do, and I would go crazy. At least at home I could do something!"

"And you think I like to sit in waiting rooms? That I enjoy having nothing to do but worry? How is that fair that you expect me to do it all by myself today while you enjoy pancakes and YouTube? And after you said you were coming!" I spit the words out with venom.

"Your dad was with you. You weren't alone," he retorts.

"Yes, but I needed *you*. Not my Dad. I needed my husband. I needed Charlotte's dad."

He falls silent. A tear slips down his cheek and he flicks it away in frustration. He's sitting forward on the edge of the foldable red rocking lawn chair, which we brought from home out of our camping supply stash in an attempt to provide some kind of sitting space in our otherwise sparse Ronald McDonald bedroom. His elbows on his knees, he rubs his temples with his right-hand thumb and middle finger.

He stares at the floor. I know that look. It's the one where I think he's checked out completely but in reality he's in deep thought and trying to rein in his emotions so he can have a constructive conversation. I'm not ready for a constructive conversation.

323

My defenses tell me to hold strong and stay angry, but then I remember—what is my goal? To be right or to reconcile? Feeling the same pull to end this face-off, he reaches across the firm full-size bed I'm sitting on and fumbles for my hand. His fingers entangle with mine. Both our eyes follow, and we find ourselves staring at our intertwined hands, not quite ready to make eye contact, but making progress.

"I didn't mean to make you feel alone. I should have told you I wasn't coming right away. I'm sorry," his tone softens and his eyes finally look pleadingly over at me, begging me to understand.

For the first time in a long time, I look at him and really see him. The lines of worry carve deep crevices around his lips and forehead. Big dark circles encase his tired eyes. His face is weighed down with weariness and anxiety. His hair has more gray peppered around his ears than I remember.

He continues to say, "But I hope you understand I thought you were okay today. Your dad was coming, and I needed a break. I thought it was okay to come up later."

Of course, he didn't *mean* to abandon me. I still *feel* abandoned. I needed him today and he didn't show. But then, I probably didn't accurately convey my desperation to him this morning. As usual, I assumed he would know.

I should know by now that if I don't clearly explain expectations, I cannot expect him to know. It's only fair. It's not like I can read his mind either. Why do I expect him to read mine?

I sit in silence, ringing a Kleenex in my hands while I try to humble myself and come to grips with the fact that Dan's not the only one at fault here. I handled today poorly, very poorly, with our daughter, with our nurse and with my husband. I wish I could go back and start the day over. There are so many things I'd do differently. Better yet, I'd skip today all together if I could.

I've overlooked the fact that Dan might process his emotions differently than I. While anxiety and fear thrusts me into action, gluing me to our daughter's side trying to improve the situation even in the slightest, that same anxiety and fear sends Dan into the need to do something with his hands. To do something he can personally affect, even if it's totally unrelated, like designing a pocketknife. It's as if he's saying, "Excuse me for not coming to your rescue today, but I'm trying hard not to have a nervous breakdown myself."

Couples Handle Trauma Differently

Couples rarely, if ever, process trauma, stress and emotions the same. Raising a child with medical complexities can place a great deal of stress on a marriage. Speaking strictly from Dan's and my experience, a critical aspect to getting through the medical trauma together is recognizing each other's unique way of processing and coping with stress. Learning to appreciate these differences and working together through them was a huge turning point in our relationship. A turning point for the better.

I waffle between my flaring anger at him and disappointment in myself for not recognizing this sooner. For assuming his absence and distraction equaled his disinterest. Why am I quick to trust others' positive intent and yet I jump to negative conclusions about the man who promised his life, his heart, to me?

I suppose it's because he's the one who can hurt me the most. Strangers can only hurt me a little and only from a distance, but Dan, he has the power to wound me so, so deeply. That's the way of love, isn't it? Those you love the most are the ones who can hurt you the most, and vice versa.

While I certainly would never intentionally hurt him, I know I have the ability to trample his heart. I already have, back when I broke up with him all those years ago.

But I've since made a commitment at the altar, before our friends, family, and God to have and to hold him all the days of our lives, in sickness and in health, through good times and bad, and I intend to see those vows through. He does, too. I need to trust that.

Thinking about our bumpy dating story jogs my memory. Haven't we been down this road before, finding ourselves at odds with each other over miscommunication and unspoken expectations— unrealistic expectations? Countless times to be sure, and we discussed this very thing before we reunited and started dating the second time around. I remember talking about how the first time we dated, we subconsciously expected each other to fill our every need, for him to be my everything and I to be his long sought-after perfect other half. In the end, we only disappoint each other when we hold such high expectations. Of course, we cannot satisfy each other's every need. We are only human.

I recall sitting on bar stools in the Akron, Ohio Thirsty Dog Brewery on our second, second date, acknowledging that this time around, if we were going to make this relationship work, we had to put God first and turn to him to fill our every need. Only then could we appreciate each other for who we are, rather than hold grudges toward each other for who and what we are not. Just like Dan said back when we were pregnant, "If we were trying to find 100% comfort in each other this would be really hard."

I realize now I've slipped into my old habit of expecting Dan to be my everything, and not surprisingly, I've found myself disappointed. Not because he doesn't love me. Not because he isn't trying. But because he's only human. And how much more have I let Dan down?

Oh Lord, help me.

"I'm sorry I didn't better communicate what I needed," I finally whisper. "And I'm sorry I haven't stopped to notice what you need in the midst of all this."

To be honest, I haven't thought much about how Dan is handling things or how he is doing. I've been focused on our child and with what little energy I have left, on my own survival. I mean, I am still bleeding from giving birth to our baby. How could I have mental or physical space left for Dan when it still hurts to walk, sit and stand?

My body is taking forever to heal from Charlotte's abrupt delivery, seemingly punishing me for not doing the self-care everyone keeps talking about.

In the midst of my own pain, physical and emotional, I've had blinders on to what's happening with Dan. I suppose subconsciously

I've assumed he's an adult and can take care of himself. Of course, he can, but having a little sympathy and mindfulness from his wife couldn't hurt.

Now that he's back to work, we hardly see each other. I'm lucky to see him for a half an hour a day as we pass each other in the halls of the hospital or quickly kiss each other goodbye in the mornings before his long commute. Our phone calls consist of practical things like Charlotte's latest bloodwork results. I have no idea how he's really doing. I'm disappointed in myself for not being a more loving and present wife. But then, how could I be in a time like this? We are clearly in survival mode, both individually and in our marriage.

 ## Survival Mode

There comes a time in situations like these when you look up and notice your partner again. It's then that a lot of hard healing starts to happen. The road is long and bumpy, but with both committed to each other, it can be a healing and beautifully strengthening journey for a relationship.
That is, with a lot of help, a lot of time, and a lot of intentionality.
Dan and I both had to see individual therapists and do couples therapy for several years before we felt strong again. But I'm humbled and grateful to say we are now (four years later) the strongest we've ever been, and it is through that trial and cleanup process that we gained trust in each other and a whole new level of emotional intimacy we never reached prior to this journey with our daughter.

He sighs. He cautiously ventures to meet my eyes. "I think we are both just tired and stressed and we need a break from it all. I go to work and at least have that outlet, but you don't even have that. I had this morning for myself at home, now I think tomorrow you need to go and do something for yourself. Get away from the hospital. I will be with Charlotte while you go," he says.

Resistance rises in my throat. After a day like today, I can't imagine leaving Charlotte tomorrow.

I swallow my rebuttal. He's right. I need to step away and clear my head, for everyone's sake.

"I saw a flyer for a free Zumba class tomorrow at the gym next door. I was thinking of going to it. I could use a good laugh at my two left feet trying to keep up with the instructor," I agree with Dan.

The mood in the room lightens and the lines around his eyes relax as he gives me a half smile. "That should be fun," he chuckles, giving my hand a playful squeeze. "Then take your time getting back to the hospital. You need time away."

Chapter 37 Self Care

Saturday, January 20, 2018

This morning I went to the gym across the street from the Ronald McDonald Room and joined a Zumba class, like I told Dan I would last night. Another NICU mom came with me, whose premature twin girls share a room with Charlotte. We laughed our way through the class as we both tripped over our own feet and tried to learn how to shake our hips like Shakira.

My body is so stiff from sitting in waiting rooms for the last couple months. It was comical trying to get it to move like our instructor showed us. Some of the dances I and the other mom couldn't even attempt because we are both still healing from childbirth. But it was good to laugh at ourselves and do something that had zero consequences to life and death.

I'm still sweating from the effort as I sit at the end of our Ronald McDonald bed typing the remainder of my thoughts in the blogpost. It's the first time I've written a blog for my ministry website since Charlotte was born. Satisfaction grows as each thought spills onto the page and begins to make sense of my experiences of late. For the first time in a long time I feel peace deep within my soul. To Dan's point, I've needed this time of rejuvenation.

I upload the post to my site and take a drink of water. My phone buzzes with a text from Dan. "Charlotte is doing great this morning. Nurses said she slept so sound through the night they didn't wake her for a weight check."

Then a second buzz, "Lab results show blood bacterial infection is negative. She pulled her NG tube out. We had to pry it out of her death grip. Our nurse replaced it easily. Now she's sleeping again. She seems comfortable."

Then a third, "I love you, Babe. I'm glad you're taking care of yourself this morning. Take your time. Our girl is doing great."

A rush of conflicting emotions floods my brain—gratitude Charlotte is doing well today, love for Dan for being with our daughter so I can take care of myself, annoyance that Dan gets to be with her when things are going well, guilt that I wasn't more supportive of Dan's need for time away like he's supporting me now—and a whole host of other emotions I cannot identify.

"Thank you, Babe," I simply reply. "Zumba was fun. Now I'm writing."

Many people tell me to take care of myself. "Self-care is so important," they say. Everyone means well, but how do I take care of myself when my child is critically ill and there is hardly time to breath much less do anything else?

When I first heard the term self-care, I thought it meant things like getting nails done, getting a massage, taking long baths, going on leisurely walks, working out, reading a book, etc. Now I'm realizing self-care in situations like this looks more like peeing when you need to pee and not hours later when you're nearing bladder infection status. Sitting when you need to sit and not forcing your over exhausted body to stand any longer than necessary. Refilling your water bottle when it runs empty and not ignoring it until you're so thirsty you think you might pass out. Taking the time to wash your clothes before you have to re-wear dirty underwear. Basically, recognizing that you're not superhuman and you have needs, too. That is self-care on a normal day in the hospital.

On rare occasions when time allows, like today, self-care means doing something that brings you joy and peace. For me, that is laughing at myself at a workout class, and writing.

It may sound odd for some, but writing is therapeutic for me. It orders all the jumbled thoughts in my head and externalizes them, so I don't have to mull them over any longer. It's like once I've written something, I can lay it to rest and move on because it no longer claws at me internally. Maybe that's why I love journaling my prayers so much, too. Each sentence I write brings peace to my soul in a way I crave and helps me shed the weight of the day so I can put on my armor of God for the next day to come. It's like I shed the yoke I've been carrying when I write out my prayers and thoughts, and pick up the yoke of God, which is much lighter than any yoke I put on myself.

This is a marathon, not a race, I remind myself. I need to start intentionally carving out time for myself like this on a more frequent basis, so maybe I can be better armed to handle battles like the raging one from yesterday.

I hit post on the blog and watch it go live on my ministry website before closing the laptop and heading to the shower. It's time to join my family in the hospital, and this time I feel equipped to handle the day with a bit more grace, peace, and confidence than the day before.

Chapter 38 Life After the NICU

Tuesday, January 23, 2018

My thumbs work quickly and quietly as I draft a CaringBridge post on my phone. CaringBridge has been our voice to the world throughout our stay in the NICU, informing what started out to be just our closest circle of family and friends of Charlotte's latest medical updates, but has now grown to thousands of people who follow Charlotte's progress and pray with us that we could go home with Charlotte as a complete family.

 ## Keeping Family Informed

We chose CaringBridge, a free online tool for sharing health updates, as our avenue to keep family and friends informed about Charlotte's medical journey. There are many ways you might keep others informed like a private group on social media, public posts on social media, specific websites, a texting chain, email, etc. I highly suggest if you find yourself in a position where multiple people are asking how things are going or reaching out for updates, find a way to streamline the communication via one avenue. Otherwise, you find yourself repeating things over and over and spending countless hours on the phone.

  If you're not too interested in being the one who communicates to others, you can always ask a family member or friend if they'd be willing to be the point person to provide updates for your inner circle, to take the pressure off of you.

How much you choose to share is entirely up to you. You might want to keep things more private, which is perfectly admirable. Or, you might want to keep your 'people' more informed so they can rally around you. There is no right or wrong way to handle it, so whatever seems right for you and your family is what's best. One thing to consider, however, is the more people are informed of what's going on, the more they are able to support you through this very difficult time.

And now, the moment we've been praying for is here. This morning the D word—Discharge—was mentioned during rounds. Dr. Rick suggesting discharge would likely be in the next few weeks once Charlotte recovers from her fifth procedure—the double ureter implant—which is scheduled for tomorrow, and once she is able to eat full feeds on her own.

After Dr. Rick shared the hard reality of our long-term inpatient status back in early December, I dreamt I would be overjoyed when he finally planned on sending us home. But, surprisingly this morning, I do not feel overjoyed so much as paralyzed with worry about the logistics.

How are we going to care for our daughter at home when she currently requires an entire medical team to keep her alive?

I continue writing the post on CaringBridge titled: *Looking for Child Care Options*. The beginning of the post reads, "Now that we know what kind of home care Charlotte needs, we are searching for childcare options when we both return to work. If you know of someone in the area that is looking for childcare work, please let me know." I list what kind of skills we are seeking in the person we hire.

But this is the thought that stops me from hitting the post button: how am I ever going to be able to leave Charlotte with a babysitter and return to work, when all I've done so far is leave her with doctors and nurses? The thought shatters me. I just hung up the phone with my work HR contact a few moments ago and we discussed my return to work at the end of March, after Charlotte is hopefully home from the hospital and has a couple additional out-patient surgeries under her belt.

I try to edit the post on my phone through blurred vision. A tear slips down my cheeks and splashes on the screen. I wipe it away and chastise myself. I should be full of gratitude. First of all, my work is being more gracious than I could ever dare ask. HR informed me today that my coworkers wanted me to be able to stay with Charlotte as long as possible, so they pooled their vacation days together and donated them to me. Donated vacation days! Who does that? Simply amazing.

Second, we are talking about going home. Home. That's what I've yearned for all this time, isn't it? To take my baby home? Why then am I so sad?

Bethanie, our nurse today, notices my turmoil and pulls out her phone. She walks next to where I'm sitting and scrolls through her pictures. A few silent moments pass before she finds the one she wants. She turns the iPhone screen to face me. I see a picture of a little girl running through a yard with a birthday cap on her head. She's smiling from ear to ear, exposing a missing front tooth. Her brown hair is blowing in her face with a kind of freedom and joy that is tangible. Envy runs through my veins before I can stop it. Good for this girl, she can run and smile and hide teeth for the tooth-fairy and play. Will my daughter ever be able to do those things? Why is Bethanie showing me this girl?

"It might not feel like it now, Emily, but there is life after the NICU," Bethanie says, a quiver in her voice gives away her deep compassion. "This little girl was very, very sick several years ago, much like Charlotte. I took care of her as her nurse and just the other day I got this picture from her mother saying she's celebrating her eighth birthday."

Bethanie looks at me intently and gently but firmly repeats, "There is life after the NICU."

Her tenderness surprises me. Bethanie is a fabulously skilled nurse but not one to show gentleness. She is a rough-around-the-edges kind of lady who is typically a no-nonsense type. We often are assigned Bethanie when Patty is unavailable. While I've grown to really appreciate her talent, I've never found her to be particularly sympathetic. Her compassion now reaches into my soul and soothes a place that aches so very deeply.

The future is so unknown. I can hardly see past tomorrow, when I know my eight-week-old baby is about to undergo yet another hopefully life-saving procedure. I can't make sense of how we will be able to manage her care at home or try to resume any sense of normalcy in our lives, between work, childcare and medical care.

I close out of CaringBridge on my phone without posting the update about childcare. I simply cannot bring myself to admit I will be leaving my daughter under someone else's care.

Leaving Charlotte again.

I can't even imagine how life is going to carry on once we are on our own outside of this institution's walls. I hope Bethanie is right. I hope there is life after the NICU. I'm not so sure.

Chapter 39 Running Interference

Journal Entry - Thursday, January 25, 2018

Good morning God,

Praise your name! Charlotte came through her fifth procedure amazingly. Thank you for the incredibly skilled surgeon who worked diligently for six-plus hours on joining Charlotte's ureters to her bladder. Praise your name.

Lord, you have answered every prayer so far. You will answer every prayer here and after. Center me on your truth and your steadfast love. Forgive me for my unbelief. Wrap me in your confident grace to remain focused on your love and your hope alone. Teach me, Lord, to rise above my fears, my worries, my anxiety, my selfishness, to only embrace your hope and confident love.

Amen.

Thursday, January 25, 2018

"We just took her blood pressure when we got her vitals an hour ago. Are you sure we need to do it again?" I ask the cardiologist whom I've never seen before today.

"Yes, I need to take it myself. I need an upper and lower blood pressure to make sure the narrowed aorta isn't compromising blood flow," Dr. Hecht replies while she untangles the tiny blood pressure cuff from the myriad of wires, now including an epidural line for pain management and a foley catheter, in Charlotte's isolette. She velcros the cuff to Charlotte's right arm and hits a button on the monitor. The cuff expands with air, making a popping noise as it squeezes Charlotte's tiny bicep. Charlotte squirms and lets out a sleepy defiant squawk. Her hoarse cries are muted in her medicated fog.

Where is Dr. Elias, our usual cardiologist? He's not nearly as forceful and frenzied as this lady. I miss his calming demeanor. Seemingly reading my mind she says, "I'm newly assigned to this case. I need to evaluate the patient myself so I can better understand what we are dealing with."

The problem with this doctor assessing Charlotte herself is that *every* doctor wants to assess Charlotte for themselves. With more than twenty specialists involved in her care, that makes for nonstop evaluations, repeat blood pressures and pokes and prods all day long. Don't doctors realize healing requires rest, too? How is our barely two-month-old supposed to heal from her fifth surgery, which happened yesterday and took more than twice as long as it was supposed to, if she is constantly being assessed? Isn't that what nurses and doctors notes are for?

"Can you check the system to read Dr. Elias's notes instead? Charlotte just fell asleep, and she *needs* to sleep." My frayed nerves need my daughter to rest and for all the doctors to go away. I feel like a mama bear again, fighting off anyone and everyone who wants to come pester my child in the name of healing.

"No, I need to do this right now. I need to know how her heart is handling post-op," says Dr. Hecht, hitting the button again for a repeat blood pressure because the first one didn't give her a clear reading. I stand back and helplessly watch as the baby I worked so hard to put to sleep a few moments ago is now awake, yet again, angrily crying that hoarse, heartbreaking cry.

Her cries seem directed at me saying, "Do something, Mom!"

Do I interfere and ask Dr. Hecht to leave? But Charlotte's heart is very compromised, and it does need to be closely monitored. I can't rightly argue that.

I watch helplessly as she hits the button for a third time, expanding the blood pressure cuff again. The monitor beeps with inconclusive numbers. "Ugh. These monitors are awful," Dr. Hecht says, exacerbated. She removes the cuff and switches it to Charlotte's other arm. I peer around the cardiologist's shoulders and see Charlotte's poor bicep covered in little bruises where the cuff popped blood vessels. My anger swells. If I could bare my teeth and growl, I would.

Dr. Hecht continues hitting the button several times with similar results on the other arm. How long must I stand idle before I interfere?

In frustration, Dr. Hecht says, "I'll try it manually." She pulls out her tiny infant stethoscope and begins squeezing air into the cuff herself. Charlotte is now screaming, though even her screams are faint because her vocal cords are sore from being intubated all day yesterday for her big ureter implant surgery.

I muster courage and step forward. "I know blood pressures are important, but the nurse just got a good reading an hour ago and Charlotte really needs rest. Unless you think she could face further complications *right now* if we don't get another blood pressure, I'd like you to stop," I say firmly.

Dr. Hecht looks at me, obviously debating her options. "Well, now the patient is mad so the reading will be off anyway," she reasons, draping her stethoscope around her neck and stepping back. "I'll come back when I'm able."

With that, she walks out. Charlotte's little bruised arms are flailing and grasping for anything she can get hold of. Anything she can control in this world she has little to no control over. Her hand finds the orange NG tube and her long fingers clench down, pulling angrily. I quickly and gently grab her hand and pry her long skinny fingers off the tube before she can yank it out of her nose. The girl's grip is surprisingly strong.

Patty hands me a rolled-up cloth which I gently slide into Charlotte's hand. She grasps down tight on the rag while Patty slips a pacifier in her mouth. Charlotte chomps aggressively and slowly fades back into a drugged sleep.

"It's so hard to know when to interfere with doctors. They are all trying to take care of Charlotte but when is enough enough?" I lament to Patty, who I am so grateful is assigned to us today.

The sound of a drill comes from the neighboring NICU room and Charlotte squirms again in irritation. I poke my head through the glass window between rooms to see a maintenance man fixing an isolette. Really? Now we are fixing a broken isolette with a noisy drill when my daughter is barely twelve hours post-op? I take the liberty to close the window and lock it, muffling the sound as best as I can.

A group of doctors and medical staff are gathered outside Charlotte's room conversing. One bursts out in laughter at something someone said, and Charlotte lets out a simultaneous screech. Clearly every little sound is painful for this poor baby.

"Can we close those?" I ask Patty, nodding toward the glass doors that are almost always left open to the hallway.

"Absolutely," Patty says. "And pull the curtain too to help make the room dark," she adds as she dims the overhead lights.

After doing so, I return to Charlotte's bedside and open a drawer to pull out two small orange foam disks. "These earmuffs should help, Sweet Girl," I say as I gently place them over Charlotte's tiny ears.

"The NICU is a noisy place, and a quiet, calm environment is what our little Sweet Pea needs right now," Patty says, encouraging me. "There are a lot of things we cannot interfere with, but there are still a lot of things we can. You're doing a great job, Emily. Charlotte is lucky to have you."

The doors reopen behind us and another doctor walks toward Charlotte's bedside. He's obviously here to evaluate Charlotte for who-knows-what. Bolstered by Patty's encouraging words, I stand between him and the isolette. "She's resting now, is this urgent or could it wait?" I whisper so as to not agitate Charlotte any further.

"Oh," he says in surprise. "I can come back later," he quietly replies and turns to walk out. Is it really that easy?

I look over at Patty and she smirks. "That's exactly what Charlotte needs from you."

Running interference. That's my role today as Charlotte's mom. I'm gaining the confidence to do it well.

Journal Entry - Friday, January 26, 2018

"When you go out to war against your enemies ... and you face illness and surgeries and IVs ... you shall not be afraid of them; for the Lord your God is with you, who brought you up from the land of Egypt." (my version of Deuteronomy 20:1)

"'Hear, O Israel! Today you are drawing near to do battle against your enemies. Do not lose heart, or be afraid, or panic, or be in dread of them; for it is the Lord your God who goes with you, to fight for you against your enemies, to give you victory.'" (Deuteronomy 20:3-4)

Amen! Hallelujah! Help me to accept and embrace this kind of fearless faith today, Lord.

Chapter 40 Empowerment

Journal Entry - Saturday, January 27, 2018

Oh God,

You know the depths of my heart and you understand the hurt. You hear my cries of injustice. Lord, having Charlotte in the NICU means I have to leave at shift change and it means I have to leave her overnight. It means I can't console her when I'm gone, and it means nurses have primary care of her. Plus, she's on pain meds and neurological meds for irritability. I HATE the neurological meds. And I hate that her dose went up today.

God, help me. Help us to get out of the hospital as soon as it is safe for Charlotte to leave. Help me to make it that long without losing my mind. Help the nurses to take great care of her and to understand a parent's hurt. Oh God, help me to not take my hurt out on Daniel.

Help us, Oh God.

Tuesday, January 30, 2018

"She's doing great with feeds. Weaning the morphine is bolstering her appetite," Dr. Rick says at rounds this morning as he skims through the night nurse's notes. "Her urine output seems adequate overnight, even with the nephrostomy tubes removed. Let's remove the foley cath today too and monitor inputs and outputs closely," he tells today's nurse.

He looks at me and asks, "Did you and Dan receive training to catheterize Q6?"

I nod yes. Dr. Fuhrman showed us how to use a special catheter designed specifically for Charlotte's unique anatomy.

"Great, once the foley cath is out you can help nurses catheterize until you're comfortable. We want to send you home feeling confident," he says.

Before this latest surgery, Dan and I had to sign a waiver stating we understood the outcome of the surgery would likely require catheterization every six hours until surgeons could do a full reimplantation of the ureters into the bladder when Charlotte is one year old. Until then, we're told her bladder will likely be unable to drain on its own.

Now that the two nephrostomy tubes are no longer in Charlotte's back, and soon she will not have a cumbersome foley catheter either, I will have a much easier time picking Charlotte up on my own and holding her without needing extra hands to juggle all the lines. Each day it seems a line or two is eliminated and soon she'll be down to an IV, heart and pulse ox monitor leads. So, I muster the courage to say what I've been practicing for the last couple of days.

"I am going to start feeding her whenever she is hungry, rather than waiting Q3 for the next scheduled feed at Hands on Care," I state matter of fact. My demeanor calm, collected, confident. My palms are sweaty. Oh God, what have I done?

Dr. Rick looks at me, surprised. "She is gaining well and eating more and more at each feed. It's unnecessary to feed her more," he says, confused.

"I know but she almost always starts crying two hours after her last feed. She's hungry and there is no reason to wait another hour while she cries, if I'm the one here to feed her anyway. At home I would feed her whenever she is hungry, I wouldn't make her wait for a scheduled feed. I understand when I'm not here she has to stay on the three-hour nurses schedule, but when I'm sitting here holding her anyway, I might as well nurse her when she's hungry," I explain my logic, hoping Dr. Rick agrees.

It's driving me crazy, this waiting for the scheduled feeding time while my hungry baby cries needlessly. I have the milk. Why shouldn't I give it to her when she wants it? It's only logical. It's not like more milk is going to hurt the kid, so long as her kidneys and bladder are dispelling the appropriate output.

I was tempted to ask Dr. Rick for *permission* to feed Charlotte when I see she's hungry. But the reality is, unless there's a valid medical reason for withholding feeds until the scheduled time, I cannot go one more day letting it happen. Especially when I'm the source of

Charlotte's food and I'm standing right here! I was intentional in my word choice, not asking permission but stating my plan of care. He can tell me no if there is a medical reason not to. Otherwise, I am feeding my baby.

"Are you sure you want to do that to yourself? It might put a lot of demand on your time and the NICU schedule is already demanding," Dr. Rick reasons.

"Yes, but I'm here anyway. My child is hungry. I want to feed her. That's how it will be at home so I might as well start now," I confirm.

Dr. Rick gives me that familiar smile I've grown to appreciate as his approval. He looks at the nurse and says, "Let's make a note that Mom will feed Baby on demand, but we will also feed Q3. Mom can tell you how much she thinks Charlotte is getting between scheduled feeds. Let's keep track of it all." Then he looks at me. "Charlotte is one lucky lady."

I release the breath I didn't know I was holding. Pride swells. I stand a little taller. I am slowly but surely gaining my feet under me, doing this mom thing. I'm starting to understand where I can have a positive impact on my child's care and I'm gaining the confidence to do it, rather than constantly seeking permission and guidance from medical staff. I'm starting to feel like maybe, just maybe, I am her mother, not just her visitor.

Journal Entry - January 30, 2018

Oh God,

I'm getting so impatient. We are so close to being able to take Charlotte home and I just want to take her now. Leaving her at night is getting increasingly hard. I want to be her mom 24 hours a day, not the nine hours that I can be in the hospital. I want to rock her at night and love on her during the day. I want to create a routine of our own and feel like her mom, not her visitor. I want her to have consistent care and not someone new every 12 hours.

Oh God, help me be patient. Help me to focus on all of our progress and not on our hold up. She's made amazing progress that is nothing short of a miracle. Only you can heal her like she has. Oh God, praise your name. Help me to never take her or you for granted.

Chapter 41   Transition Room

Journal Entry - Monday, February 5, 2018, 9:00 a.m.

God, you are so good. You hold true to your promises. Lord, Charlotte is healing beautifully, and I know it's because of you. Thank you God. I cannot thank you enough.

I have fallen sick (since Friday, February 2, with strep throat) and I wonder if it's your way of forcing me to rest before Charlotte comes home. And maybe it's your way of protecting Charlotte by giving her my antibodies through breast milk. I know you make all things work for good and so I praise you.

I cannot complain because Charlotte, Dan and my parents have remained healthy which is nothing short of a miracle. Oh God, I want to be back with my daughter. Please help me to heal and strengthen so I may be there for her. Praise your name for keeping her and those around me healthy.

Help me to see you today. Help me to know you. Help me to serve you. Amen.

7:30 p.m.

I feel so much better. You are a loyal God. Praise your name. How will I ever thank you for all you've done and all I know you'll do?

Wednesday, February 7, 2018

"Look Dan, I am standing farther than three feet from her bed!" I laugh, jubilant. I lift Charlotte close to my face and kiss her forehead repeatedly. "I'm not attached, either!" I do a slow spin to demonstrate.

He looks at us, his girls, with a huge grin on his weary but happy face. "Freedom!" he exclaims. There is a knock at the door to the Transition Room.

"Come in," I say, rocking Charlotte back and forth while I stand, reveling in this newfound liberty to move about the room without limitation. The last week has been a slow weaning process off all the attachments Charlotte's sported since day one.

The orange NG tube no longer hangs from her nose. There was talk last week of needing to surgically insert a longer-term gastrostomy feeding tube, referred to as a G-tube, into Charlotte's stomach in preparation of her going home and needing supplemental feeds beyond what she could consume on her own from the bottle or from breastfeeding. But, as each day went by, and more and more pain meds were weaned, Charlotte's appetite caught up to her and doctors are now satisfied enough with her oral intake that they opted to hold off on the G-tube surgery, and even experiment without the NG tube before sending us home.

The longer-term IV PICC line that was in Charlotte's arm is now removed, too, since she no longer needs intravenous pain medications.

What medications she is still on, we've worked hard to transition to oral administration.

The foley catheter is long gone.

All drains are eliminated.

For the sake of spending the night in the Transition Room, nurses even allowed us to remove the three heart monitor leads from her chest and the pulse ox from her big toe. "You won't have these to rely on at home, so you might as well start weaning yourselves off them now," they said.

I never foresaw needing to wean ourselves off monitors. But the nurses are right. We've formed a dependency on the reassurance monitors provide, knowing if anything goes south, they will alert us. It's much like weaning off Google Maps and learning how to read a real map. You can no longer glance at Google Maps every few seconds to make sure you're on the right route. You have to use common sense and look for landmarks and signs.

Similarly, we have to learn how to watch Charlotte for signs of distress rather than depending on machines to tell us. It's simultaneously thrilling and terrifying. Monitors no longer babysit our daughter's heart rate, breathing rate and blood oxidation levels. It's uncharted territory for Dan and me. But it's so nice to hold my baby without worry of tangles and snags in Charlotte's web.

The Transition Room door swings open and an unfamiliar face walks in with a large brown bag and box in his hands. He drops them with a thud next to the stiff pullout couch that is Dan and my makeshift bed for the night. "I have 300 specialized catheters for you. Just sign here," he pushes a clipboard toward Dan.

I smile and squeeze Charlotte in a little closer. "You might not ever need one of those," I whisper to her.

Though we thought her bladder would not drain on its own after the last surgery, it seems her body has other plans. Her diapers continue to fill and we haven't had to catheterize her for a few days. It's wild to think her bladder literally never cycled before her urology surgery, and now it's functioning well enough to void on its own.

The Urologist recommends we take the catheters home just in case things change, which we will gladly do. "If you go six hours without getting a wet diaper, just use one of these catheters and drain her," he said.

Still, miracles abound.

Discharge is only two days away. This morning we had the greatly anticipated Discharge Meeting during Rounds. We reviewed the plan for Dan and me to take Charlotte home on Friday morning. We went over the long list of specialists and follow up appointments Charlotte will need, including Neurology, Nephrology, Urology, Endocrinology, Audiology, Pediatric Surgery, Cardiology, Cranio-Facial Plastics, Occupational Therapy, Physical Therapy, at home therapies, oh, and her General Pediatrician, too.

One of the residents who often attends Charlotte's Rounds took it upon herself to create a binder for us, helping capture all the schedules, notes and records we need to manage Charlotte's care at home and with all these outpatient specialists. She shared it with us this morning and everyone agreed we would need to stay very organized to keep it all straight.

As Rounds finished, Patty reviewed Charlotte's medical schedule with me for the tenth time, per my request. "Now the Synthroid needs to be given one-and-a-half hours after her morning bottle and at least thirty minutes before her next bottle. You'll want to cut the pill in quarters and give her ¾ each morning, dissolved in 1mL water. The goal is to give it to her on an empty stomach so it can fully absorb. You don't want to give her the Iron at the same time as the Synthroid. They'll bind and the Synthroid won't fully absorb."

She went on, "The Neurotin is on a slow weaning schedule, so you'll want to follow Dorie's plan to decrease the dose every week. Don't wean her any faster than the plan prescribes, or Charlotte will start showing withdrawal symptoms. The prophylactic antibiotic needs to be administered daily and you'll need to refill the script every two weeks when it expires …" She went on to explain each drug, the timing for each dosage and the specified amounts to administer.

"Also, you'll want to fortify two feeds a day to bring it up to 24 k-cal per 30mL breast milk. We are using Gerber Good Start Soothe, so you'll want to make sure that's the kind of formula you use at home. You don't want to introduce anything new because that will add variables to her care and make it hard to tell what's causing any symptoms you may see at home."

My head is calculating how and when we are going to source this, in our "spare time" once we get home.

Patty seemed to know what I was thinking, because she followed with, "We will send you home with this container to get you started," showing me the formula can.

"Can you please write all this down," I asked, my head spinning. There were a lot of things I helped with in Charlotte's care during her hospital stay, but never medication administration nor feed fortification. Those were the nurse's jobs. I found myself confident that I would accidentally overdose my kid, underfeed her, or perhaps worse, skip a medication that would send her body into shock or delay her development. The responsibility seemed more than any one person could handle, let alone me.

Dorie, the pharmacist, who lingered with us after the rest of the Rounding crew left, saw my distress and reassured me she would help even once we left the NICU.

"Here's my cell number," she said as she wrote it down in my new binder. "You call or text anytime, day or night, for any reason. My only request is that you send me photos of Charlotte. That'll be my payment," she smiled.

Looking at Charlotte now while I gently swing her back and forth, I know I will be calling Dorie often, as well as Dr. Rick, Patty, and others whenever needed. They've become more than Charlotte's medical team. They are part of our family, just like Dr. Rick warned us would happen. I never imagined I'd mourn leaving them behind when we left the NICU, but part of me will certainly miss their constant, reassuring presence.

And that is the purpose of the Transition Room, too, to spend a day and night with Charlotte on our own, while still being just down the hall from doctors and nurses so we can call with any questions or concerns. It seems Dan and I need to wean from their constant presence and support just as much as Charlotte needs to wean from her pain medications.

"How are you feeling?" Dan asks, interrupting my thoughts.

"Much better, just tired," I say, grateful the antibiotics kicked in and my strep throat is a thing of the past.

"I'm tired too. Give me that baby. We are going to take a nap," Dan says, sitting down in the rocking chair and stretching his arms toward me, signaling me to pass Charlotte to him. I gently lay Charlotte on his chest and the two settle in for their first nap together.

Nurses say Charlotte is content during the day when we are here but then screams her way through the night unless someone is holding her. "She has her days and nights mixed," they tell us. "It'll take her a few weeks but once she's exposed to daylight and a typical routine at home, she'll settle in."

That makes sense. She has never even seen the sunshine before. Of course, her circadian rhythm is wonky.

I cannot wait to take her out in the fresh air. To watch her take in daylight for the first time. To see her reaction when a breeze touches her skin. To rock her in our own rocking chair. Introduce her to her dogs and cat. Lay her in her own crib. Help her adjust her days and nights. I cannot wait to take her home.

Chapter 42 Home

Friday, February 9, 2018

"Dr. Rick, look in Charlotte's pocket," Patty smiles and giggles, pointing to the tiny decorative chest pocket on Charlotte's pink button sleeper. There is a piece of paper sticking out. He reaches into Charlotte's crib and slides the paper out of the sleeping baby's outfit. It is folded into a hand-crafted book, no larger than his thumb, with medical tape binding the pages.

He reads the cover of the book out loud so everyone can hear, "Charlotte's Calendar." He grins and opens it to the first page. "2/9 Home Sweet Home," he holds the book up to show the rounding staff the red hearts drawn all over the pages. He flips the book to the back cover and reads, "Made with love by nurse Patty."

"Charlotte needs her own calendar and notebook to keep track of things, just like her mommy," Patty explains, and everyone laughs.

"That is cute," he chuckles.

I hold up the leather notebook I'm using right now for our 73rd and final NICU rounds this morning and say, "We match! She's learning young." I've clearly left a lasting impression on the NICU staff as the mom who is constantly taking notes, and Charlotte's left an impression as the baby who has lots of medical needs to track.

The room is joy filled as Dr. Rick reviews his own final notes before we are officially discharged.

"Now, you know how to reach me," Dr. Rick says. "Don't ever hesitate to call." He adds, "Don't forget all your frozen milk in the freezer. You're going to need that."

Dan nods and opens the large blue cooler to show Dr. Rick he has packed all the milk to take with us.

"And don't forget to take all the medications home. Did Pharmacy bring them, yet?"

Dan holds several white paper bags up, "Here they are."

"Great! And I see you're lined up for your first out-patient visit with your pediatrician in a couple of days. The lip adhesion surgery is scheduled with the Cranio-facial team for March 7," Dr. Rick says, thinking through final details we need to discuss before saying goodbye.

"She passed the car seat test, and you have it here, that's good. The roads were slick on my way in this morning so be careful on your drive home, you'll have precious cargo with you now," he adds, lingering at Charlotte's bedside longer than usual.

It feels like the day a dad drops off his baby girl at college for the first time. When he checks the oil in her car three times just to make extra sure she's all set. Dr. Rick clearly cares so deeply for his patients, and we have grown to love him like a father figure in our family.

He looks at Patty and asks, "Can I keep that calendar? I'd like to put it in my wallet as a token of our little fighter Charlotte." I love this man. He has shepherded Charlotte's medical care so diligently for the past two-and-a-half months and has empowered me to step into the role of mother and medical manager that I find myself now filling. He is an absolute treasure.

"Yeah, of course," Patty says. "I'll make another one to send home with Charlotte and Mommy and Daddy." She pulls out the medical tape, some paper and a pen to craft another keepsake book. She, too, is like a mother figure to us in her tireless care for our family and her attention to details, big and small.

She dolled Charlotte up today for her big going-home debut. She adorned Charlotte's head with a pink bow. She put fresh tape on Charlotte's lip and nose, and she removed all the monitors before putting her going-home outfit on which is white and soft pink with an embroidered heart made of roses. Inside the heart, the sleeper reads, "Thank Heaven for Little Girls." I've waited so long to put her in this outfit and walk out the NICU door, this time with my baby, going home together as our little family unit—Mom, Dad and baby.

We load Charlotte into her car seat which seems way oversized for her now 7.62-pound body. Dan lowers the car seat with Charlotte into the crib, which is already stacked with all Charlotte's supplies to go home. Medications, her clothes, taping supplies, the catheters, diapers, wipes, bottles, pump parts, all the decorations from family and Child Life specialists that garnished her bedspace, the cooler of milk, discharge paperwork, the books we read to her during her hospital stay and everything else we lugged into the NICU over the course of the last ten weeks.

"Our receptionist will wheel the crib with Charlotte in her car seat down to the front lobby doors where Dan can pull the car up for loading," Dr. Rick explains discharge protocol. "Try to keep Charlotte covered on your way out so gawkers don't get too close. She is super cute, and everyone will want to see but she doesn't need exposure to any germs on her way out of the hospital."

Then he gives Dan and I each big hugs and takes a minute to say goodbye to Charlotte. "You come back and visit us as a NICU grad," he tells Charlotte. "That's the joy of our job, seeing our kids growing and thriving."

Then he and others line the M31 Neonatal Intensive Care Unit Hall to wave goodbye to us. As the receptionist wheels the crib ahead of me, I turn around to snap a picture on my phone of this hospital floor and these people who have dedicated their time and energy so diligently to saving our daughter's life. I want to remember them. I want to remember this hard, holy, and healing space.

Exhilarating thrill and deep sadness tugs at me. I cannot wait to get out of here, but I will miss these people who were mere strangers flooding the delivery room just a few months ago.

We enter the elevator and go down to the main floor. I help steer the mobile crib as the receptionist pushes. We cross the same lobby Dan and I walked the night we came in for induction. The same lobby I've walked through every day since, wishing my baby was with me.

The space is abuzz with activity, patients and staff coming and going. Some joy filled with healing progress and others burdened with prognoses and setbacks. My heart throbs for everyone I see, now having an insider's experience of what it's like living the front lines of the battle for life itself. The hospital that used to be like a foreign culture to me is now forever a part of who I am. I will never look at a human person the same. My recognition of their value, their dignity and the sheer fragility of their lives is like nothing I've experienced before. Empathy for each of their individual stories, though I don't know any of them, exceeds a level I thought possible. I sense God is going to do something big with this stirring of love in my soul, though I have no idea what.

Dan pulls the car up to the pickup area. Once loaded, Dan climbs in the driver's seat and I slide in the back next to Charlotte. I squeeze Dan's shoulder in excitement, and he grins at me in the rearview mirror. As each mile melts past us, leaving Cleveland Clinic further and further behind and growing closer and closer to our house, the joy of the day fills our car as if tangible.

Charlotte is still sound asleep, enjoying the gentle rocking and bouncing motion of highway driving. I watch her little chest rhythmically pop up and down, obsessively ensuring she is still breathing with each passing mile. The hour drive flies by and before we know it, we are pulling into our driveway in our quaint, quiet little town. Our abandoned house has clearly had visitors of late, because the driveway and sidewalks are cleared of all snow and there is salt on the walkway to the door. I heard rumblings that our uncle was going to stop by to plow. Amazing.

I get Charlotte's car seat out of the car and follow Dan to the front door. He unlocks it and pushes it open saying, "Welcome home, Charlotte Jo!" We both grin and walk in, feeling like the wedding night when the groom carries his bride over the threshold into their newly shared home. We are finally all under one roof, at our home. For the first time since Charlotte was born, this house truly feels like our home.

As we enter, we are hit with a fresh scent of cleaning supplies. I smile, remembering my aunts had asked how they could help us prepare for coming home. I took them up on their offer to help and suggested they clean our abandoned home in preparation for us arriving. I can't imagine how gross it must have been after being closed up for so long. They must have just finished cleaning recently because the smell of bleach and citrus lingers.

Dan begins unloading the car of everything we've used to survive since delivery day. I unstrap Charlotte from her seat and carry her into the kitchen to begin sorting through the piles of medications, bottle and pump parts with my free hand.

I look around the squeaky-clean kitchen and my eye catches on the decorative chalkboard hanging on the wall. Aunt Hannah's handwriting reads, "Home is where Charlotte is."

Journal Entry - February 12, 2018

Good morning, Lord,

My heart is overwhelmed with gratitude, God. I'm sitting in my glider, holding my baby, sipping on coffee and spending time with you at HOME. *Oh God, praise your name for all your goodness. You have pulled us through these last ten weeks (eleven now actually) and you have remained loyal and unwavering even as I waivered. Praise your name.*

Oh God of Israel, God of Jacob, God of me, God of Charlotte, praise your name. I am forever grateful.

I knew you were preparing me for something big in life, I just didn't know what. Now I know and I'm forever grateful you trusted me to take on the challenge of being Charlotte's mom and Daniel's wife. Neither are easy and I fail often, but you redeem me in my weakness and you will lead us all to healing and eternal relationship with you. My cup overflows!

Praise you God.

Chapter 43 Beautifully, Wonderfully, Fearfully Made

Friday, February 16, 2018

She's perfect.

Her soft baby skin has that after-bath glow, washing all the hospital away with Johnson's baby shampoo. The tape is all removed from her face, including remnants of the adhesive and the nasal elevator. She's wrapped comfortably in a pink fleece swaddle and her eyes are closed in a peaceful sleep. I rock back and forth in the green glider Dan and I carefully picked out for just this purpose, rocking our baby girl, at home.

I haven't seen her face completely tape-free since we took those professional photos in the hospital weeks ago. We removed it tonight to give her sweet skin a much-deserved break.

It's shocking to see her naked face. Shockingly beautiful.

There is no doubt she is beautifully, wonderfully, fearfully made. Her little bilateral notched upper lip almost looks like it's how the lip is supposed to be.

Man, I'm going to miss this. I don't want to go through with the lip adhesion surgery in a couple weeks. She's perfect just the way she is.

Not only that. I know what pain she will be in post-op. I know her hands will have to be held away from her face in braces called No-No's so she can't pull on the sutures. I know she will not be allowed to have a pacifier or even a bottle for four whole weeks after the surgery. The few things she counts on for comfort will be taken from her. I don't think I can handle it.

A tear slips down my cheeks and lands on the swaddle, absorbing quickly into the soft fabric. Charlotte's so peaceful now, sleeping comfortably with a full belly of fresh milk. I have a sense that all is well in the world tonight, all is calm, all is perfect. But this sixth surgery looms. Sixth of many more to come. She has at least four more all before she celebrates her first birthday. Then at least another four more by the time she's an adult. Perhaps more. Must we go through with them? She appears just fine to me. More than fine. Perfect.

But she can't have a cleft lip for the rest of her life. I know this. She can't have a cleft palate for the rest of her life. I know this. She can't go on with ureters merely grafted to the bladder. They must be fully inserted. I know this.

Looking at her tonight though, it's as if the world has stopped and everything and everyone is in awe at the perfection that is my daughter, if only in my mind's eye. It's only me, Dan, the dogs and the cat in the house tonight, but I get the sense that the universe sees her alongside me and sees her as very good. God himself is looking on her with the kind of love that burns deeper than human words express. Dare I mess with her beauty with a lip surgery?

All logic says yes, it must be done. But my heart screams no. I love Charlotte's lips just the way they are. And she's just beginning to attempt to smile. Oh how her smile lights up my world. Many cleft support groups talk about a baby getting their forever smile at that lip adhesion surgery. Why can't this be Charlotte's forever smile? I will forever miss it.

The plastic surgeon repeatedly reassures me, "Once we are done, you'll never know she even had a cleft lip." She means it to encourage me. But each time she or anyone else says this I am surprised by my reaction.

I really don't care if we know she had a cleft lip. It's part of who she is, and she is beautiful.

Chapter 44 The Embrace

Journal Entry - Thursday, February 22, 2018

"Because you did not serve the Lord your God joyfully and with gladness of heart for the abundance of everything, therefore you shall serve your enemies whom the Lord will send against you ..." (Deuteronomy 28: 47-48)

Lord,

You have abundantly blessed us with countless blessings. Help me to never forget your loving work and help me to always remember your loyalty.

You answer every prayer, big and small. Even as small as asking for help to spend time with you, that Charlotte may nap peacefully while I pray. Even as big as supplying the funds so we can cover Charlotte's expenses and ours and still be able to live comfortably. Oh God, I am in awe at your abundant blessings.

I fear my own weakness that I may start feeling independent and as if I could do this without you. I know I can't. I need you every minute of every day and I can't fathom survival on my own let alone thriving like you provide. God, keep me humble. Teach me to need you even more than I do now. Remind me that you are the reason for all that is good. Oh God, praise your name.   Lead me.

Monday, April 30, 2018

Music quietly plays in the background as I wash pump and bottle parts for what feels like the 75th time today. Charlotte is propped on her Boppy nursing pillow on the kitchen floor. The dog whines to be let outside.

My phone rings and a number with a Cleveland area code pops up on my screen. It's Cleveland Clinic, again. I've spent most of the morning talking with schedulers, therapists, pharmacists, insurance and billing, in between bottle feeds, nursings, pumping and diapers.

I answer. It's the feeding clinic wanting to schedule a consultation with a dietician, per Charlotte's pediatrician's orders. After we find an appointment time and date that works, I hang up to find Charlotte squirming and squawking on the floor.

"Do you have a burp, Sweet Pea?" I ask as I bend down to scoop Charlotte up and begin gently bouncing her.

I grab a pen and paper with my free hand and start noting Charlotte's latest medication schedule for my mom to follow tomorrow when she watches Charlotte. Tomorrow is my first full day back at work in the office, and Mom has graciously offered to babysit so I can be at ease this first week.

I hear the lyrics of one of my favorite worship songs come on my streaming bluetooth device that's sitting on top of the fridge.

"Let the King of my heart be the mountain where I run, the fountain I drink from, Oh he is my song ..." I smile and put my pen down,

recognizing the Bethel Music and Steffany Gretzinger song, *King of My Heart.*

"I listened to this song on repeat while you were in the hospital. It pulled me through some of my darkest moments," I whisper to Charlotte as I pull her up to my chest, her ear close to my lips.

I start to sway to the slow beat, rocking Charlotte along and taking her in. Breathing in her scent. Feeling the weight of her in my arms.

"And let the King of my heart, be the shadow where I hide, the ransom for my life, oh he is my song,"

As the melody picks up and the lyrics tug at the depths of my soul, I start to gently swing and spin around the kitchen, holding Charlotte close.

"Cause you are good. You're good. Oh oh. You are good. You're good. Oh oh."

I sing along with an eruption of joy, bouncing and swaying Charlotte with me, recognizing I'm holding a miracle in my arms right now. She smiles her now-surgically scarred smile at me and watches wide-eyed in wonder as her mother is swept up in the melody.

I spin and spin and spin, reveling in the freedom of no wires, no leads, no lines, no hospitals. Just me and my daughter, in our home, dancing in the kitchen like we have no care in the world. Dancing for the countless miracles that have led up to this moment.

"You're never gonna let, you're never gonna let me down."

My soul is on fire and every movement and lyric is a joyous cry of praise to our Lord. It bubbles out of me until the crescendo of the song. As the music fades, *"Cause you are good. You're good. Oh oh."* I waltz to the living room and collapse on the couch laughing and crying, clinging Charlotte to my chest with so much gratitude I think I might explode.

Charlotte is alive. She is home. She is free. And she is with me.

Afterword

Journal Entry - Friday, May 4, 2018

Oh God, you are so good. You inspire me to continue pursuing your calling. You flood my brain with ideas. You fill me with passion. You overwhelm me with support from family and friends. And today Daniel reached out and asked me to schedule time to discuss your calling and how to feasibly accomplish it together.

Oh Lord, lead us. Bless our conversation that it may be fruitful. Oh God, lead me. Help me to use my time wisely to serve you best.

While at the hospital yesterday we visited the NICU to say hello to the staff and I saw one of the baby's mom's walking by. My heart leapt and all I wanted to do was be there for her.

Teach me how, Lord.

Be there for others as they navigate this wild, beyond hard, yet sometimes surprisingly beautiful journey of raising a medically complex child—that is my heart's cry. Now that I've walked quite literally to the edge of life and back, I simply cannot imagine doing anything else with my life besides walking with others as they make the journey themselves, with their own kids.

I knew I needed to do something with our experience that would benefit those coming after us and around us. The need is great, the void tangible. Who will walk with these parents and caregivers and help them embrace their new and unexpected roles, validating their experiences and empowering them to care for their beautiful children who have complexities?

There is a critical transition that happens somewhere along the way in this journey, that takes you from not only accepting the reality of your situation but also embracing it. Taking it head on and seeking the good out of it, and from there, using it for the betterment of others. This is where the gold lies—where great purpose is born through immense suffering.

The Lord's purpose, his call, tugged on me day in and day out—*See my people. Love my people.* And with each step the vision for how I could use this for others slowly became more visible, albeit still fuzzy.

It started with me resuming ministry talks.

Six months after leaving the NICU, while in and out of the hospital on a weekly basis with Charlotte, still with many more surgeries ahead, I announced to my ministry followers and fans that I was back to speaking and that if anyone was looking for a speaker at their next event, I would be honored to come. Of course, I had my original talk topics in mind regarding relationships, faith, sex.

My followers had something else in mind. I received a surprising response of speaking requests, but they weren't for my prepared talk topics. They were for the story of our experience with Charlotte.

At first, I balked. That was not what my ministry was about. I didn't set out to tell people about my daughter's health challenges and her fight for her life. But the requests came flooding in nonetheless.

I recalled a ministry coach at the 2017 She Speaks Conference, just weeks before that fateful 20-week ultrasound, telling our auditorium filled with eager speakers like me, "When the Lord opens doors for your ministry, your job is to walk through them, even if they are unexpected doors leading you in unexpected directions." So, when the requests came, I said yes.

I was blown away at the results. So many people approached me after my talks, sharing their own stories of caring for medically complex children. People asked if they could connect me with so-and-so who had a child with complexities. Before I knew it, I was on the phone and meeting over coffee with other parents, being with them in their struggle for their child's life.

I found myself lending a listening ear and words of encouragement to families in all kinds of situations—parents who lost their child, parents in the NICU, parents arriving home from the hospital and not sure how to integrate back into normalcy with their anything-but-normal parenting situation.

I found myself sharing our story on podcasts, one of which was for families in crisis. After the interview, the podcast host, Anne DeSantis, said, "I have the contact of a publisher, Bathsheba Monk at Blue Heron Book Works, who I think would love your and Charlotte's story. You have to write this story, Emily. It could help so many people. I'm going to connect you with her."

I didn't plan to write a book on this topic, but I met with Bathsheba nonetheless. After talking with her I just knew that I did, in fact, need to write this book. Charlotte's story was clearly not meant for me to keep to myself. God's glory in her story obviously shone bright and who was I to keep it to myself? The verse from Matthew 5:15 comes to mind, *"No one after lighting a lamp puts it under the bushel basket, but on the lampstand, and it gives light to all in the house."* That was Charlotte's story—light for others. God was inviting me to put the lamp on the stand.

One mom, Ashlyn Thompson, who had followed Charlotte's story as it unfolded, and who supported us through our many surgeries and recoveries, called me after receiving a devastating diagnosis for her own daughter. I was honored to walk with her through her daughter's traumatic surgery and healing and then was so humbled when she called me saying, "I'm going to start a podcast for parents going through similar things with their kids. I just know I'm supposed to do it with you."

Okay Lord, you keep opening unexpected doors. I'm walking. Lead me.

One door led to another, which led to this book in your hands, the Empowered by Hope podcast going live, and the nonprofit Charlotte's Hope Foundation, Inc., launched, cofounded with Ashlyn. The Foundation mission is simple: to support, encourage and educate parents and caregivers of children with medical complexities, embracing each family's reality with an outlook of hope and empowering them as capable advocates for their child's optimal quality of life.

I can't think of a more personally fitting and appropriate way to see and love God's people.

If you'd like to join us in sharing hope with others, or if you are looking for support and encouragement yourself, visit us at CharlottesHopeFoundation.org to learn more. We cannot wait to see what God will do through you and us, to see his people, love his people.

ACKNOWLEDGEMENTS

I have long debated and wondered how I could possibly thank the countless family members, friends, and even strangers, doctors, nurses, and medical staff who have helped us through this wild journey. You are the ones who covered us in prayer, shared a word of encouragement, brought us meals, sent us checks, cleaned our house, fed our dogs, shoveled our snow, changed our daughter's dressings and IV medication bags, rocked her in the wee hours of the night when we couldn't be there with her, performed miraculous surgeries, coached me on how to care for her after countless surgeries, replied quickly to my desperate calls for help on Fridays at 10 p.m., and the list goes on.

And how do I thank all the people who've guided me in ministry efforts, writing and speaking? You are the ones who encouraged me when I was afraid, coached me when I didn't know which way to turn or how to proceed, helped me build a website and social presence, taught me how to let the Holy Spirit lead, connected me to your networks, reviewed my talks and writings and shared constructive feedback, coached me to write this book, trusted me to speak at your events and so much more.

You know who you are, the very people who have been God's hands and feet for me and my family. The body of Christ.

The best way I can think to appropriately thank you is to share your gifts, what you've done for us, with others. This book is my attempt to do just that. This is my thank you letter to each of you and a note of encouragement and love to all readers, passing on your gifts. I may not be able to thank you each individually, but I pray this book expresses my gratitude.

To Bathsheba Monk, who guided, encouraged, and coached this book into fruition. Our weekly calls, even while nursing a baby and rocking napping toddlers, kept me on task amidst ongoing medical challenges and relentless schedule upheavals. Your belief in me and this story fueled my resolve to write.

To our amazing parents, Daniel's and mine. You hold us upright when we can't stand on our own. You show up every time we need you. You provide a shoulder to cry on when needed, cookies always, and love and laughter even amidst heartbreak. You bring light to an otherwise often dark situation. Without you, our young family would not have survived this storm, let alone thrived. I can never thank you adequately.

And to my beloved husband, Daniel. You take your role very seriously, helping me get to heaven. When I told you I felt called to write this book, your response was, "If that's what God's asking you to do, I'll support you however you need." You took over childcare on evenings and weekends so I could have writing time, you encouraged me when I was riddled with anxiety, and you cheered me on through the entire process. Without you, none of this is possible.

About Charlotte's Hope Foundation, Inc

Charlotte's Hope Foundation, Inc. is a 501(c)(3) non-profit organization whose mission is to support, encourage and educate parents and caregivers of children with medical complexities, embracing each family's reality with an outlook of hope and empowering them as capable advocates for their child's optimal quality of life. The organization is co-founded by Executive Hope Directors Ashlyn Thompson and Emily K. Whiting, who both are raising daughters with rare medical complexities.

Charlotte's Hope Foundation offers one-on-one support for families with children with medical complexities, a podcast called Empowered by Hope, community support, educational resources, public speaking opportunities, and so much more.

To learn more about Charlotte's Hope Foundation and to join the movement of hope, visit www.CharlottesHopeFoundation.org and connect on Instagram and Facebook.

Where hope is found.™

About the Author

If the saying is true, that you are what you eat, then Emily is mostly comprised of coffee and cookies. If it were up to Emily, she'd have 20 children. Okay, maybe not 20, but a lot. And if her book, *She is Charlotte*, and work helps people navigate the hardships of life and provides some hope for them at their time of need, then she will be greatly satisfied.

Emily K. Whiting is the co-founder of Charlotte's Hope Foundation, Inc. Emily also speaks and writes about God's design for relationships and true intimacy, an intimacy meant to be so deep and fulfilling it leaves the world's idea of romance lacking.

She holds a Bachelor of Science degree in agriculture communications and minors in animal science and psychology. A farm girl at heart, she used this professional training to build a career in beef brand marketing and loved it. But as life continues to evolve and circumstances change, this unlikely background proves perfect for preparing Emily for her career today, which is first and foremost, raising her sweet babies, secondly, coordinating care and advocating for her eldest child's medical needs, and third as Executive Hope Director for Charlotte's Hope Foundation.

Emily lives in Ohio with her husband, Dan, her three children and possibly the largest most loving extended family in the world.

To get to know Emily and her work more, visit www.CharlottesHopeFoundation.org and www.EmilyKWhiting.com

Made in the USA
Monee, IL
03 December 2022

19492089R00225